Culturally Responsive Teaching

Culturally Responsive Teaching

Lesson Planning for Elementary and Middle Grades

Jacqueline Jordan Irvine

Emory University

Beverly Jeanne Armento

Georgia State University

with

Virginia E. Causey, Columbus State University
Joan Cohen Jones, Eastern Michigan University
Ramona S. Frasher, Georgia State University
Molly H. Weinburgh, Georgia State University

Boston Burr Ridge, IL Dubuque, IA Madison, WI New York San Francisco St. Louis
Bangkok Bogotá Caracas Lisbon London Madrid
Mexico City Milan New Delhi Seoul Singapore Sydney Taipei Toronto

McGraw-Hill Higher Education

A Division of The McGraw-Hill Companies

CULTURALLY RESPONSIVE TEACHING: LESSON PLANNING FOR ELEMENTARY
AND MIDDLE GRADES

 This book is printed on recycled, acid-free paper containing 10% postconsumer waste.

1 2 3 4 5 6 7 8 9 0 QPD/QPD 0 9 8 7 6 5 4 3 2 1 0

ISBN 0–07–240887–1

Vice president and editor-in-chief: *Thalia Dorwick*
Editorial director: *Jane E. Vaicunas*
Sponsoring editor: *Beth Kaufman*
Developmental editor: *Teresa Wise*
Marketing manager: *Daniel M. Loch*
Project manager: *Rose Koos*
Media technology producer: *Lance Gerhart*
Production supervisor: *Laura Fuller*
Coordinator of freelance design: *Michelle M. Meerdink*
Freelance cover/interior designer: *Maureen McCutcheon*
Cover images: Foreground: © *Phil Borges/Tony Stone Images*
Background: © *Aldo Tutino/Art Resource, NY*
Senior photo research coordinator: *Carrie K. Burger*
Photo research: *LouAnn K. Wilson*
Supplement coordinator: *Brenda A. Ernzen*
Compositor: *Carlisle Communications, Ltd.*
Typeface: *10/12 New Baskerville*
Printer: *Quebecor Printing Book Group/Dubuque, IA*

Photo credits:
Chapter Opener 1: © Jim Cummings/FPG, International; **2, 5, 6:** © D. Young-Wolff/PhotoEdit;
3, 4: © Elizabeth Crews; **Conclusion:** © Education/Corbis CD

Library of Congress Cataloging-in-Publication Data

Culturally responsive teaching : lesson planning for elementary and middle grades /
[edited by] Jacqueline Jordan Irvine, Beverly Jeanne Armento. — 1st ed.
    p. cm.
    Includes bibliographical references and index.
    ISBN 0–07–240887–1 (alk. paper)
    1. Multicultural education—United States—Curricula. 2. Education, Elementary—United
States—Curricula. 3. Lesson planning—United States. I. Irvine, Jacqueline Jordan. II. Armento,
Beverly Jeanne.

LC1099.3 .C84 2001
372.19—dc21   00–055422
                                                                        CIP

www.mhhe.com

Contents

Preface

This textbook provides teacher education students with comprehensive and extensive culturally responsive lesson units in language arts, mathematics, science, and social studies. Although there are increasing numbers of text-books and materials on the history and culture of specific minority groups (i.e., African American, Asian, Latino, and Native American), there is a scarcity of materials that translates this cultural and historical knowledge into examples for instructional use. Too often students are provided theoretical concepts about cultural diversity in foundations courses and lesson planning and pedagogical tools in their methods courses. Seldom are significant linkages made in teacher education between the two courses of study.

This text moves beyond cursory and often stereotype-reinforcing instructional examples of cultural diversity, such as the contributions approach discussed by Banks (1999) in which teachers focus on foods, festivals, heroes, and holidays. Irvine's Chapter 1, "The Critical Elements of Culturally Responsive Pedagogy," outlines for teacher education students the definitions, theoretical constructs, and high standards associated with culturally responsive pedagogy. In Chapter 2, Armento explains the four major components of culturally responsive classrooms—the beliefs, content and instructional examples, student engagement principles, and learning assessment principles. The principles defined by Armento are then illustrated and coded in each of the four lesson units in language arts, mathematics, science, and social studies.

In developing this text, the authors identified instructional challenges that student teachers face as they design teaching/learning experiences aimed at helping their students. These challenges include helping elementary and middle school students learn meaningful, flexible, and important conceptual knowledge. There is also the challenge of promoting higher-order thinking skills and the ability to locate relevant information using relevant technological tools.

In addition, student teachers must learn how to use state-of-the-art teaching materials that are also culturally and ethnically diverse. These teaching materials must include multiple perspectives and worldviews and at the same time illustrate the commonalties that unite us as a country.

It is also important that the elements of culturally responsive pedagogy reflect high standards. The lesson topics included in this volume reflect typical units used across the country at the elementary and middle-grade levels. Each unit includes references to national standards in the content area.

Ramona Frasher's language arts unit, "Stories, Stories, Stories," provides integrated language arts experiences that build on students' cultural background and experiences and are based on the premise that young children love stories and are natural storytellers themselves. In this unit, students tell, write, and read stories from their own experience and that of their families and communities. Folk literature and contemporary stories representing many cultures are provided as models for extending children's awareness of cultural diversity.

Joan Jones's math unit, "Craft Patterns and Geometry," allows students to explore informal geometry within the context of geometric patterns found in Navajo rugs, African textiles, Mexican pottery, and other ethnic tapestries and artifacts. Students study perimeter and area of polygons, symmetry, tesselations, and pattern recognition. In addition to learning powerful math concepts, the unit teaches students that patterns are universal and geometry and mathematics are used in our everyday lives. This unit has an interdisciplinary focus and uses art, literature, and history to heighten students' interest in mathematics.

Molly Weinburgh's science unit, "Weather," provides students with opportunities to learn about weather in a pedagogical approach that relates students' prior knowledge about weather to their home and community. Students construct their own knowledge of weather as they collect original data, create instruments used in weather forecasting, interpret their own and class data, connect weather experiences to cultural folk myths and sayings, and plan and evaluate a social action project.

Virginia Causey's social studies unit, "The Constitution: Voting Rights," is based on the principles of inquiry approach and learner construction of knowledge. The unit is an investigation of the evolution of American democracy by examining changing requirements for voting. Students role-play simulations of presidential elections through U.S. history and interpret documents related to changing suffrage requirements. During the unit, students also design and carry out an investigation of local voting patterns and create a voter education project as the culminating activity for the unit.

The four units model different lesson formats and approaches to effective instruction. The authors chose to illustrate a variety of lesson formats that depict the many ways that effective lessons can be planned and implemented. Each chapter has different instructional objectives, is written for different grade levels and content fields, and serves different purposes. For example, Virginia Causey's social studies chapter uses a detailed teacher script to demonstrate transitions and linkages between sections. The math unit by Joan Jones employs a more typical lesson plan format that uses cultural artifacts and examples to teach geometric concepts. The language arts unit by Ramona Frasher is a detailed version of the evaluation of student-constructed stories and writing experiences. Molly Weinburgh's science unit on weather and climate, also an inquiry lesson, models the use on active, hands-on lesson planning and implementation.

The reader should be aware that the lessons are not intended to represent every ethnic group or every aspect or category of multicultural education. There are significant differences between and among different ethnic groups that have the same labels. For example, groups labeled Hispanic include Mexicans and Brazilians. Mexicans speak Spanish; Brazilians speak Portuguese rather than Spanish. Although Japanese and Filipino students are both called Asian, their cultures and geographic origins are very different. Hence, these lessons should be considered examples that can be adapted by teachers to represent many cultures. Jones's math unit could be adapted to include the weaving and rugs of some Central American or Islamic cultures. The possibilities are endless, and teacher educators should encourage their students to experiment with many different cultural representations in their lessons.

The lessons were developed through a comprehensive and systematic curriculum development process that took place over a three-year period. The lessons were reviewed by teachers and curriculum specialists in school systems. The lessons were piloted by teachers in middle school classrooms and teacher educators in colleges of education. In addition, the lessons were presented at local, state, and national teacher education professional organizations. This process was very helpful to the authors of this book, and the feedback from teachers, curriculum specialists, and teacher educators was invaluable.

The units developed for this publication are intended to serve as examples of culturally responsive pedagogy as defined by the principles of inclusion, active student engagement, and individual assessment. The coding that appears in the units is the authors' interpretation of the principles applied to their work. However, there are other culturally responsive principles that could reasonably apply. Consequently, the writers recommend that teacher education faculty not use these lessons and the category labels in exercises that require students to "match" the authors' coding. Rather, the units should be viewed as general examples of sound instruction based on the principles of culturally responsive pedagogy.

Jacqueline Jordan Irvine

Jacqueline Jordan Irvine

Beverly Jeanne Armento

Beverly Jeanne Armento

References

Banks, J. A. 1999. *Introduction to multicultural education.* Boston: Allyn & Bacon.

Acknowledgements

This book was produced from a project, Perfecting Educational Practice: Culturally Responsive Curriculum Development, funded by the American Association of Colleges of Teacher Education (AACTE) through a grant it received from the Philip Morris Companies, Inc. Mary Dilworth and Mwangaza Michael-Bandele of AACTE were very helpful during this entire process. There were numerous teachers, teacher educators, curriculum specialists, and state department educators who assisted us in pilot testing and refining these lesson units. Thanks to Gwendolyn Williams, Catherine Turk, Jennifer Williams, Deborah Mills, Elizabeth Blackmon, Diane Klinect, LaTonya Brown, Billie Earl Sparks, Christine Thomas, Carole Tilley, Nancy Schwartzhoff, Robyn Greer, Sharron Hunt, Nannette McGee, Shelia Cooper, Loretta Burton, Patricia Daniels, Carole Rutland, Jean Murrell, John Finley, and Fran Watkins.

We gratefully acknowledge the feedback and wise counsel offered by the following reviewers: Norvella Carter, Texas A & M University; Lana M. Danielson, The University of South Dakota; Adele Ducharme, Valdosta State University; Jane E. Hughes, Ball State University; Madge Kibler, Piedmont College; Doni Kobus, California State University–Stanislaus; Barbara Nelson, St. John's University; Julia Rothenberg, The Sage Colleges.

Finally, we appreciate the assistance of Patricia Bell and William West, former graduate research assistants at Emory University and Georgia State University.

About the Authors

Jacqueline Jordan Irvine

Jacqueline Jordan Irvine is the Charles Howard Candler Professor of Urban Education in the Division of Educational Studies at Emory University. Her areas of specialization are multicultural education and urban teacher education, particularly the education of African Americans. Professor Irvine's books include *Black Students and School Failure, Growing Up African American in Catholic Schools,* and *Critical Knowledge for Diverse Students.* Professor Irvine has also published numerous articles and book chapters. In 1991, Professor Irvine's book *Black Students and School Failure* received the 1991 Outstanding Writing Award from the American Association of Colleges of Teacher Education (AACTE). Currently, she works with public school teachers in a center she founded and directs, the Center on Urban Learning/Teaching and Urban Research in Education and Schools (CULTURES).

Beverly Jeanne Armento

Beverly Jeanne Armento is currently Research Professor in social studies education and chair of the Middle/Secondary Education and Instructional Technology Department at Georgia State University in Atlanta. She holds a doctoral degree in social studies education from Indiana University. Professor Armento's major areas of professional research and writing are economic education, diversity issues, and excellence in teaching and learning. Dr. Armento's works include chapters in the *Handbook of Research on Teaching,* the *Handbook of Research on Teaching and Learning in Social Studies,* and the *Handbook of Research on Teacher Education.* She is actively leading efforts to reform the nature of teacher education programs and the quality of teaching and learning in urban schools in the Atlanta area.

Virginia Causey

Virginia Causey is an assistant professor of social science education at Columbus State University in Columbus, Georgia. She received her Ph.D. in history from Emory University. A secondary social studies teacher for eleven years, she has developed curriculum focusing on women and minority groups for K–12 social studies classrooms. Professor Causey's special interests include history education and diversity issues in education.

Joan Cohen Jones

Joan Cohen Jones is currently an assistant professor of mathematics at Eastern Michigan University. Professor Jones received her Ph.D. in mathematics education from Georgia State University, where she was on the faculty from 1993 to 1995. A former middle and secondary school teacher with over fifteen years experience teaching in culturally and ethnically diverse schools, she has made numerous presentations on multicultural mathematics. Her special interests are curriculum development in multicultural mathematics, teacher education, and teacher attitudes and beliefs.

Ramona Scheiderer Frasher

Ramona Scheiderer Frasher, now retired, was a member of the Middle-Secondary Education and Instructional Technology Department at Georgia State University from 1974 to 1998. Prior to her work in teacher education, she spent ten years as an elementary and secondary school teacher and librarian. Professor Frasher was an active member of professional organizations in her areas of specialization, English language arts and children's and young-adult literature, and authored and coauthored many articles, papers, and presentations.

Molly Weinburgh

Molly Weinburgh is currently a member of the Early Childhood Education Department of Georgia State University and a Ph.D. graduate of Emory University. Professor Weinburgh taught science in the Atlanta metropolitan area schools prior to her work in higher education. Her research interests include equity issues in science, student attitudes toward science, and teacher/student epistemology. She is coprincipal investigator on a NSF-funded Local Systemic Change grant (Elementary Science Education Partners) and is the author of eleven refereed papers, seven proceedings, and twelve manuals/textbooks.

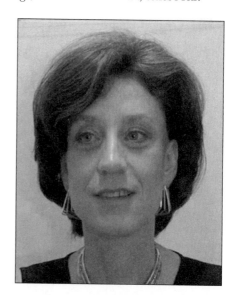

The Critical Elements of Culturally Responsive Pedagogy: A Synthesis of the Research

Jacqueline Jordan Irvine

Emory University

The school failure of culturally diverse students, particularly African American, Hispanic, and Native American students, is well documented. On most indicators and measures of academic achievement, African American and Hispanic American students' performance lags behind their white and Asian peers. Although African American students have shown some increased performance on standardized test scores, the gains have been relatively small and inconsistent over time. The data from the National Assessment of Educational Progress (NAEP) reveal that only 19 percent of white twelfth graders scored below basic proficiency level in reading as compared to 48 percent of African Americans and 42 percent of Hispanic students. Similar achievement discrepancies were found in mathematics, writing, and history (Nettles 1997).

In addition to the disproportionate school failure of culturally diverse students, there are other compelling data that speak to the significance and urgency of implementing a culturally responsive pedagogy. Demographic data confirm that by the year 2020 about 40 percent of the nation's school-age population will be students of color, and students of color already represent 70 percent of the student population in the 20 largest school districts. However, as the number of culturally diverse students increases, the number of teachers of color is decreasing. The American Association of Colleges of Teacher Education reports (1995) that 80 percent of preservice teachers are white females who are unfamiliar with the cultural experiences of their diverse students. Consequently, these teachers often feel unprepared to deliver effective instruction for the multicultural student populations they instruct. Inexperienced teachers particularly need classroom materials that will assist them with planning and implementing meaningful lessons for their diverse students. New teachers often struggle with addressing the needs of most of their students, but these issues become even more challenging when faced with students from diverse cultures.

Will this problem of increasing diverse student populations and decreasing numbers of culturally diverse teachers increase in the future? The answer is definitely yes. The Department of Education has projected that 2.1 million teachers will be hired in the next ten years to replace an unusually high number of expected retirees. These new hires will also be mostly white females who will be placed in classrooms of culturally diverse students. If the past data are instructive, 17 percent will leave within three years.

This chapter has three primary purposes. First, it defines culturally responsive pedagogy as presented in the literature. Second, the chapter proposes four critical elements that support culturally responsive pedagogy:

1. Culture is a powerful variable that influences teaching and learning processes.
2. Effective teaching research is compatible with and supportive of the principles of culturally responsive pedagogy.
3. Teacher knowledge and reflection are important considerations when designing and implementing a culturally responsive lesson.
4. High standards and high expectations are important components of culturally responsive pedagogy.

Third, the chapter counters some myths and misperceptions associated with culturally responsive teaching styles.

Definitions

The term *culturally responsive pedagogy* is used interchangeably with several terms such as culturally responsible, culturally appropriate, culturally congruent, culturally compatible, culturally relevant, and multicultural to describe a variety of effective teaching approaches in culturally diverse classrooms. These terms all imply that teachers should be responsive to their students by incorporating elements of the students' culture in their teaching. In fact, there is general agreement that all teachers should be responsive to their students. *Responsive* simply means reacting appropriately in the instructional context. The teaching effectiveness research literature informs us that a responsive teacher is sensitive to the needs, interests, learning preferences, and abilities of their students. Responsive teachers do not blindly follow one teaching method or use the same teaching methods and materials for all students. Instead, these teachers modify their knowledge and training, paying attention to classroom contexts and to individual student needs and experiences. For example, responsive teachers provide the correct amount of structure for those students who need structure. They use appropriate classroom materials and methods such as peer tutoring and cooperative learning for students who prefer to work with others. Students who have difficulty with abstractions are provided with models, manipulatives, and other concrete representations.

Culturally responsive teachers spend considerable classroom and nonclassroom time developing a personal relationship with their students (Irvine 1990b). These relationship-building exchanges are recurrent and spontaneous daily events. These teachers understand that teaching is a social interaction that involves the development and maintenance of relationships as well as more widely accepted activities such as the planning, delivery, and evaluation of instruction. Culturally responsive teachers listen patiently to their students and allow them to share personal stories and anecdotes during classroom time. Teachers ask students, for example, to share stories about their family, weekend activities, hobbies, and so forth. Students are encouraged to express themselves openly, and storytelling and comments delivered with high affect and positive emotions are not prohibited. Responsive teachers also share appropriate stories about their personal lives and connect their own and their students' lives to the content of the instruction.

For example, one teacher in language arts assigned her students the homework task to write a story about their family. She was careful to include examples in her instructions that referenced traditional as well as nontraditional families and immediate and extended family members. The following day, the students turned in their stories, and the teacher was disappointed with the results as well as the enthusiasm of the students about the assignment. Remembering the culturally responsive principle that states teachers often share stories about their personal lives with their students, the teacher decided to write a story about her family and brought pictures to share. In her story, she modeled the writing process that she wanted her students to understand, and she discovered that this exercise contributed to an improved classroom climate and interpersonal relationships with her pupils.

Although there is agreement on some of the essential elements of teacher responsiveness, writers use the term *culturally responsive* for teachers who have very different teaching styles and philosophies. Some teachers believe they are being culturally responsive when they organize cultural celebrations during Cinco de Mayo or Black History Month. Culturally responsive teachers, however, attend to the principles of effective teaching each day, not just holidays and celebrations. Others, like King (1991), believe a culturally responsive pedagogy must be more closely related to issues such as antiracism, social justice, and activism. King suggested that teachers must assist students to change the society, not simply exist or survive in it.

Various conceptions and definitions of culturally responsive pedagogy are found in the works of Bowers and Flinders (1990), Smith (1998), Villegas (1991), and, most popularly, Ladson-Billings (1994). Bowers and Flinders (1990) posit that "being responsive means to be aware of and capable of responding in educationally constructive ways to the ways in which cultural patterns influence the behavioral and mental ecology of the classroom" (p. vii). Villegas (1991, p. 13) expands the definition of Bowers and Flinders by acknowledging the purpose of culturally responsive pedagogy is the maximization of learning for culturally diverse students. She states, "A culturally responsive pedagogy builds on the premise that how people are expected to go about learning may differ across cultures. In order to maximize learning opportunities, teachers must gain knowledge of the cultures represented in their classrooms, then translate this knowledge into instructional practice." Examples of this can be found in the language arts lesson by Frasher who suggests the students interview members of the community and invite them to tell stories to the class. Smith's (1998, p. 20) definition extends the Villegas interpretation by noting that student achievement is not the only purpose of a culturally responsive pedagogy. He believes, like King, that a culturally responsible pedagogy also helps teachers to understand their "commitment to the common good means the reconstruction of society to be fair, just and free of oppression."

Ladson-Billings (1992) notes that

> Culturally relevant pedagogy prepares students to effect change in society, not merely fit into it. These teachers support this attitude of change by capitalizing on their students' home and community culture. These teachers . . . empower students intellectually, socially, emotionally, and politically by using cultural referents to impart knowledge, skills, and attitudes. Unlike critical pedagogy that emphasizes an individual critique of the social environment, culturally relevant pedagogy urges collective action grounded in cultural understanding, experiences, and ways of knowing the world. (pp. 382–383)

In her book *The Dreamkeepers*, Ladson-Billings (1994) compares culturally relevant and assimilationist teaching in the areas of conceptions of self and others, social relations, and conceptions of knowledge. An assimilationist believes that ethnic groups should change and adopt the values, beliefs, and behaviors of the dominant culture and not preserve their own culture. For example, she noted that culturally relevant teachers believe that all students can succeed; however, assimilationalist teachers tend to believe that failure is inevitable for some. In social relations, culturally relevant teachers encourage community building as contrasted to assimilationist teachers who encourage competitive achievement. Knowledge for culturally relevant teachers is viewed critically; for assimilationalist teachers, knowledge is thought to be infallible.

In summary, as a developing field of research and practice, there is growing consensus about the definitions of culturally relevant pedagogy and how it differs from more traditional, assimilationist teaching. As the number of culturally diverse students increases, it becomes more compelling that all educators become more attentive to ways to adapt their practice to meet all students' needs.

Critical Elements That Support Culturally Responsive Pedagogy

The theoretical foundation of a culturally responsive pedagogy is related to four critical elements that have guided and supported its development:

1. Culture is a powerful variable that influences teaching and learning processes.
2. The effective teaching research is compatible with and supportive of the principles of culturally responsive pedagogy.
3. Teacher knowledge and reflection are important considerations when designing and implementing a culturally responsive lesson.
4. High standards and high expectations are important components of culturally responsive pedagogy.

The inclusion of these elements assists teachers to view culturally responsive pedagogy in nonstereotypic and non-formulaic ways and helps them to think deeply and reflectively about their teaching and the needs of their diverse learners.

CULTURE IS A POWERFUL VARIABLE THAT INFLUENCES TEACHING AND LEARNING PROCESSES

What Is Culture? Cultural variables are powerful, yet often overlooked, factors that help to explain the school failure of diverse, nonmainstream children. In summarizing the influence that cultural variables have on teaching and learning, Irvine and Irvine (1995) note that culture is the sum total of ways of living. Hoopes and Pusch (1979) believe that culture is a way of life that is shared by members of a population (Ogbu 1988). Culture is an important survival strategy that is passed down from one generation to another through the processes of enculturalization and socialization, a type of roadmap that serves as a "sense-making device that guides and shapes behavior" (Davis 1984, p. 10). Culture includes forms such as rites, rituals, legends, myths, artifacts, symbols, language, ceremonies, and history and is best characterized by the statement, "It's the way things are done around here" (Kilmann 1985, p. 5). Everyone, not just members of ethnic groups, has a culture, and institutions such as schools have cultures as well. Schools have rituals, for example, the pledge of allegiance, awards ceremonies at assemblies, artifacts such as computers, calculators, and book bags, and Standard English as the valued language.

How Does a Students' Culture Influence Teaching and Learning? Culture (Owens 1987) is what one thinks is important (values); what one thinks is true (beliefs); and how one perceives how things are done (norms). Many teachers disregard the fact that schools themselves have a culture that has implicit values, beliefs, and norms that are related to school success. Bennett (1999) uses Hall's conception of high- and low-context cultures to illustrate some of the implicit cultural characteristics of mainstream schools. For example, schools operate on tight time schedules as opposed to flexible ones. Knowledge gained through analytical reasoning is valued over intuitive reasoning. Individual achievement and competition are valued over group achievement through cooperation. Cushner, McClelland, and Safford (1992, p. 105) summarize the culture of schools by noting that "the particular symbols used, the knowledge made accessible to others, and the preferred method of imparting that knowledge have been agreed upon by the majority of the members of a particular cultural group: in the case in the United States, dominant white middle-class males."

African American, Hispanic, Asian, Native American, as well as some poor and working-class white students often bring to the school setting a distinctive set of cultural values, beliefs, and norms that is often incongruous with middle-class cultural norms and behaviors of schools. This conflict results in cultural discontinuity or lack of cultural synchronization between the student and the school (Irvine 1990a). What happens to students when their culture is rejected or not recognized by schools? Psychologists (Lambert 1989) believe that students of color suffer from psychological discomfort and low achievement when they perceive that the school setting is hostile and incongruous. When there is a cultural mismatch or cultural incompatibility between students and their school, the inevitable occurs—miscommunication; confrontations between the student, the teacher, and the home; hostility; alienation; diminished self-esteem; and eventual school failure (Irvine 1990a).

It must be emphasized that all students have a culture, not just students of color. Mainstream white middle-class students bring to school cultural beliefs, values, perceptions, behavior, verbal and nonverbal language, worldview, community expectations, and learning styles. The difference between the school experiences and success of students from ethnic groups and lower social economic-class students and mainstream students is that the mainstream students' culture is more likely to be compatible with the culture of the school. Unfortunately, some female students, students of color, and poor white students have ways of doing and knowing that often conflict with and are antithetical to the ways in which schools expect them to do and know. If these types of students are to succeed, schools must become places where schools, families, and communities work cooperatively and the school and home cultures are not conflicting and contentious.

Wilma Longstreet (1978) identified five aspects of ethnicity that are useful guidelines for understanding how cultural differences are manifested in classrooms and how they influence teaching and learning. The five aspects are (1) verbal communications, (2) nonverbal communications, (3) orientation modes, (4) social values, and (5) intellectual modes. The following examples demonstrate Longstreet's aspects in three of the five areas—verbal communications, nonverbal communications, and intellectual modes.

Verbal Communications Padron and Knight (1990, p. 177) state that "language and culture are so inextricably intertwined that it is often difficult to consider one without the other." Not only are there obvious differences in ethnic students' pronunciation, vocabulary, and phonology (rhythm, tempo, pitch) but differences in assumptions regarding what is spoken and left unspoken, whether one interrupts, defers to others, or asks direct or indirect questions (Erickson 1986). Gollnick and Chinn (1998) add that teachers need to understand how semantics, accents, dialect, and discussion modes manifest themselves when they communicate with their diverse students. For example, some urban teachers claim that many of their students do not follow mainstream school behavior when participating in classroom discussions. Some of the students do not raise their hands to be recognized. Some do not want to speak in public.

Culturally diverse students whose spoken and written language does not match the requirements of mainstream language experience academic difficulties in school because their language is not compatible with the language of the school. Students who are not native speakers of English encounter barriers in school because their language is not valued and is perceived as a cultural deficit rather than an asset. Many English as a Second Language (ESL) students are misdiagnosed and placed in special education because they do not speak English. Some researchers even believe that the Navajo language has influenced Native American students' mastery of mathematics since there are no agreed upon meanings for concepts such as multiply, divide, if, cosine, and sine (Bradley 1984; Moore 1982).

Nonverbal Communications   Research by Byers and Byers (1972) provides some help in understanding the significance of nonverbal communications between teachers and diverse students. Byers and Byers investigated nonverbal communication by filming the interaction between a white teacher and two black and two white girls in nursery school. They found that one of the white girls was more active and successful in getting the teacher's attention. She looked at the teacher 14 times, and the teacher reciprocated 8 of these times. On the other hand, the more initiating black girl looked at the teacher 35 times but caught the teacher's eye only 4 times. The researchers concluded that the black girl, unlike her white counterpart, timed her glances inappropriately. She made inappropriate moves at crucial times, pulling when she should have pushed or pushing when she should have pulled. The black girl, unlike the white girl, did not share with the teacher an implicit understanding of cultural nuances, gestures, timing, verbal and nonverbal cues. For the white child, interacting and learning with the teacher was productive and enjoyable; the black child had the opposite experience.

Sixty-five percent of all communication is related to nonverbal language (Bowers and Flinders 1990). Nonverbal language includes proxemics (interpersonal space), kinesics (body language), haptics (frequency of touching), and paralanguage (voice pitch, tone, and rhythm). This area in the teacher-student relationship often produces miscommunication and eventual conflict in schools. Feldman (1989), for example, stated that black students' "back-channel" behaviors are different from mainstream school behaviors. *Back-channel* behaviors are the short sounds and nonverbal moves that students use to signal the teacher that they are attentive and listening. In addition to issues like back channel behaviors, there are differences in the ways some cultural groups either maintain or avoid eye contact with authority figures. For example, mainstream middle-class students are more likely to look directly at the teacher and nod with an accompanying verbal affirmation. Some African American and Native American students do not look directly at the teacher and are assumed to be inattentive and off task.

Styles of walking, eye glances, dress, and style of personal presentation are also included in Longstreet's aspects of ethnicity and culture. Johnson (cited in Bennett 1990, p. 62) noted:

> Young Black males have their own way of walking. Observing young Black males walking down ghetto streets, one can't help noticing that they are, indeed, in Thoreau's words "marching to the tune of a different drummer." The "different drummer" is a different culture. . . . The young Black males' walk is different. First of all, it's much slower—it's more of a stroll. . . . The gait is almost like a walking dance, with all parts of the body moving in rhythmic harmony.

Inexperienced teachers often overreact to these nonverbal cultural manifestations by imposing unenforceable rules and prohibitions. Unfortunately, the predictable vicious cycle occurs. The diverse students become more tenacious in their efforts to maintain their identity and culture, and teachers and administrators are caught in the proverbial no-win situation.

Intellectual Modes The most popular and widely researched category of Longstreet's intellectual modes is learning styles or learning preferences. Learning styles is a preferred way in which students perceive, process, store, and retrieve information. A summary of the research on African American and Hispanic students (Baruth and Manning 1992; Boykin and Toms 1985; Castañeda and Gray 1974; Cushner, McClelland, and Safford 1992; Grossman 1984; Hale-Benson 1986; Ramírez and Castañeda 1974; Shade 1989) suggests that these diverse students are field-dependent learners as contrasted to field independent (some writers prefer to use the terms relational, field-sensitive, or global learners) and tend to

- respond to things in terms of the whole instead of isolated parts;
- prefer group learning situations;
- prefer inferential reasoning;
- approximate space and numbers rather than adhere to exactness or accuracy;
- focus on people rather than things;
- prefer learning by doing;
- be more proficient in nonverbal than verbal communications;
- prefer learning characterized by variation in activities;
- prefer kinesthetic, active, hands-on instructional activities.

Irvine and York (1995) conclude that learning-styles research is a useful beginning point in designing appropriate instruction for culturally diverse students. They emphasize that the learning-preference research, if not carefully interpreted and implemented, can be dangerous when assumptions limit students' experiences or infer negative characteristics about ability. For example, students thought to be field dependent may be discouraged from participating in solo performances or leadership roles. Negative teacher expectations can be fueled if teachers incorporate generalized and decontextualized observations about children of color without knowledge of the limitations of learning-styles labels. Research in which conclusions are unsupported or insufficiently supported by the data may be not only misleading but also harmful. For example, one author (Cureton 1978), describes African American students' auditory skills as, "They are not accustomed to listening for long periods" (p. 752). Dunn et al. (1990) stated that whites, in comparison to African Americans, prefer bright lights while learning, a trait correlated with a successive-analytic-left processing style and concluded that "Euro-Americans may be more analytical than Afro-Americans" (p. 73). These types of statements encourage stereotyping and lead teachers to categorize students' learning preferences based on their ethnicity alone.

Culturally diverse students, like all students, can master various intellectual styles if provided the proper psychological and instructional support. Hilliard (1992, p. 373) adds, "All students have an incredible capacity for developing the ability to use multiple learning styles, in much the same way that multiple language competency can be accomplished." However, teachers who understand the preferred style of a student can use that knowledge to design and plan instruction and to encourage their students to experiment with a wider repertoire of learning approaches.

THE EFFECTIVE TEACHING RESEARCH IS COMPATIBLE WITH AND SUPPORTIVE OF THE PRINCIPLES OF CULTURALLY RESPONSIVE PEDAGOGY

Culturally responsive teachers use the best of what we now know about good teaching. Cruickshank (1990) summarizes that body of literature by indicating that effective teachers are identified by (1) their character traits, (2) what they know, (3) what they teach, (4) how they teach, (5) what they expect from their students, (6) how their students react to them, and (7) how they manage the classroom. The extensive teacher effectiveness research informs us that successful teachers of students of color exhibit behaviors that are compatible with the instructional behaviors of any effective teacher. These basic principles of good teaching should be addressed in the culturally responsive research. Culturally responsive pedagogy has a strong theoretical base that emphasizes some familiar characteristics of the teaching effectiveness research.

Examples of some of these effective instructional strategies include

- connecting students' prior knowledge and cultural experiences with new concepts by constructing and designing relevant cultural metaphors and images;
- designing appropriate transfer devices;
- setting high expectations;
- instituting positive classroom climates and positive relationships with parents and community;
- understanding students' cultural knowledge and experiences and selecting appropriate instructional materials;
- helping students find meaning and purpose in what is to be learned;
- using interactive teaching strategies;
- seizing the "teachable moment";
- allowing students to participate in planning instructional activities;
- using culturally familiar speech and events;
- preparing students to effect changes in society;
- helping learners construct meaning by organizing, elaborating, and representing knowledge in their own way;
- using primary sources of data and manipulative materials;
- aligning assessment with teaching through activities such as teacher observations, student exhibitions, and portfolios.

In summary, culturally responsive teachers use best teaching practices in their classroom, and they construct their understanding of the effective teaching research based on their students' instructional needs as well as their own beliefs, experiences, perceived role efficacy, and philosophy of education.

TEACHER REFLECTION AND KNOWLEDGE ARE IMPORTANT CONSIDERATIONS WHEN DESIGNING AND IMPLEMENTING A CULTURALLY RESPONSIVE LESSON

Culturally responsive teachers do not use the teacher effectiveness research as a set of rigid prescriptions to be modeled. Instead, they contextualize this body of research and use it to inform and guide their teaching practices. Culturally responsive teachers recognize that the effective teaching research is instructive yet often limited by its static, generic, and decontextualized nature. These teachers recognize that they do not instruct culturally homogenized, generic students in generic school settings, and teachers armed with a repertoire of these generic teaching skills often find themselves ineffective and ill-prepared when faced with a classroom of culturally diverse students. Consequently, the process of reflection must inform the effective teaching research.

What Is the Process of Reflection?   Reflective practice as summarized by Cadray (1999) is associated with terms such as *inquiry teaching* and *action research*. It is the "iterative process of thought and action that is based on profession experience" (p. 33). Through reflection, teachers are able to evaluate their teaching and seek appropriate professional development for continued growth.

Reflective teachers are open-minded, astute observers and problem solvers who monitor, evaluate, and continually revise their own teaching practices (Schon 1987).

They have a thorough and well-grounded knowledge of their content field and understand that good teaching often emerges from situations of high ambiguity and frequent experimentation. In other words, these teachers learn to make informed choices that result in achievement for their students. Eisner (1983) called this skill "educational connoisseurship, the ability to appreciate what one has encountered" (p. 11).

Because there are no quick and simple solutions, no single program or packaged intervention to train teachers to teach culturally diverse students, the issue of reflection becomes critically important. Any attempt to generate "tricks of the trade" must be avoided because of the complexity of the issue and because of the individual needs, motivations, experiences, and abilities of children of color. Reflection enables teachers to examine the interplay of context and culture as well as their own behaviors, talents, and preferences. Reflective teachers are inquirers who examine their actions, instructional goals, methods, and materials in reference to their students' cultural experiences and preferred learning environments. The teacher probes the school, community, and home environments, searching for insights into diverse students' abilities, preferences, and motivations.

Several of the lessons in this textbook illustrate this principle. Chapter 6 discusses how social studies classrooms must provide opportunities for social action in the students' community and home environment. In the social studies unit, students analyze neighborhood voting patterns. The Chapter 4 unit in mathematics suggests that students find cultural and ethnic patterns in the home and neighborhood to explore geometric concepts such as perimeter.

HIGH STANDARDS AND HIGH EXPECTATIONS ARE IMPORTANT COMPONENTS OF CULTURALLY RESPONSIVE PEDAGOGY

The authors of the lesson units in the four content areas of language arts, mathematics, science, and social studies in this textbook document how the elements of culturally responsive pedagogy support the standards of the National Council of the Social Studies (NCSS), the National Council of Teachers of Mathematics (NCTM), the National Science Education Standards (NSES), and the National Council of Teachers of English (NCTE) and the International Reading Association (IRA). For example, the language arts lesson written by Ramona Frasher (Chapter 3) is consistent with NCTE and IRA standards. *Stories, Stories, Stories* provides rich and meaningful activities that build on students' personal and cultural knowledge while emphasizing written and oral communications, vocabulary building, and literature. In the mathematics lesson (Chapter 4), author Joan Jones designed a lesson unit to teach challenging geometry concepts using craft patterns from different cultural groups. The lessons reinforce NCTM standards, such as reasoning, communications, and connections. Molly Weinburg's science unit on weather (Chapter 5) is an example of an inquiry, hands-on, culturally responsive learning experience that also meets the National Science Education Standards. Finally, the social studies unit by Virginia Causey (Chapter 6) is a social reconstructivist unit that allows students to become involved in a voter education project. In keeping with NCSS standards, this unit is an example of educating students for responsible citizenship and social action.

In addition to meeting the standards of the various content areas, the essential elements of culturally responsive pedagogy have been found to be compatible with the standards and performance indicators of the Interstate New Teacher Assessment and Support Consortium (INTASC). INTASC standards define what all beginning teachers should know and be able to do. The following chart developed by Joseph Cadray of Emory University (1999) outlines the culturally responsive practice and references the INTASC standard that is addressed.

INTASC Standard	Culturally Responsive Practice
Standard 1 The teacher understands the central concepts, tools of inquiry, and structure of the fields of knowledge she/he teaches and can create learning experiences that make these aspects of subject matter meaningful for students.	The teacher integrates professional, content, and pedagogical knowledge to create learning experiences that make the content area meaningful for all students. The teacher uses multiple representations and explanations and links them to students' prior understandings.
Standard 2 The teacher understands how children learn and develop and provides learning opportunities that support their intellectual, social, and personal development.	The teacher understands and appreciates cognitive processes involved in academic learning, including diverse learning styles.
Standard 3 The teacher understands how students differ in their approaches to learning and creates instructional opportunities that are adapted to diverse learners.	The teacher knows and is sensitive to diverse cultural groups globally, and understands how ethnicity, class, gender, and other sociocultural factors influence students' learning and classroom climate. The teacher understands students' families, cultures, and communities and uses this information as a basis for connecting to students' experiences.
Standard 4 The teacher understands and uses a variety of instructional strategies to encourage students' development of critical thinking, problem solving, and performance skills.	The teacher implements a variety of instructional and assessment strategies appropriate to diverse learners.
Standard 5 The teacher uses an understanding of individual and group motivation and behavior to create a learning environment that encourages positive social interaction, active engagement in learning, and self-motivation.	The teacher diagnoses and builds upon the personal, cultural, and historical experiences of learners from a variety of socioeconomic and ethnic backgrounds and develops meaningful instructional activities and positive, productive learning environments.
Standard 6 The teacher uses knowledge of effective verbal, nonverbal, and media communication techniques, including technology, to foster active inquiry, collaboration, and supportive interaction in the classroom.	The teacher communicates in ways that demonstrate sensitivity to cultural and gender differences.
Standard 7 The teacher plans instruction based on knowledge of subject matter, students, the community, and curriculum goals.	The teacher plans learning opportunities that meet the developmental and individual needs of diverse learners.
Standard 8 The teacher understands and uses formal and informal assessment strategies to ensure the continuous intellectual, social, and physical development of the learner.	The teacher uses a variety of assessment techniques, including observation, portfolios, self-assessment, peer assessment, and projects, as well as teacher-made and standardized tests.

INTASC Standard	Culturally Responsive Practice
Standard 9 The teacher is a reflective practitioner who continually evaluates the effects of his/her actions on others.	The teacher reflects on his/her personal background and life experiences in order to develop culturally responsive curricula and instructional practices.
Standard 10 The teacher fosters relationships with school colleagues, parents, and agencies in the larger community to support students' learning and well-being.	The teacher understands the influence of family participation on students' learning and involves families in students' learning. The teacher identifies and uses community resources in the classroom and understands teaching as situated in schools and communities.

In summary, the research on culture, effective teaching, reflection, and high standards are essential elements in culturally responsive pedagogy. These four elements are well-known and accepted fields of study in teacher education. So why is this seemingly reasonable and practical addition to the knowledge base so perplexing for so many teachers? Part of the answer is related to the fact that educators often hold myths, misperceptions, and misunderstandings that are associated with culturally responsive pedagogy. The following section explores some of these erroneous ideas.

Myths and Misperceptions

Myth One: Culturally responsive pedagogy is a new and special type of pedagogy that is relevant only to low income, urban students of color.

Reality: Traditional pedagogy has always been culturally responsive, that is, responsive to the culture of students who are primarily middle class and Euro-American. This type of culturally responsive pedagogy emphasized the importance of individual achievement, strict adherence to time schedules, knowledge through analytical reasoning, self-sufficiency, and little reliance on nonverbal or contextual cues (Bennett, 1990). There was common agreement among educators that Euro-American cultural values and their accompanying pedagogical teaching styles were appropriate for all students. Students who did not adapt and change their cultural perspectives simply failed in school. A culturally responsive pedagogy is, in fact, helpful to all students— mainstream and minority. Elliot Wiggenton's Foxfire teaching principles, first used with white rural Appalachian students, have now been implemented in mainstream schools across the country. His work is a form of culturally responsive pedagogy.

Myth Two: In schools with diverse student populations, only teachers of color are capable of demonstrating the essential elements of a culturally responsive pedagogy.

Reality: AACTE reports that approximately 80 percent of all elementary and secondary teacher education students are white (AACTE 1995). Consequently, the typical preservice teacher is a white female from a small town or suburban community who intends to return to her provincial surroundings, expecting to teach children from a background similar to her own (Zimpher and Ashburn 1992). The reality is that most teachers of students of color are and will continue to be white females, and there is evidence that their inability to teach students of color effectively may have more to do with their lack of training than their race. All teachers, regardless of their ethnic and racial background, have to be multiculturalists. They must be thoroughly knowledgeable, sensitive, and comfortable about culturally diverse children's language, style of presentation, and community values. In addition, as they respect and acknowledge their students' home/community culture, they must help them to learn the dominant school culture as well.

Myth Three: Culturally responsive pedagogy is a "bag of tricks" that minimizes the difficulty of teaching some students of color.

Reality: As previously discussed, culturally responsive pedagogy has its foundation in the concept of reflection and not in simplistic solutions and "quick fixes." Unfortunately, some writers have reduced culturally responsive pedagogy to a mere teaching method. It is clearly more than that. Culturally responsive pedagogy is not just a teaching method, but it is also an attitude about children and schools and an impetus for redefinition of teacher and student roles. It is a vehicle for social change, an empowering device, through which students of color gain access to knowledge previously denied them.

Myth Four: Culturally responsive pedagogy requires teachers to master the details of all the cultures of students represented in the classroom.

Reality: Not only is the mastery of multiple cultures an unrealistic expectation for experienced teachers, it is impractical for novice teachers who are striving to define personal and professional roles in reference to their school's culture and curriculum, administrators' and community expectations, and students' individual learning needs. The acquisition of cross-cultural competence is time intensive and complex, and questions remain as to whether teacher training should be culture-general (training for a broad spectrum of cultural differences) or culture-specific (training for interaction with one culture only) (York 1993). It appears that a more developmentally sound approach involves the creation of long-term and continuing internships that incorporate in-school and out-of-school cultural immersion experiences where prospective teachers can acquire the necessary pedagogical and anthropological skills to make reasonable instructional decisions. These classroom decisions are based not on stereotyped cultural profiles of ethnic groups but rather on how culture may or may not contribute to an understanding of an individual student's behavior.

Myth Five: Culturally responsive pedagogy reinforces stereotypes about children of color because this pedagogy categorizes and labels children based on their race and ethnicity.

Reality: Culturally responsive pedagogy, in fact, leads to less, not more, stereotyping because teachers are trained to focus on individual students' needs, prior experiences, knowledge, and learning styles. Responsive teachers adjust their professional knowledge and training to address their students' needs. In helping learners make sense of new concepts and ideas, culturally responsive teachers create learning opportunities in which students' voices emerge and knowledge and meaning are constructed from the students' perspectives. This liberating teaching and learning process is likely to decrease, not increase, instances of stereotyping and labeling.

Conclusion

Because the concept of culturally responsive pedagogy is so logically and emotionally appealing, teachers must be particularly cautious in their interpretation and application of this type of teaching. In the process of creating authentic discourse and culturally relevant examples, inexperienced teachers might resort to a style of teaching that further isolates diverse students from mainstream society. Giroux (1992, p. 9) notes that cultural responsiveness does not mean that the "experiences that students bring to school be merely affirmed. On the contrary, one begins with such experiences but does not treat them as undisputed nor allow them to limit what is taught. Knowledge needs to be made meaningful in order to be made critical and transformative." It is important that teachers understand the goal of culturally responsive pedagogy is student achievement of high academic standards. Some teachers believe that their goal is simply to celebrate their students' diverse cultural traditions. Although the celebration of diversity is a welcomed and laudatory goal, teachers must always place student achievement as the primary and essential goal.

Teachers who embrace culturally responsive pedagogy should also attend to the concept of culturally responsive schools. A culturally responsive classroom located in a culturally insensitive school does not facilitate maximum student achievement. Culturally responsive schools are a necessary condition for culturally responsive pedagogy. These are schools that employ sensitive and caring teachers, use a multicultural curriculum, eliminate inflexible systems of tracking and rigid and confining school structures that stifle both teachers and students. Shanker (1990, p. 349) reminds us that "the rigidity of the traditional structures forces us to try to fit diverse children into the same mold. Given the way we organize schools, children must learn in lockstep or not at all."

Culturally responsive teachers work in schools that are supportive and that reward them appropriately. In addition, parents, teachers, and community members in culturally responsive schools are involved in governance, decision making, and the recruitment and selection of school personnel. Smaller schools, schools within a school, flexible course schedules, team teaching, and multiple-age groups are some examples of schoolwide strategies that are frequently implemented. Culturally responsive schools are communities of learners where all students are respected and recognized as individuals and where they feel a sense of connection, intimacy, visibility, and self-worth. Martin (1995) calls these responsive schools "school homes, not schoolhouses," where the three C's (care, concern, and connection) are as important as the three R's.

This chapter presents a theoretical foundation of culturally responsive pedagogy related to four critical elements that have guided and supported its development. They are culture, the effective teaching research, reflection, and high academic standards. A culturally responsive pedagogy addresses students' cultural knowledge, history, personal style, language and dialect, and learning preferences. In addition, cultural responsive pedagogy incorporates the students' parents and community. The pedagogy forces a redefinition of teacher roles and an understanding of how these roles are enacted within the political, social, and economic structures of society.

In an effort to facilitate the discussion, future development, and evolution of culturally responsive pedagogy, there are some compelling questions that teachers should consider. How should schools be reformed to accommodate culturally diverse students? How can schools better use the cultural resources of the students' community and home? Is the purpose of a culturally responsive pedagogy to prepare students to transform and challenge the system or to succeed in it as it currently exists? In addition, this chapter also raises some issues related to definitions and myths surrounding the concept of culturally responsive pedagogy and encourages teachers to participate in professional growth activities that advance the theoretical and practical development of this concept.

Finally, research in the attributes and outcomes of culturally responsive pedagogy is called for as the number of children of color increases in our schools and as disproportionate numbers of them fail to achieve. This research is needed because any premature attempt to package, label, and simplify this culturally specific teaching style will result in yet another failed attempt to convince teachers that, indeed, "all children can learn."

REFERENCES

American Association of Colleges for Teacher Education. 1995. *Survey of teacher education enrollments by race/ethnicity and gender.* Washington, DC: Author.

Baruth, L. G., and M. L. Manning. 1992. *Multicultural education of children and adolescents.* Boston: Allyn & Bacon.

Bennett, C. I. 1990. *Comprehensive multicultural education.* 2nd ed. Boston: Allyn & Bacon.

Bennett, C. I. 1999. *Comprehensive multicultural education.* 3rd ed. Boston: Allyn & Bacon.

Bowers, C. A., and D. J. Flinders. 1990. *Responsive teaching: An ecological approach to classroom practices of language, culture, and thought.* New York: Teachers College Press.

Boykin, A. W., and F. D. Toms. 1985. Black child socialization. In *Black children: Social, educational, and parental environments,* eds. H. P. McAdoo and J. L. McAdoo. Beverly Hills: Sage.

Bradley, C. 1984. Issues in mathematics education for Native Americans and directions for research. *Journal for Research in Mathematics Education* 15 (2): 96–106.

Byers, P., and H. Byers. 1972. Non-verbal communication in the education of children. In *Function of language in the classroom,* eds. C. Cazden, V. John, and D. Hymes. New York: Teachers College Press.

Cadray, J. E. 1999. *The field experiences handbook.* Unpublished manuscript, Emory University, Atlanta, Georgia.

Castañeda, A., and T. Gray. 1974. Bicognitive processes in multicultural education. *Educational Leadership* 32: 203–207.

Cruickshank, D. R. 1990. *Research that informs teachers and teacher educators.* Bloomington, Indiana: Phi Delta Kappa.

Cureton, G. O. 1978. Using a black learning style. *The Reading Teacher* 31 (7): 751–756.

Cushner, K., A. McClelland, and P. Safford. 1992. *Human diversity in education.* New York: McGraw-Hill.

Davis, S. M. 1984. *Managing corporate culture.* Cambridge, MA: Ballinger Press.

Dunn, R., J. G. Gemake, and F. Jalali. 1990. Cross-cultural differences in learning styles of elementary-age students from four ethnic backgrounds. *Journal of Multicultural Counseling and Development* 18 (2): 68–93.

Eisner, E. W. 1983. The art and craft of teaching. *Educational Leadership* 40 (4): 4–13.

Erickson, F. 1986. Culture difference and science education. *The Urban Review* 18 (2): 117–124.

Feldman, R. S. 1989. In *Culture, style, and the educative process,* ed. B. J. R. Shade. Springfield: IL: Charles C. Thomas.

Giroux, H. A. 1992. Educational leadership and the crisis of democratic government. *Educational Researcher* 21 (4): 4–11.

Gollnick, D. M., and P. C. Chinn. 1998. Multicultural education in a pluralistic society. Columbus, OH: Merrill.

Grossman, H. 1984. *Educating Hispanic students.* Springfield, IL: Charles C. Thomas.

Hale-Benson, J. E. 1986. *Black children: Their roots, culture, and learning styles.* Baltimore: John Hopkins University Press.

Hilliard, A. G. 1992. Behavioral style, culture, and teaching and learning. *Journal of Negro Education* 61 (3): 370–377.

Hoopes, D. S., and M. D. Pusch. 1979. Definitions of terms. In *Multicultural education: A cross-cultural training approach,* ed. M. D. Pusch. Yarmouth, ME: Intercultural Press.

Irvine, J. J. 1990a. *Black students and school failure: Policies, practices, and prescriptions.* Westport, CT: Greenwood Press.

Irvine, J. J. 1990b. Beyond role models: An examination of cultural influences on the pedagogical perspectives of black teachers. *Peabody Journal of Education* 66 (4): 51–63.

Irvine, J. J., and R. W. Irvine. 1995. Black youth in schools: Individual achievement and institutional/cultural perspectives. In *African-American youth: Their social and economic status in the United States,* ed. R. L. Taylor. Westport, CT: Praeger.

Irvine, J. J., and D. E. York. 1995. Learning styles and culturally diverse students: A literature review. In *Handbook of research on multicultural education,* eds. J. A. Banks and C. A. Banks. New York: Macmillan.

Kilmann, R. H., M. J. Saxton, R. Serba and Associates. 1985. Introduction: Five key issues in understanding and changing culture. In *Gaining control of the corporate culture,* eds. R. H. Kilmann, M. J. Saxton, and R. Serba and Associates. San Francisco: Jossey-Bass.

King, J. E. 1991. Unfinished business: Black students alienation and black teacher's emancipatory pedagogy. In *Qualitative investigations into schools and schooling*, ed. M. Foster. New York: AMS Press.

Ladson-Billings, G. 1992. Liberatory consequences of literacy: A case of culturally relevant instruction for African American students. *Journal of Negro Education* 61 (3): 378–391.

Ladson-Billings, G. 1994. *The dreamkeepers*. San Francisco: Jossey-Bass.

Lambert, J. W. 1989. Accepting others' values in the classroom. *The Clearing House* 62: 273–274.

Longstreet, W. C. 1978. *Aspects of ethnicity*. New York: Teachers College Press.

Martin, J. R. 1995. A philosophy of education for the year 2000. *Phi Delta Kappan* 76 (5): 355–359.

Moore, C. G. 1982. *The Navajo culture and the learning of mathematics*. Washington, DC: The National Institute of Education. (ERIC Document Reproduction Service No. ED 214 708).

Nettles, M. T. 1997. The African American data book: Preschool through high school education. Fairfax, VA: The Frederick D. Patterson Research Institute.

Ogbu, J. 1988. Cultural diversity and human development. In *Black children and poverty: A developmental perspective*, ed. D. T. Slaughter. San Francisco: Jossey-Bass.

Owens, R. G. 1987. *Organizational behavior in education*. Englewoods Cliffs, NJ: Prentice Hall.

Padron, Y. N., and S. L. Knight. 1990. Linguistic and cultural influences on classroom instruction. In *Leadership, equity, and school effectiveness*, eds. H. P. Baptiste, Jr., H. C. Waxman, J. W. deFelix, and J. E. Anderson. Newbury Park, CA: Sage.

Ramírez, M., and A. Castañeda. 1974. *Cultural democracy, bicognitive development, and education*. New York: Academic Press.

Schon, D. 1987. *Educating the reflective practitioner: Toward a new design of teaching and learning professionals*. San Francisco: Jossey-Bass.

Shade, B. J. 1989. Afro-American cognitive patterns: A review of the research. In *Culture, style, and the educative process*, ed. B. J. Shade. Springfield, IL: Charles C. Thomas.

Shanker, A. 1990. The end of the traditional model of schooling and a proposal for using incentives to restructure our public schools. *Phi Delta Kappan* 71 (5): 345–357.

Smith, G. P. 1998. *Common sense about uncommon knowledge: The knowledge bases for diversity*. Washington, DC: American Association of Colleges for Teacher Education.

Villegas, A. M. 1991. *Culturally responsive pedagogy*. Washington, DC: ERIC Clearinghouse on Teacher Education.

York, D. E. 1993. *At home anywhere*. Unpublished doctoral dissertation, Emory University, Atlanta, Georgia.

Zimpher, N. L., and E. A. Ashburn. 1992. Countering parochialism in teacher candidates. In *Diversity in teacher education*, ed. M. E. Dilworth. San Francisco: Jossey-Bass.

Principles of a Culturally Responsive Curriculum

Beverly Jeanne Armento

Georgia State University

Just what does a culturally responsive classroom look like? How do culturally responsive teachers act? What do they believe? How do the students relate with one another, with the teacher, with their learning goals? How do students and teachers feel in a culturally responsive classroom?

Imagine a classroom where all students and educators feel a sense of caring, security, trust, and genuine value; where each person is treated with a sense of dignity and an expectation for outstanding performance; where each person truly wants to be present and is excited about learning and teaching; where all persons feel proud of their growth, are curious about the world, are adventuresome and aggressive about their own learning.

Is this possible? Not only is this image of a classroom possible, but it does exist in many classrooms around the world where children of different ethnicities, religions, languages, socioeconomic status (SES) levels, and beliefs meet daily to learn, play, and work together. Achieving a culturally responsive classroom is a way for educators to think about the best practices that promote maximum learning and personal growth for all children. It also is a way for educators to move closer to the twin goals of *equity* and *excellence* in education.

Educators can no longer tolerate low achievement scores, student and teacher boredom, high dropout rates, and general apathy toward learning and school by so many students, especially those students in large urban centers and those students who are from poor and culturally diverse backgrounds (Education Trust 1998; Irvine 1990). Students of color and those who are poor are entitled to an excellent education and to the full development of their academic and personal potential, as are all students. As today's world becomes more complex, as the demands of a modern education increase, and as today's students become more diverse, educators must find better ways to provide a meaningful and empowering education for *all* children.

The demographic changes in today's schools alone (Shinagawa and Jung 1998) demand new ways of organizing and implementing instruction. Diverse students bring a range of learning preferences, a range of life experiences and typical ways of relating to other people and their teachers, and basic beliefs about learning and school that may be different from the teacher's knowledge, beliefs, and views and certainly different from the dominant norms of the school.

In order to achieve the dual goals of equity and excellence in education, educators will need to pay attention to at least four major questions:

1. What do I believe about students, learning, and my responsibilities as an educator? (basic beliefs)
2. What materials, examples, and content will I use to achieve educational goals? (content and instructional examples)
3. How will I actively and meaningfully engage students' minds and hearts? (student engagement principles)
4. How will I assess student learning and growth? How will I use this information to improve teaching and learning? (learning assessment principles)

In this chapter, we will discuss and give examples of each of these four major components of a culturally responsive classroom, and we will draw upon the latest theoretical and empirical work to derive basic principles that characterize a culturally responsive classroom.

Basic Beliefs of a Culturally Responsive Educator

A culturally responsive educator is one who thinks in certain ways about students, about themselves as "teacher," and about the entire teaching-learning process. This person is one who believes in the worth, value, and competency of every child and who believes that it is the responsibility of the school and educators to ensure the maximum development of each and every student. The culturally responsive educator believes that each child should have full access to the best learning opportunities and that educators and parents are partners in the education and development of the child. Prospective educators who hold such beliefs are well on their way to developing a culturally responsive classroom and a healthy learning environment where young people feel, and are, capable and empowered.

There are at least ten basic beliefs that underlie the development of a culturally responsive learning environment. Since these beliefs form the foundation of any curriculum development or implementation, it is important to reflect on these basic ideas and think about ways we might nurture these attitudes in ourselves:

1. Culturally responsive educators hold high academic and personal expectations for each child and believe that each child can learn and should be able to develop to the maximum level of his/her potential (Darling-Hammond 2000). Holding high expectations implies having a high level of confidence in each child, believing that each child has great human potential, and believing that each child wants to learn and to be successful.
2. Culturally responsive educators provide equitable access to the necessary learning resources and sufficient opportunities to learn for each child. It is not enough to hold high standards for students; it is also necessary to build the foundation so that each child can indeed learn. Since many students have gaps in their learning, it is critical that educators know "where their students are" in their knowledge and skills and that they are able to provide the correct "next steps" so that students can effectively learn in all areas. Diagnosis and

remediation are often necessary in order for students to reach high standards in their academic studies. Watering down the curriculum or not adequately addressing gaps in knowledge and skills are unacceptable practices for culturally responsive educators.

3. Culturally responsive educators ensure that learning outcomes are meaningful, relevant, useful, and important to each child. This is done, in part, by knowing and understanding students so that personal and relevant examples can be used to illustrate content ideas (Ladson-Billings 1994; Nieto 2000). In addition, educators should help students see how their studies relate to their present lives as well as to the future. There are many linkages and applications for any area of learning, so students and teachers should become facile with thinking about "how" this learning relates to their lives. If students see no relevance for studying algebra, for example, it will be difficult for them to persist and to select other advanced mathematics courses.

4. Culturally responsive educators nurture learning-support communities for each child (families, peers, homework hotlines, community centers). Families play important roles in helping students see the value of education; in addition, families can support learning by monitoring homework, assisting with and checking homework, and by making sure the student has the necessary help to succeed (Armento and Scafidi 1999). Educators can assist families by making information available about community resources, homework hotlines, or study groups. In addition, educators can assist parents and family members in their own learning, thus increasing the enthusiasm for new ideas and new skills. Educators and caregivers should believe that it is their common goal to support the education of the child and only by working together can they enhance the growth of the student (Hoover-Dempsey and Sandler 1997).

5. Culturally responsive educators facilitate the maximum growth of each learner by making informed academic adaptations that match and build upon the learner's prior knowledge, experiences, skills, and beliefs (Au 1993). This is an important aspect of enabling each child to succeed. If learning is really a reconstruction of prior knowledge and experiences (Wittrock 1974, 1986), then educators must have some idea of what students are thinking, what they know, the misconceptions they hold (Cooper 1993), and the nature of the skills they have at their disposal. Having this knowledge and being able to make appropriate teaching and learning adaptations are very difficult professional skills. Being able to make academic adaptations means that the teacher is able to diagnose learner's strengths and weaknesses and then is able to figure out what to do next to prompt learning. This is particularly difficult if there are many struggling learners in a class; however, it is impossible to promote real learning if the learner is not actively building on their prior knowledge and skills to create new ideas.

6. Culturally responsive educators build positive and supportive school and classroom learning environments that are grounded in mutual and genuine respect for cultural diversity (Cochran-Smith 1995). This belief implies learning about and valuing customs, beliefs, traditions, and mores that are unfamiliar to the teacher and to other students. It also implies basing the human interactions in the school and classroom on human dignity principles, on a sense of respect for each person, and on attitudes of optimism and hope. People are treated with civility, with gentleness, and with support, and students learn how to relate to one another with these basic principles. Disagreements are handled with discussion and with respect for alternative positions, not with attitudes of dogmatism and anger.

7. Culturally responsive educators promote classroom climates built on social justice, democracy, and equity (Delpit 1988; Villegas 1991). In other words, students play critical roles in the development of the classroom and school community, its rules, consequences, and ways people relate to one another. Students are treated as individuals, are provided with equal access to learning resources, and are nurtured as special and creative young people. In a democratic classroom, educators and students discuss the issues and problems that arise and make consensus decisions about how these matters will be handled. As developmentally appropriate, students must be encouraged to make choices and decisions that have increasing degrees of difficulty and importance.

8. Culturally responsive educators promote individual empowerment, self-efficacy, positive self-regard, and a belief in societal reform (Banks 1993). Education is viewed as a vehicle for empowerment, for it brings not only knowledge about the ways things are, but also ideas about the issues and the ways things could be. Students are encouraged to feel strong and as though they can influence policy decisions. In order for such feelings of self-efficacy to develop, students should have experiences with real-life problems and should move past decision making to action. Taking social action on issues that are within the life span of the child is an important aspect of feeling that one has important ideas and that one can make a difference in the community. Students in culturally responsive classrooms not only learn "how" the world is but also look beneath the surface to investigate hidden issues. They are encouraged to reflect on important matters, such as equity issues, and to act in proactive ways at school and in the community.

9. Culturally responsive educators value diversity as well as human commonalities (Greene 1993). As *Homo sapiens sapiens,* all humans share certain essential human qualities. As members of a democratic society, we share certain core values such as respect for the individual and our common entitlement to liberty, equality, and justice. These aspects of our common traits and values leave plenty of room for the full range of diversity and individuality to flourish. Diversity refers to culture, ethnicity, race, gender, language, religion, values, and physical/mental abilities/disabilities that characterize each person. Culturally responsive educators promote respect for the uniqueness of each person as well as for the ways we are similar.

10. Culturally responsive educators believe that it is their role and responsibility to provide effective and empowering instruction for each child (Oakes and Lipton 1999). Educators must believe it is their role to address the learning needs of each child, regardless of the academic gaps or issues of the child; this might mean ensuring that the child has the necessary learning resources, making important instructional adaptations for the child, or spending extra instructional time with the child to guarantee success. This belief is a very important one for culturally responsive educators to hold, even though it is not a popular value. Many educators believe that if a child has major learning issues, it is someone else's job to address the needs of the child. Thus, students who are several grade levels behind their classmates in reading or mathematics are often left to try to figure out how to adapt by themselves. These students are the ones who become lost in the system, bored, and frustrated because they cannot comprehend their studies. These are the students who will be absent from school, become behavior problems, and eventually drop out with a minimal education and few academic and technical skills. Culturally responsive educators believe that they themselves are responsible for each child and his/her learning and academic growth, and they take this role seriously as they seek the resources needed by each child to fully succeed.

Culturally Responsive Educators
1. Hold high academic and personal expectations for each child.
2. Provide for each child equitable access to the necessary learning resources and sufficient opportunities to learn.
3. Ensure that learning outcomes are meaningful, relevant, useful, and important to each child.
4. Nurture learning-support communities for each child (families, peers, homework hotlines, community centers).
5. Facilitate the maximum growth of each learner by making informed academic adaptations that match and build upon the learner's prior knowledge, experiences, skills, and beliefs.
6. Build positive and supportive school and classroom learning environments that are grounded in mutual and genuine respect for cultural diversity.
7. Promote classroom climates built on social justice, democracy, and equity.
8. Promote individual empowerment, self-efficacy, positive self-regard, and a belief in societal reform.
9. Value diversity as well as human commonalities.
10. Believe that it is their role and responsibility to provide effective and empowering instruction for each child.

These ten basic beliefs of culturally responsive educators form the foundation for effective teaching and learning for all students and are the basis of equity and excellence in the classroom. Educators who hold these basic beliefs are well on their way to establishing wholesome classrooms where each child is able to flourish and where students will learn the essence of democratic ways of behaving and thinking.

Let us now consider the essential elements of teaching and learning that characterize a culturally responsive curriculum. There are many aspects of this issue that could be addressed. We have chosen three critical areas: (1) the content of the curriculum and the content of the instructional examples that are used, (2) the ways we engage students in the learning process, and (3) the ways we assess student learning. For our purposes, we have used the following terms: instructional examples (IE); student engagement (SE); and assessment (A). The question we asked is, What is it about diversity, equity, and excellence that interacts with the choices we make when we select instructional examples, when we decide what pedagogy to use to engage learners, and when we decide how to assess learning and how to use that information? We will discuss each of these three major areas of teaching and learning and from the discussions, derive basic principles that could be used by culturally responsive educators to make curricular and instructional decisions.

We turn now to consideration of the curriculum and the instructional examples that allow the teacher to address the needs of today's diverse student body.

Content Principles/Instructional Examples (IE)

What content should be included in the curriculum studied by students? How are curricular examples selected, by whom, and with what criteria? These questions are among the most controversial in education today.

In this section, we will discuss the principles that should guide our thinking about the content of curriculum. These principles are selected to highlight here because of their relevance to a culturally responsive curriculum: *inclusiveness, alternative perspectives, commonalities as well as diversity, and student-constructed examples*. There are several factors that influence our thinking about the content of the curriculum;

among the most important are these: the nature of scholarship in all areas is changing rapidly, prompting us to consider new interpretations and new information; the world is "shrinking," prompting new considerations about what students should know; and the nature of our diverse society is prompting us to consider just what is a democratic curriculum. Let's discuss each of these factors.

THE NATURE OF SCHOLARSHIP IS CHANGING

Scholars in all areas have uncovered new data and thus have made new interpretations about so many topics and issues over the last few decades that the body of knowledge has become very large. Therefore, it is more difficult to decide what content should be studied at various developmental stages. The changing nature of the knowledge base is more obvious in some fields than in others. For example, social studies knowledge has expanded rapidly as more diverse scholars joined the ranks of historians, political scientists, and anthropologists; asked new questions; and sought data in new or recently uncovered data sources. These scholars helped to develop the fields of African American history, Native American history, and Latino history, and these fields have gained increasing acceptability and more inclusion in the mainstream history of the country and the world (Nash 1992). We now recognize the history most of us studied in school was one interpretation of the way things were. As we look at issues and events from different perspectives and with new data in front of us, the events and issues may take on new meanings. As we know more about what did happen in the past, the study of history, for example, becomes more complex and perhaps more controversial. However, it also becomes more accurate, more complete, more honest, and a more in-depth study than ever before. Academic studies also become more interesting as we read the stories of the actions, struggles, and contributions of more members of society and as we ask more critical questions about the causes and effects of events.

Technological advances such as space exploration, the development of computer technologies, and advances in the biological and other natural-science fields have prompted discoveries in almost all areas of life. Knowledge of the human body and research in space have enabled the development of new and more powerful ways of treating human illness; research has brought about major technological changes in the ways we grow our food, develop our resources, defend ourselves, and construct our buildings and cities. Along with these advances have come new issues and problems as we struggle with the value choices imbedded in such trade-offs as the competing demands of development and conservation, wellness and animal experimentation, and technological know-how and the quality and ethics of life. In many ways, technological advances have proceeded at a faster rate than our ability to deal with the ethical and value issues these advances have brought about. Thus, the study of science has changed dramatically as we try to facilitate thoughtfulness and critical thinking in today's youth on important scientific and social issues.

Today, we have more knowledge in all fields, and we are also faced with new issues that are perplexing and complex. These facts make it more difficult for educators to decide *which* knowledge students should learn and *when* they should study certain topics and issues. As we know that the body of knowledge will continue to increase and shed new light on major issues as new discoveries are made, it is important for students to learn how to learn, how to stay abreast of changes in the knowledge base, and how to critically assess the accuracy and validity of new information. These skills and abilities must also become an integral part of any relevant curriculum for today's young people.

THE WORLD IS SHRINKING

Today, we can travel to almost any part of the world in record time and can communicate with friends and strangers in seconds using computer technologies. Migration has changed the face of most nations in the world as people move voluntarily or involuntarily to seek better lives for themselves and their families, as they settle in new areas, work alongside diverse colleagues, and send their children to schools that are now more diverse than ever, in more countries than ever. In addition, most countries in the world are interdependent because of their economic and political linkages with one another. We depend upon other countries for many of life's necessities, trade extensively with many countries, and citizens of one country often own resources and businesses in other countries. Even the most isolated countries in the world today, such as Cuba and North Korea, must engage with others in order to survive.

Today's young people must learn more about the world in order to better live and work alongside others who come from lands and cultures that are very different from their own. In today's global and interdependent world, and in a world where information is accessed instantaneously, it is imperative that educators rethink the content of the curriculum and the critical thinking processes needed by today's youth. In order to better understand our new friends, classmates, coworkers, and fellow citizens, we should know something of their culture, basic values and beliefs, their customs and ways of living. Schools and school systems must address questions of diversity and find better ways to educate all children and better ways to communicate with their parents, many of whom will speak only one language, and that will not be English. In some classrooms in the world today, we find students who are facile with four to five different languages, in classrooms where educators know only their mother tongue. Such situations pose new and exciting challenges for educators who believe in equity and excellence goals for all students.

CREATING A DEMOCRATIC CURRICULUM IS A CHALLENGE

In a democratic society such as our own, we pride ourselves on telling young people that this is a nation "of the people, for the people, and by the people." If so, then, should not all the people see themselves and their ancestors and their cultures represented in the pages of the curriculum? Should not all students see their own reflection in the curriculum, not merely to help them "feel good" but because their ancestors really did play integral roles in the history of this country? Should not young people read literature from all parts of the world, not only to "increase their self-esteem" but because such literature is important in its own right, is part of the richness established by the human mind, and because such literature informs us of the beliefs and traditions of others? Should not educators use cultural examples to illustrate important concepts and ideas, not to "improve self-identity" but because such examples are familiar to students and promote more meaningful learning? In other words, inclusion of diversity in the curriculum makes pedagogical and content good sense. Inclusion of diverse peoples, ideas, and cultures also contributes to making a curriculum that is more complete, honest, and accurate and that better represents the full picture of the past and of any field of study.

Even if we believe in inclusion of diversity in the curriculum, we are still faced with the problem of just how much inclusion? Can all persons be equally represented? Can all points of view be represented? Is it possible to build a curriculum that is honest and based on current scholarship and yet promotes good citizenship and attitudes of civic participation? Can a curriculum raise controversial issues and yet enable students to become analytical and thoughtful, not cynical and dogmatic? As an educator, you will continue to grapple with these and other important curricular issues throughout your career, for you will soon see that there are a range of opinions on these matters today and that these issues are complex and not easily addressed. Yet, we do believe that it is possible to build a more balanced, honest, and inclusive curriculum than ever before and that culturally responsive educators who hold the beliefs we discussed earlier can indeed implement such a democratic curriculum to promote thoughtfulness, civic responsibility, and civic action in young people.

From these considerations, we have derived four basic principles that address the content choices we have as we develop a culturally responsive curriculum. The question for the educator is, What materials, instructional examples, and content will I use to achieve learning goals? The content principles we will highlight are (1) inclusiveness, (2) alternative perspectives, (3) commonalities as well as diversity, and (4) student-constructed examples.

Culturally Responsive Curriculum Principles

Instructional Examples (IE)
IE 1 = Cultural examples used in the curriculum; Inclusion
IE 2 = Alternative perspectives
IE 3 = Diversity and commonalities
IE 4 = Culturally relevant and student-generated images/metaphors/examples

Student Engagement (SE)
SE 1 = Purpose/curiosity/anticipation
SE 2 = Multiple learning preferences
SE 3 = Individual/unison/team communications
SE 4 = Cooperative/competitive/individual goals
SE 5 = Student choices/decision making

Assessment (A)
A 1 = On-going assessment, using a range of materials
A 2 = Assessment information to provide feedback and inform instruction
A 3 = Special accommodations for special learners

(IE 1) INCLUSIVENESS

The child's voice and heritage should be heard and represented in content examples. Authentic cultural data, literature, music, art, artifacts, primary source materials, and cultural history should be used in the curriculum to represent the full range of relevant persons and groups that should be included in historical or other studies. An inclusive, rich, and varied array of instructional examples should be used to portray the fullness, accuracy, and completeness of life in the past and present. The question is not, Who is in my class this year, and how can I represent them in the curriculum? (Such a question will yield limited and narrow definitions of inclusion.) Rather, educators must ask, During the time period we are studying, or the event, or the issue, or the genre, or the scientific theme, who is relevant and should be included in this study? When we ask this question, we are implying that the teacher knows the answer. It will be the case that each of us will need to do some research on many of the topics we are asked to teach, for our own knowledge of diversity is limited. However, the first step is to ask the question and then to inquire about the answer. Students can and should become inquirers along with the teacher, for they must learn that any one source will usually not provide all the necessary information.

(IE 2) ALTERNATIVE PERSPECTIVES

Alternative views should be presented, especially on controversial issues or with topics that look different from different perspectives. When we step out of our own shoes and examine an issue or topic from the view of another person who holds different beliefs, we can see why there is so much controversy and disagreement over so many matters. It is difficult to see the other person's point of view, for we do not have much practice taking on alternative perspectives. Yet, this skill of *perspective taking* is perhaps one of the most important analytical tools in the modern person's repertoire. Unless we are able to see issues from a range of perspectives, we will have trouble reaching a consensus and will have less tolerance for those with differing views.

From a historical perspective, it is easy to see that most of us learned the stories of the past from one main view, a Eurocentric view. When one examines topics such as slavery, discovery of North America, "Westward Expansion," or labor unions from the views of African Americans, Native Americans, or the working class, however, new facts and new issues arise, and the topic takes on a new complexity. It is through the analysis and interpretation of the entire body of data surrounding an issue that the full story can be known. Looking at an issue or event from the vantage point of different people and groups who were invested in the issue for different reasons gives the student a more complete view. In a culturally responsive approach to curriculum, students study about history, literature, and the humanities through the eyes of different groups of people and are challenged to address the conflicting interpretations. In the natural sciences, people also hold different interpretations about a number of important topics; here also, as developmentally appropriate, students should examine data in light of alternative interpretations.

(IE 3) DIVERSITY AND COMMONALITIES

Culturally responsive curriculum and educators stress diversity as well as the commonalities that unite all humans. It is important that students realize the bonds that unite all humans and the members of particular societies. As members of the same species, *Homo sapiens sapiens,* each of us shares common human traits and characteristics. As members of particular societies, we are bound together by the common values of the society. For example, basic principles of justice, equity, the value of the individual, and the importance of democratic ideals form the foundation of the United States and guide policy decisions and practical choices.

It is also important that the full range of human diversity be recognized as the factor that makes each person unique and interesting. Understanding the groups to which we belong brings a certain amount of pride, self-esteem, and self-knowledge. These positive feelings are critical to the development of a wholesome self-concept and pride in one's identity. By the same token, such feelings of pride in one's group do not have to conflict with one's respect for others who identify with different groups. For example, my pride in being an Italian American should only enhance my respect for others who are different from me. It is also critical that students and educators learn to not overgeneralize about the members of any particular ethnic, gender, cultural, or religious group; members of any group are unique and may not hold similar beliefs, values, or patterns of behavior as others in the group.

(IE 4) STUDENT-CONSTRUCTED EXAMPLES

Concrete representations, images, metaphors, examples, and graphic organizers (Wittrock 1974, 1986) should be culturally and experientially relevant and should be generated by students and teachers to give meaning and depth to learning tasks. Especially when students are learning new ideas, they should be presented with examples of the concept that they recognize. It is particularly important that vocabulary, references, and examples are familiar to the students. Starting with what students know enables the teacher to build a bridge from the known to the new knowledge. Building from the known examples, teachers can introduce information, examples, and ideas that are new to the student.

Conceptual learning is demonstrated when learners are able to apply ideas to new examples and when they are able to provide examples from their own experience.

It is important to encourage students to construct their own examples of new ideas for a number of reasons. First of all, the student is able to see that the new idea has relevance and does exist in his/her own life and is able to verbally name examples in a range of ways. In addition, the teacher is able to test for understanding of new ideas when students are able to provide examples that match the meaning of the new idea.

Student Engagement Principles (SE)

Active student engagement (Wittrock 1986) lies at the heart of meaningful learning and effective teaching. From the learners' perspective, they are actively engaged in learning when their curiosity is aroused and they see a *purpose* in learning; when the instructional tasks appeal to the full range of *learning modes* (Irvine and York 1995); when they are able to practice *comfortable communication patterns;* when they are able to *relate to other learners* in meaningful ways; and when they are given *choices and decisions* while learning.

Learning is a complex and quite an amazing phenomenon that involves a wide array of cognitive and affective processes. We believe that learning is a reorganization of prior ideas, a process wherein the learner must tap into memory and recall ideas and information that are related to the new learning (Wittrock 1974, 1986). Learners must pay attention to the new examples, must make active comparisons with their old ideas, and must make judgments about the similarities and differences of the new ideas with the old. In many cases, the learners will literally "throw out" old ideas that are no longer useful. If the learner recognizes that old ideas are inaccurate or incomplete, the learner makes active adjustments in the brain and stores the new and improved ideas (Vosniadou and Brewer 1987). This active and dynamic process of adding, refining, retiring, and reconstructing ideas and information is a lifelong process that characterizes human learning. The learning process is facilitated by motivation, curiosity, interest, and purpose. In other words, learners generally have some genuine reason or driving force or purpose that motivates them to want to learn. All things being equal, one might expect that the stronger the sense of purpose and the deeper and more intense the cognitive and affective engagement, the greater will be the learning outcomes. In addition, learning is maximized if the new ideas and information are matched to the prior knowledge and skills of the learner and if the learner is able to see the linkages between what is already known and what is to be learned. In other words, if there is a large skill or knowledge gap between prior knowledge and the new learning, learners are apt to feel confused, frustrated, and lost, for they will be unable to make meaningful linkages between what they know and what they are trying to learn. In such cases, the teacher must "build a bridge" or "scaffold" the transition from prior knowledge to new learning. This can be done by using advance organizers, vocabulary linkages, and visual connections between the new and prior knowledge.

Cultural diversity influences learning in a number of significant ways. A culture represents a total way of life, a set of values and norms for behaving and thinking, a set of shared experiences and beliefs. To a great extent, *culture influences what is held in prior knowledge* by the group members. To the extent that experiences, language, roles, and beliefs differ among groups (whether these groups are defined by ethnicity, gender, class, religion, language, or disability), one would expect that people in these groups know different things, see the world in different ways, and prioritize things differently. It is important that educators recognize this important notion, think more consciously about the rich prior knowledge held by each child, and find creative ways to incorporate children's current knowledge into the learning experience.

CULTURAL AND RELIGIOUS BELIEFS INFLUENCE WHAT IS VIEWED AS IMPORTANT AND MAY ACT AS A LENS FOR FILTERING NEW IDEAS AND INFORMATION

Group values may influence the weight a person gives to certain kinds of information and to the value one gives to a formal education itself. Persons holding certain beliefs may dismiss data if they believe the information is not in keeping with their values. Extreme examples of such persons might be viewed as dogmatic, closed minded, or unable to see other points of view.

CULTURE INFLUENCES THE WAYS PEOPLE RELATE TO ONE ANOTHER AND THE WAYS PEOPLE COMMUNICATE IN DIFFERENT SETTINGS

In some cultures, people relate to one another in hierarchical, lineage ways, with generational respect given to the elders. Such respect may be communicated in a range of ways, from dropped eyes and head in the presence of adults to deference to the adults in speaking, taking turns, and in queuing behavior. Many Asian cultures are organized in primarily hierarchical ways. In other cultures, people relate to one another in collateral or group ways, with age groups often taking on equal status. These societies tend to be cooperative, especially within equal status groups, and value the group highly. Many Native American, African American, and Latino cultures are organized in primarily collateral ways, with values that promote cooperation and group decision making. Some other societies are primarily individualistic; here, the individual is seen as the primary focus of attention. The dominant European American orientation is individualistic, and values of competition and individual achievement are evident in many arenas, including education. For example, it is the individual who is expected to succeed, to respond to questions, and to perform academic tasks by oneself. The individualistic pattern has been the dominant one used in classrooms in the United States; this has resulted in patterns of individualistic response modes and individualistic goal structures. That is, teacher talk leads to a question directed to one student; that student responds to the teacher. This individualistic pattern of talk dominates most classrooms today.

One must be careful to not overgeneralize when making statements like those we just made about the dominant patterns of groups. It must always be remembered that individuals within any group may differ dramatically from these dominant patterns and that we cannot know about individuals, their beliefs, their behavior, and their preferences simply because of their membership in certain groups.

In addition, it is important to recognize that in any society, people relate to one another and communicate with one another in a range of ways. The more diverse the society, such as ours, the more variation one will find in roles, values, modes of communication, and ways of behaving and relating with one another. Thus, students should have opportunities in their classrooms to develop and practice the skills and interactive patterns they will experience in their society and in the world. It is through such practice and skill development that students will be able to interact successfully with others in the complex and diverse world.

How is it that educators can most effectively engage students in the tasks of learning, while taking into consideration the variations in their students? How might students' minds, bodies, and affect best connect and interact with their learning tasks? How can we facilitate students' active construction of new ideas and the reorganization of prior knowledge, especially when we know that students bring a wide range of knowledge and skills into the classroom? How should we relate with and communicate with students in today's diverse classrooms in order to build on the strengths already existing and develop within students the full range of possibilities?

We propose five major dimensions of teacher-student interaction and engagement that should be considered when constructing effective teaching-learning situations: (1) creating a purpose for learning; (2) addressing the full range of learning modes; (3) considering the oral and written communication patterns of the students; (4) considering the range of interactive patterns possible for goal attainment; and (5) addressing the power relationships in the classroom and the ownership of learning by students through the choices and decisions they make. Let's discuss the five student engagement principles.

(SE 1) CREATING A PURPOSE FOR LEARNING, OR "WHY SHOULD I BOTHER LEARNING THIS?"

Students should see the value of accomplishing the task at hand, and should have a sense of curiosity, purpose, and anticipation about learning. Teachers should develop a reason for learning, a reason for reading, a reason for watching a video, a reason for reading a poem or original data source, as well as a sense of puzzlement, investigation, excitement, and energy for learning. Without such motivation (Kohl 1994), it is going to be difficult for students to pay attention, to be fully engaged in the learning tasks, and to relate their prior understandings to the new ideas. Educators often have to be creative in the ways they invite their students into a learning situation; in the highly stimulating world of today's children, it is becoming ever more challenging for teachers to capture the attention of their students. However, without full student engagement, learning cannot be maximized.

(SE 2) ADDRESSING THE FULL RANGE OF LEARNING MODES, OR "MY MIND IS COMPLEX AND UNIQUE."

Educators should appeal to the full range of student learning preferences and modes (Irvine and York 1995). In order to build on the knowledge and skills students bring to the classroom, teachers must explore the prior knowledge, the ideas, misconceptions, and beliefs of the students. It is helpful to believe that each child is unique and comes to the classroom with a wealth of experience and knowledge. In addition, learners are different in the ways they like to learn and have certain preferences when it comes to visual, verbal, kinesthetic, interpersonal, or other modes of seeing and doing. It is important to build on the areas of strength but also to extend and enlighten the other modalities of learners. In other words, if a student prefers gaining information through reading and verbal means, this area should be strengthened; however, since all humans possess the full range of learning modes and abilities, other areas should also be developed.

(SE 3) CONSIDERING THE ORAL/WRITTEN COMMUNICATION PATTERNS OF STUDENTS, OR "ME . . . TALK?"

There are many ways of communicating, and educators should become familiar with the communication and language patterns of their diverse students and the ways the values of their cultures set standards for communicating. Many classrooms are fairly unidimensional in their communication patterns: the teacher asks a question to one student, the student answers; the teacher asks another question, and another student answers. This individualistic mode of responding is the dominant pattern and is comfortable for many students. However, there are other methods. Students could respond in unison to questions; students could work in pairs or teams and could respond collectively in these small groups; students could enact responses or could create essays, poems, or letters to the editor. Giving students choices in the ways they respond to questions and tasks allows students to select their own individual cultural and academic comfort zone.

(SE 4) CONSIDERING THE RANGE OF INTERACTIVE PATTERNS, OR "WITH WHOM SHALL I WORK TO ACHIEVE THE LEARNING GOALS?"

Students can achieve learning goals by working cooperatively with a partner or with a team; by working individually, or by competing against another student or students. Students have different individual, cultural, and academic comfort zones with these various goal and interactive structures, as do teachers. In a highly individualistic and competitive society such as ours, it is often difficult for teachers, parents, and students to learn to cooperate in group endeavors. Yet, in the world of work and in so many aspects of life, students will need to work successfully in cooperative groups. However, there are times when working alone or in competitive situations is not only healthy but can result in meaningful learning.

(SE 5) ADDRESSING THE POWER RELATIONSHIPS IN THE CLASSROOM AND PASSING THE OWNERSHIP FOR LEARNING TO THE STUDENT, OR "MUST I DO IT THAT WAY?"

Teachers can provide opportunities for students to make choices and decisions about alternative assignments that represent achievement of the learning goals. Allowing student choice and decision making shifts the ownership and responsibility for learning to the student and can serve as an empowering mechanism. Students, though, should be allowed to make meaningful choices, not merely whether they will prepare an essay or a short story. Opportunities for student choice and decision should be developmentally appropriate and should increase as students mature.

Learning Assessment Principles (A)

How do we know if students have indeed mastered specific academic and social goals? How do we know where to begin instruction with students in a diverse classroom? How do we know how much progress students have made toward the learning goals? Assessment of learning is an integral component of any teaching-learning situation and if performed with skill and sensitivity, should yield important information for the student, the parent, and the teacher (Oakes 1990). There are three fundamental learning assessment principles: (1) assessment should be ongoing and should occur in a range of contexts; (2) assessment should provide valuable information to the student and teacher and should indicate areas for reteaching or refinement; and (3) assessment should be modified for students with special needs.

(A 1) ASSESSMENT SHOULD BE ONGOING AND SHOULD OCCUR IN A RANGE OF CONTEXTS, WITH A RANGE OF MATERIALS AND TECHNIQUES

One cannot rely on one or a few measures to tell us anything reliable about what and how much a student knows. A range of data sources will give a more complete picture of the child's knowledge and skill. Assessment can and should be happening in many contexts, with the teacher alert to unobtrusive data sources as well as the more formal tests and evaluation measures.

(A 2) ASSESSMENT INFORMATION SHOULD PROVIDE FEEDBACK TO INFORM INSTRUCTION

Teachers should recognize skill and knowledge gaps and should supplement and enrich learning tasks, as needed. It is critical to address the learning gaps of students prior to going on with the normal instruction. If students have major reading issues or learning difficulties, these issues must take priority over any attempt to cover the material. Successful teachers make many adaptations in the course of a day to address the information they are continuously gathering on the levels of comprehension of their students. This ability is difficult to develop, for it demands a sound knowledge of the content and a good grasp of child development. In addition, the knowledgeable teacher is able to make inferences about a child's misconceptions from the child's oral and written work.

(A 3) SPECIAL ACCOMMODATIONS SHOULD BE MADE FOR SPECIAL LEARNERS

Special assessment accommodations should be made with learners who need particular assistance with learning. This might include students with linguistic, intellectual, or cultural issues that interact with the learning tasks in such a way as to demand a special approach. It is the teacher's responsibility to either make these special accommodations or to see that the services are provided for the student. Some students will need more time to take tests or will need assistance with translation or reading. In addition, some students need more structured tasks than other students and can perform well when given prompts.

Conclusion

We have presented a framework for thinking about decisions educators make in order to promote high expectations for all students and learning opportunities that will allow students to achieve to their maximum potential. We have discussed the necessary beliefs an effective educator must have in order to successfully develop and implement a culturally responsive curriculum. In addition, we have thought about the content of the curriculum and the ways we can build a more accurate and honest curriculum. Since learning is the focus of this discussion, we focused on the ways students become meaningfully engaged with learning and the aspects of this engagement that might interact with aspects of diversity. In addition, we addressed the issue of assessment.

There are many ways to implement the culturally responsive principles developed here. In the following chapters, you will find a unit in language arts, one in mathematics, one in science, and one in social studies. Each chapter demonstrates different approaches to unit construction and to the application of the culturally responsive principles. For example, the language arts unit challenges young children to respond to a real situation—their need to communicate with another class. This "real purpose" is an important driving force in the *Stories* unit, for students know they have an audience for their writing. In turn, the students will have opportunities to take on the role of the reader or recipient of the story. Students have opportunities to tell stories aloud, to dictate stories, and to write stories. If accessible, cameras make a wonderful addition to a unit like this, for students can capture visual images in their lives to accompany their stories.

The math and science units emphasize the inclusion of cultural examples (patterns and stories about weather). The math unit calls upon learners to examine and compare cloth, rugs, and other cultural artifacts to learn geometry and measurement concepts. The science unit actively engages students as they conduct experiments and make hypotheses about weather patterns. Since everyone experiences weather, it is easy to arouse student interest and excitement in this topic. Students are actively engaged in prediction, analysis of data, and investigations of weather patterns.

Other cultural examples could be used in either the math or science unit, depending on the class access to these examples. In both the math and science units, students have opportunities to interact with one another and with the content in a range of ways, with assessment occurring daily. In addition, both the math and science units provide opportunities for discussions about social and historical issues.

The social studies unit actively engages students in an important social issue: the rights of the citizens in a democracy to express their opinion and to vote. This unit is an *additive inquiry* unit, or one in which new data are "added" to each lesson to help students see patterns and to help them raise important questions. The social studies unit demonstrates inclusiveness by addressing the rights of people of color, women, and others to vote. In each lesson, students examine the reasons for change and the ways the issue might look to different groups. In addition, students are called upon to address the ways all people are similar in a democracy; that is, each is entitled to certain rights and has certain responsibilities. There are many opportunities in the social studies unit for students to generate their own historical or contemporary examples of voting/representation issues. Since each lesson is structured in a similar pattern, this repetition serves to scaffold the learning experience for students. This structural scaffolding frees the student to concentrate on the new primary sources added to each lesson and to reflect on the substantive issues of the unit.

The social studies unit aims to actively engage students' curiosity by having them take on the roles of people with different characteristics. Such role taking is an effective technique for engaging students and also for helping them to see other points of view. In addition, the social studies unit encourages students to work individually and in teams/groups to achieve learning goals. Students can also express their ideas in a range of ways and have opportunities to make meaningful choices.

The teacher has many ongoing opportunities to assess student understanding, using the information to make instructional adaptations in pacing, questioning, and complexity of data sources.

As you read the four units, try to identify the *content* and *student engagement principles* and the modes and range of assessment techniques used. Think about other ways you could apply the principles of a culturally responsive curriculum to each unit. What adaptations would you make for your own class? How would you implement these units to demonstrate your basic beliefs about *equity* and *excellence* in education?

REFERENCES

Armento, B., and B. Scafidi. 1999. *Promoting parental involvement in middle school*. Research Atlanta, Inc. School of Policy Studies, Georgia State University, Atlanta, GA.

Au, K. H. 1993. *Literacy instruction in multicultural settings*. New York: Harcourt, Brace.

Banks, J. A. 1993. Multicultural education: Development, dimensions, and challenges. *Phi Delta Kappan* 75 (1): 22–28.

Cochran-Smith, M. 1995. Uncertain allies: Understanding the boundaries of race and teaching. *Harvard Educational Review* 65 (4): 541–570.

Cooper, J. D. 1993. *Literacy: Helping children construct meaning*. Boston: Houghton Mifflin.

Darling-Hammond, L. 2000. Teacher quality and student achievement. *Education Policy Quarterly* 8 (1): 1–50.

Delpit, L. D. 1988. The silenced dialogue: Power and pedagogy in educating other people's children. *Harvard Educational Review* 58 (3): 280–298.

Education Trust. 1998. *Education watch: State and national data book*. Vol. 2. Washington, DC.

Greene, M. 1993. Diversity and inclusion: Toward a curriculum for human beings. *Teachers College Record* 95 (2): 211–221.

Hoover-Dempsey, K. V., and H. M. Sandler. 1997. Why do parents become involved in their children's education? *Review of Educational Research* 67:3–42.

Irvine, J. J. 1990. *Black students and school failure*. Westport, CT: Greenwood Press.

Irvine, J. J., and E. D. York. 1995. Learning styles and culturally diverse students: A literature review. In *Handbook of research on multicultural education*, eds. J. Banks and C. McGee Banks. New York: Macmillan.

Kohl, H. 1994. *"I won't learn from you" and other thoughts on creative maladjustment*. New York: New Press.

Ladson-Billings, G. 1994. *The dreamkeepers: Successful teachers of African American children*. San Francisco: Jossey-Bass.

Nash, G., coordinating author. 1992. *A teacher's guide to multicultural perspectives in social studies*. Boston: Houghton Mifflin.

Nieto, S. 2000. *Affirming diversity: The sociopolitical context of multicultural education*. 3rd ed. New York: Longman.

Oakes, J. 1990. *Multiplying inequalities: The effects of race, social class, and tracking on opportunities to learn mathematics and science*. Santa Monica, CA: Rand.

Oakes, J., and M. Lipton. 1999. *Teaching to change the world*. Boston: McGraw-Hill.

Shinagawa, L. H,. and M. Jung. 1998. *Atlas of American diversity*. Walnut Creek, CA: AltaMira Press.

Villegas, A. M. 1991. *Culturally responsive pedagogy for the 1990s and beyond*. Trends and Issues paper No. 6. Washington, DC: ERIC Clearinghouse on Teacher Education.

Vosniadou, S., and W. F. Brewer. 1987. Theories of knowledge restructuring in development. *Review of Educational Research* 57 (1): 51–67.

Wittrock, M. C. 1974. Learning as a generative process. *Educational Psychologist* 11: 87–95.

Wittrock, M. C. 1986. Students' thought processes. In *Handbook of research on teaching*. 3rd ed. Ed. M. C. Wittrock. New York: Macmillan.

Stories, Stories, Stories
Culturally Responsive Language Arts Lessons
K—2nd Grades
Story Writing and Storytelling

Goals and Objectives

Goals

1. Students will build upon their personal experiences and cultural background and develop and extend their knowledge and skills in reading, writing, listening, and speaking.
2. Students will develop their skills as authors and storytellers.
3. Students will appreciate the wealth of story materials in their own experiences and communities.
4. Students will enhance their self-esteem through valuing their own experiences and successfully translating these into creative oral and written outcomes.

Objectives

1. Each student will participate as speaker and listener in large and small group discussions.
2. Each student will demonstrate a sense of audience in preparing and delivering oral presentations.
3. Each student will expand listening and speaking vocabularies through practice in informal and semiformal settings.
4. Each student will plan and organize a narrative that tells a story.
5. Each student will write, revise, edit, and present a narrative in finished form.
6. Each student will expand reading and writing vocabularies.
7. Each student will read and comprehend literature.

Ramona S. Frasher

Georgia State University

with

Anne S. Crane, Georgia State University
Mary Mohead, Atlanta Public Schools
Delores Turner, Atlanta Public Schools

Introduction

The ability to use language is one of the defining characteristics of being human. Language enables one to communicate with others, to obtain and use information, to give and receive meaning, to express ideas, to solve problems, and to meet one's needs. Individuals who become skilled and effective users of language have at their disposal a means of self-empowerment that provides them access to opportunities in educational, political, and economic endeavors. In infancy and early childhood, language develops naturally, and children learn to speak and understand the language of home and community without formal instruction. The continuation of language development for most children occurs in school, in the form of literacy, or learning to negotiate written language to expand and extend the uses of oral language. Enabling children to achieve competence and confidence in oral and written language use is, without doubt, one of the most important tasks of the school. The primary responsibility for this task is assumed by the language arts teacher.

Research on the development of language in children has produced a body of knowledge with highly practical implications for literacy instruction. Early language learning is participative and interactive. Children's initial experiences with language occur in environments that are meaningful and empowering; they take place in contexts that relate to their needs, desires, and interests. Children learn very early the value and uses of language in their community. They come to school with a store of language ability and experience that can facilitate the transition from oral skill to literacy. It is important that language arts teachers capitalize on the knowledge students bring to the classroom and that they acknowledge and use the language and cultural strengths of their students in their instructional programs. Packaged language arts programs, prepared for widespread use throughout the country, cannot by themselves address the needs of youngsters in today's classrooms. Rather than bridging the gap between the student's experience and school learning, current methods and materials often widen it, sometimes so much that there is little meaningful communication between student and teacher. What language arts teachers need to support their genuine desire to open and develop the wonderful world of literacy for their students is an approach that emphasizes students' strengths—their language, experiences, culture, and values.

The framework for culturally responsive curriculum development presented in this book provides the principles for just such an approach. More specifically, the lessons in this unit give teachers permission to tailor their instruction to the children they actually work with in their classroom. Firmly based in research and teacher experience, culturally responsive pedagogy sets the stage for effective teaching and learning of the language arts. In traditional programs, the content of the language arts is often reduced to sets of textbooks and support materials for reading, writing, spelling, grammar, literature—often taught separately, with little attention to the wholeness of language and the interrelationships among its various oral and written aspects. Materials are usually selected because they represent a skill and the type of subject matter to be taught. Certainly these are criteria to be considered, for the teaching of literacy skills and relevant content is just as essential for culturally responsive pedagogy as for any traditional model. What the latter provides, however, are the overriding considerations of how the skill is to be taught and what content is relevant for the students as well as for the learning outcomes.

Culturally responsive pedagogy calls for a curriculum that recognizes and values the diversity of North America's population and its historical and cultural experiences: a curriculum that is inclusive, that incorporates multiple perspectives, that acknowledges the complexity of each culture while paying heed to the needs that are common to all citizens of a democracy. In the language arts, this implies that the linguistic integrity of every language is respected; that whatever language students bring to school is accepted as a valid means of communication; that this linguistic background serves as the foundation for literacy in the mainstream language and the acquisition of at least a regional standard variety; that the study and use of language emphasize its versatility and potential for creativity in addition to its forms and rules. Culturally responsive pedagogy implies that the literature curriculum represents diversity in content and authorship to reflect different voices and experiences; the author who has experienced an event or phenomenon tells a story from a different perspective from one who has done research or observed from a distance. It is important that all young people appreciate the contributions made by writers from their own as well as other cultures and that a new literature canon be compiled to foster this concept. In its implementation, a culturally responsive pedagogy calls for a language arts classroom that provides opportunities for students to bring their unique perspectives to any topic. Oral and written language experiences should require students to generate their own responses, to express their ideas and interpret others' in their own words. Most of all, learning experiences should require students to engage in discussions in which they listen to, understand, and respect the ideas of others.

Background Information for the Teacher

The lessons in the unit were designed for students in the early elementary grades, typically kindergarten through the second grade. The lessons assume that students have had some experience listening to and telling stories and have developed a sense of story that can be transferred to the writing of their own stories. The unit is divided into daily lessons for convenience in planning, but the actual time spent on each lesson will depend on the students' reading and writing experience. The extent to which each activity is developed will also vary according to individual and class experience and need. Teachers who wish to implement this unit with their classes should assess their students' readiness for each activity and make appropriate modifications.

It is not essential that the teacher be an expert storyteller or writer in order to teach this unit, only that he or she be willing to try. There are many excellent resources for teachers to build background for the unit and to become familiar with culturally relevant works of literature for children. Two bibliographies are provided at the end of the unit. One lists professional resources that include ideas for telling and writing stories with children; the other lists a selection of the many excellent works available from the traditional and contemporary bodies of children's literature of the major ethnic groups in North America.

In many communities, there are professional storytellers who visit schools, telling stories and sometimes conducting workshops on storytelling for students. Although certainly not essential to the success of the unit, the participation of an accomplished storyteller would prove highly motivating to the students.

There are other guidelines and suggestions for facilitation of your students' language arts skills:

1. Read to your students every day. Select works of fiction, nonfiction, and poetry that represent a broad variety of cultures, regardless of the majority culture in your classroom. Ask questions that elicit both the uniqueness of the culture represented in the text and the commonalities among many cultures.

2. Set aside time for your students to read independently their own choices. Have available and ask the media specialist to feature books that appeal to your students' developmental levels and represent a variety of cultures. Ask the media specialist to give book talks about the selections; prepare your own book talks as you become familiar with many of these books. Validate language varieties by including works that incorporate dialects into dialogue and narration.

3. Have your students keep a journal of personal stories and select some to be published in one of the formats suggested in the unit.

4. Set up projects that involve your students' interacting with those in schools representing a different cultural mix. They might write to pen pals using "snail mail" or electronic mail. Or, using the Internet, they might collaborate on science research projects, math problems, or social studies issues.

5. The families of students who have immigrated may have works of literature representing their languages and cultures. These may be included as part of a genre unit or theme unit, freely translated or told by the student, another family member, or someone else who is familiar with the language and literature. Include second- and third-generation immigrants as well as recent arrivals. If there is an ethnic cultural center within reasonable distance, ask a staff member to share literature, print or other media, by reading, telling stories, or interpreting.

6. Encourage bilingual or second language learners with appropriate skills to translate a work of literature or a part of it as a writing project. Try it both ways—from the native language to English and from English to the native language.

7. Allow all students to try their hand at translation. Collect wordbooks or simple dictionaries and very simple children's books. Have students work in pairs or small groups to write and illustrate their own versions of the children's books in different languages. Include this project with a literature or social studies unit that features one or different cultures or a historical period of cultural relevance such as immigration.

Unit Organization

LESSON 1

Students will

Work in large and small groups to establish a plan to gather information on their classroom, school, and community in order to prepare a *news story* they will send to a partner class;

Interview community and school informants and record responses;

Compile and organize the survey responses;

Participate in drafting, revising, and editing a group story, letter, and visuals that will be sent to the partner class.

LESSON 2

Students will

Use conventional criteria to evaluate their story;

Orally compose a personal narrative and share the story with peers.

LESSON 3

Students will

Write a personal narrative, using the writing process elements of planning, drafting, revising, and editing.

LESSON 4

Students will

Publish their stories in a format of their choice;

Read or tell their stories to their classmates.

LESSON 5

Students will

Engage in discussions to generate ideas for collecting family or neighborhood stories;

Identify the source of a family or neighborhood story;

Plan the story collection activity.

LESSON 6

Students will

Write the stories they have collected, using the writing process;

Read or tell their stories to their classmates.

LESSON 7

Students will

Choose audiences for storytelling;

Choose stories to tell individually or as part of a small group.

LESSONS 8 AND 9

Students will

Prepare and practice telling their stories;

Evaluate their own and one another's oral presentations.

LESSON 10

Students will

Tell their stories to their audiences;

Evaluate their story writing and storytelling unit.

The Content Standards:
IRA/NCTE Standards for English and Language Arts

The language arts unit that was developed to illustrate the principles of culturally responsive pedagogy, "Stories, Stories, Stories," was also designed to be consistent with the content standards for the English language arts. These standards, developed jointly by the National Council of Teachers of English (NCTE) and the International Reading Association (IRA) are broadly stated objectives representing the collected experience and wisdom of thousands of language arts teachers (*Standards for the English Language Arts* NCTE/IRA 1996).

Standard 1: Students read a wide range of print and nonprint texts to build an understanding of texts, of themselves, and of the cultures of North America and the world; to acquire new information; to respond to the needs and demands of society and the workplace; and for personal fulfillment. Among these texts are fiction and nonfiction, classic and contemporary works.

Standard 2: Students read a wide range of literature from many periods in many genres to build an understanding of the many dimensions (e.g., philosophical, ethical, aesthetic) of human experience.

Standard 3: Students apply a wide range of strategies to comprehend, interpret, evaluate, and appreciate texts. They draw on their prior experience, their interactions with other readers and writers, their knowledge of word meaning and of other texts, their word identification strategies, and their understanding of textual features (e.g., sound-letter correspondence, sentence structure, context, graphics).

Standard 4: Students adjust their use of spoken, written, and visual language (e.g., conventions, style, vocabulary) to communicate effectively with a variety of audiences and for different purposes.

Standard 5: Students employ a wide range of strategies as they write and use different writing process elements appropriately to communicate with different audiences for a variety of purposes.

Standard 6: Students apply knowledge of language structure, language conventions (e.g., spelling and punctuation), media techniques, figurative language, and genre to create, critique, and discuss print and nonprint texts.

Standard 7: Students conduct research on issues and interests by generating ideas and questions and by posing problems. They gather, evaluate, and synthesize data from a variety of sources (e.g., print and nonprint texts, artifacts, people) to communicate their discoveries in ways that suit their purpose and audience.

Standard 8: Students use a variety of technological and informational resources (e.g., libraries, databases, computer networks, video) to gather and synthesize information and to create and communicate knowledge.

Standard 9: Students develop an understanding of and respect for diversity in language use, patterns, and dialects across cultures, ethnic groups, geographic regions, and social roles.

Standard 10: Students whose first language is not English make use of their first language to develop competency in the English language arts and to develop understanding of content across the curriculum.

Standard 11: Students participate as knowledgeable, reflective, creative, and critical members of a variety of literacy communities.

Standard 12: Students use spoken, written, and visual language to accomplish their own purposes (e.g., for learning, enjoyment, persuasion, and the exchange of information).

Standards for the English Language Arts is available from the National Council of Teachers of English, 1111 W. Kenyon Road, Urbana, Illinois, 61801-1096 or from the International Reading Association, 800 Barksdale Road, P.O. Box 8139, Newark, Delaware, 19714-8139.

Matrix of Standards Referenced to Individual Lessons

	Lesson 1	Lesson 2	Lesson 3	Lesson 4	Lesson 5	Lesson 6	Lesson 7	Lesson 8	Lesson 9	Lesson 10
Standard 1		x			x	x	x			
Standard 2					x					
Standard 3					x	x	x			
Standard 4	x	x			x		x	x	x	x
Standard 5	x		x	x	x	x				
Standard 6	x		x	x	x	x				
Standard 7	x				x					
Standard 8		x			x	x				
Standard 9		x			x	x				
Standard 10	x	x	x	x	x	x	x	x	x	x
Standard 11	x	x	x	x	x	x	x	x	x	x
Standard 12	x	x	x	x	x	x	x	x	x	x

LESSON 1

(Note to the teacher: Before the lesson, establish a partnership with a class in another city or another part of your town. This can be done through personal contacts or via Internet pen pals. Work out arrangements with a partner teacher to have students in each class communicate with one another.)

Objectives

1. Each student will work in large and small groups to establish a plan to gather information on their classroom, school, and community in order to prepare a *news story* they will send to a partner class.

2. Each student will interview community and school informants and record responses.

3. Each student will compile and organize the survey responses.

4. Each student will participate in drafting, revising, and editing a group story, letter, and visuals that will be sent to the partner class.

Materials

Chart or board, cameras, tape recorders

Instructional Strategies

Opener

SE 1,   SE 3,   SE 4

Teacher: How can we introduce ourselves to our new partner class? What shall we tell them about us, our class, and our community? Write students' responses on a chart or board. Ask the students to identify the categories that emerge. For example, the community categories might include parks and places for play, places to study and learn, problems in the community, and places to shop.

Body

Teacher: We already know a lot about our community. How could we find out more about the things we have listed so we could introduce ourselves to our partners? Student responses will probably include looking around and asking others. **Teacher: Whom could we ask?** List the students' suggestions on the chart or board, eliciting more if they do not include key people. You would expect to include parents, shopkeepers, religious leaders, firefighters, librarians, police officers, health workers, barbers, and school personnel.

Teacher: Let's ask some of these people to give us some information and ideas about our neighborhood. But first, let's think about the questions we need to ask. At this point, you might want to have students move to work groups. Depending on the categories that emerge, student groups might be school information, community information, classroom information. Have each group identify *questions* and the people who could help them with the answers. This work could be done on large chart paper. **Teacher: Now that we have our questions and the names of the people we want to interview, what's the next step?** Have students develop a plan to work in teams to interview key people they have named. If possible, the story/letter they send to their partner class could be enhanced by the use of cameras, camcorders, or audio recorders. Depending on the level

and kind of technology available, students can also use computers to prepare their survey questions, summarize their findings, and prepare drafts of their stories.

After the information is collected, work with the students to compile it in a workable form, such as a chart with all the different responses listed under the related questions. Lead the students in writing a news story, language-experience style, with contributions from any who volunteer. Remind the students that it is a first draft, and ask them to think about whether it needs to be revised and edited. Incorporate the suggestions into the next draft. Once the class (or group) is satisfied with the story, have them pretend to be the partner class as they receive the story. **Teacher: Did we include enough information to tell our partners everything we want them to know? Is the story interesting? Will the readers get a good picture in their minds about us, our class, our school, and our community?**

Closing

As students take on the role of the reader of their story and ask these questions, have them edit and change their story as they consider ways to improve it. Drawings, pictures, photos, or videotape might accompany the story.

Actually send the story to the partner class and receive a story from them.

Assessment

A 1,   A 2

During the introductory discussion and planning of the project, note the nature and level of students' responses. During the survey, note students' willingness to participate by interacting with the respondents and taking appropriate notes. During the language experience activity, assess participation both through willingness to contribute to the story as well as the revising and editing skills exhibited.

During the final editing phase, students apply the criteria of

completeness   accuracy   interest level

to their story and revise accordingly. Students should then be able to apply these criteria to other writing experiences they have.

LESSON 2

Objectives

1. Each student will use conventional criteria to evaluate their story.

2. Each student will orally compose a personal narrative and share the story with peers.

Materials

Chart or board, display books

Instructional Strategies

Opener

SE 1,   SE 2,   SE 4,   IE 1,   IE 4,   A 1

Provide a copy of the story for each student and read it as the students read with you. **Teacher: What do you think of your story? Let's evaluate it using what we know about the stories we read. Does it answer the questions who, what, where, when, and how? Who are the characters? What is the setting? What happened in the story? How did it happen?** Allow as many volunteers as possible to respond. **Teacher: You have written a great story about our school and our community. One of the reasons it is so good is that you were writing about something you know well. Did you know that many of the stories you read also come from the experiences of the authors? Some of your favorite authors use their own experiences or those of their families and friends as a basis for their stories.**

Body

Teacher: Think of all the books you have read by Betsy Byars, Lucille Clifton, Eloise Greenfield, Johanna Hurwitz, and Gary Soto. I know their books remind you of yourselves sometimes because you talk about them in our discussion groups and conferences. Display some of the most popular books that focus on children's experiences in school, at home, or in the community. Include stories that have specific cultural relevance to the students in the class as well as cultural groups not represented in the class. Ask the students to suggest others that fall into this category. **Teacher: I also know you have experiences that are just as interesting because I overhear bits and pieces of the stories you tell one another. You know stories worth telling. If you write some of these stories, you can share them with one another, our partner class, and with your family and friends. Let's think of experiences you have had that would make good stories.** Provide a few examples such as the following, modeling a few of them with the beginnings of personal experience stories. If possible, include activities that are relevant to students in particular cultural groups, such as Chinese or Vietnamese

New Year; Cinco de Mayo; Martin Luther King, Jr., Day events.

> When my mother went to the hospital to have a baby
> My favorite adventure
> My first cooking experience
> My first day of school
> Pets, pets, pets!

Ask the children to list orally some of their memories on one of these topics. After as many children as possible offer their stories, tell them that they will be using these memories to write a story from their experience. Then ask them to make a written list of several favorite personal experiences to tell about, to make a check mark by the three they think they remember the most about, and finally to select one to tell to a small group of classmates. Before telling, they should write down the essentials of the story—the beginning, the most important things that happened, and the outcome. As children become ready to tell their stories, the teacher should help them form small groups, and they should take turns telling stories to one another.

Closing

IE 4

Teacher: This afternoon and evening, think of other stories in your life. Ask your mother, father, or other members of your family to help you recall interesting things. Look around your room; are there any objects such as an old favorite toy that help you recall an experience? Look at family pictures. Add these story ideas to the list you made today and jot down something about each one. Tomorrow, you will begin to write one of your stories. Again, refer to experiences that are likely to have taken place in their lives.

Assessment

A 1,   A 2

Some children may not think they have stories. Do not pressure them, but note who seems reluctant to relate an experience and use your judgment to encourage them to recall an experience related to some of the story starters mentioned earlier or to a school experience. Children who cannot seem to get started may join a group to get more ideas. Have students dictate their stories into tape recorders to promote fluency.

LESSON 3

Objective

1. Students will write a personal narrative, using the writing process elements of planning, drafting, revising, and editing.

Materials

Storyboard, chart, computer and software

Instructional Strategies

Opener

SE 1,   SE 2,   IE 4

Teacher: Before we begin to write our own stories, let's review the steps we followed together to make certain our class and community story would be a good one. First, we planned it; next, we wrote the first draft; then, we revised it. Finally, we edited it, making all the corrections we needed to make it easy and interesting for people to read. Let's review these steps to prepare for writing your stories.

1. Display a list of the important details of the community story. The use of a storyboard or similar device is recommended. Many children, especially those who are visually oriented, find it very helpful to draw the important parts of a story first, then write the description of the event below the picture.

2. Review the details, making sure they are in correct sequence.

3. Display the first-draft version of the story, pointing out how each of the major points was developed.

4. Display the copy on which the children revised as a group, asking them to recall the questions writers ask themselves to make sure they have included everything they can to make the story complete and interesting. Tell the students that they will also help one another revise their stories.

5. Display a chart with the editing criteria for their grade and experience level and remind them to refer to it during their writing if they need to and to use it to make corrections on their final draft.

Body

SE 4,   SE 5,   A 1,   A 2,   A 3

Ask the students to select one of their story ideas and file the other ideas in their writing folders for later consideration. Remind them to work through the steps just demonstrated. Set up an area where peer helpers may read and respond to one another's stories. Post the peer revision questions on a large chart as well as on small sheets in the helping areas. Children with writing workshop experience will be able to serve as helpful readers. Those with little such experience will require the teacher's guidance in developing their story ideas. Therefore, you should be prepared to circulate among the writers, asking the revision questions and encouraging them to write a complete story. The *Writers Express* handbook listed at the end of the lesson is also recommended for children who have developed independent reference skills.

Children love to use technology, and computer software to facilitate children's writing is now available. Three such programs are listed under Resources/References at the end of this lesson. If these or similar materials are available to the teacher, every effort should be made to allow students to use them to plan, revise, and publish their stories.

If possible, students with limited writing skills or physical impairments should be assisted at each stage requiring writing by dictating their ideas and compositions to a scribe who will write or type them into a word processor. Paraprofessionals, aides, or volunteers, including peers, could provide this assistance that would allow all children to see their work in writing. Another alternative is for some children to tell their stories through illustrations and dictated stories. It is important to include opportunities for each student to improve both their writing skills and storytelling abilities.

Closing

Students will use remaining time to work on their next drafts or will file their work for the next day. Remind them that their minds will still be processing their stories after they leave school, perhaps even in their dreams, and they should be sure to jot down other things that come to mind.

Assessment

Using the four elements of the writing process, planning, drafting, revising, and editing, evaluate each of the students' stories.

Resources/References

Story-writing software: *Storybook Weaver Deluxe, Kid Stories,* and *My Own Stories* are three possibilities.

Writing handbook: *Writers Express: A Handbook for Young Writers, Thinkers, and Learners.* Write Source Educational Publishing House.

LESSON 4

Objectives

1. Each student will publish their stories in a format of their choice.
2. Each student will read or tell their stories to their classmates.

Materials

Computers, bulletin board

Instructional Strategies

Opener

When most students have indicated that their stories are complete, call the class together to discuss publication possibilities.

Body

SE 1,   SE 5

Remind students that some of the computer programs available permit a variety of layouts and include clip art or other illustrating capability. Offer to assist those who need help with these features or have them enlist the assistance of a class member who already has these skills. For those who want to type their stories but prefer to do their own illustrations, remind them how to set up a story on the computer to leave space for illustrations. Display examples of these formats and review and display other kinds of book formats and illustrations they have used in the past. It would also be a good time to use some of the picture books available in the classroom to illustrate different ways of presenting their stories (e.g., a photo essay or collage). This is another opportunity to use books that represent various cultures, those that are not represented in the class as well as those that are. There should also be a reminder to use the editing checklist to make sure their final drafts are free of mechanical errors before publication. The degree of editing expected should be commensurate with the students' levels of instruction and experience. Tell students that the stories will be displayed in the classroom and other appropriate places in the school, including other classrooms and the library, and we can send their stories to our partner class. A bulletin board or other posting place should be designated for displaying the stories, and the students may select a title such as "The Stories We Tell" or "Once upon Our Time." The stories could also be compiled into a collection and several copies made so that they could be checked out of the library.

Closing

Students will use the remaining time to complete their stories and prepare them for publication. The teacher will monitor, provide feedback, and assist with writing and publishing as needed. As noted above, editing skills, including spelling, vary greatly among children in the lower grades.

Assessment

A 1,   A 2,   A 3

Criteria appropriate for the levels represented in the class should be used in setting expectations, providing instruction, and in making evaluations. Students who complete their stories may assist others or read one another's stories or those from the classroom collection. In addition, enough time should be reserved so that students who have completed their projects can be invited to share them with the class.

LESSON 5

Objectives

1. Each student will engage in discussions to generate ideas for collecting family or neighborhood stories.
2. Each student will identify the source of a family or neighborhood story.
3. Each student will plan the story collection activity.

Materials

Chart board, overhead transparency, tape recorders

Instructional Strategies

Opener

SE 4

If students are still working on their stories, time should be allowed for them to complete and publish them. Students who have completed their stories may assist others, read their peers' stories, or read from the collection of short stories and folktales provided by the teacher. Recommended titles are included in the

Resources/References section following this lesson. Again, time should be provided for students to read aloud or tell their stories informally. When the class is ready, the following lesson is started.

Body

IE 1,   IE 2,   IE 3,   IE 4

Select a picture storybook from the list provided or select another story that depicts a family experience, tradition, or setting to serve as an opener to discuss family stories. The following example uses a recently published picture storybook, *Family Reunion*, for this purpose. It describes the events that take place during the reunion and features several unique characters. Lead a discussion with appropriate comments. **Teacher: Not only does each one of us have our own stories to tell. In every family, there are stories and storytellers. Sometimes the stories are true, about special events and experiences. In the story I just read, I think there is a story behind why Aunt Alicia is so ladylike. I also think the storyteller has other stories to tell about this person. Did the part about how everyone eats corn on the cob remind you of your family? Think of the people in your family. In my family, my father used to retell the experience his mother, my grandmother, had when she immigrated from Germany to the United States over a hundred years ago.** (I would use a world map to indicate the locations of Germany and New York). **Teacher: Can you imagine how scared a young girl would be traveling with strangers on a ship that would take her thousands of miles across the ocean?** If some of my students were immigrants, I would look for signs that they might want to share their feelings at this time. **Teacher: A friend of mine tells the story her grandfather told about the first time he voted. Remember that at one time both African Americans and women were forbidden to vote. He just couldn't believe he could actually walk into that building and cast his ballot. When she told the story, I could just see him cautiously, even fearfully, look around as he took each step.**

Teacher: Here are a few more stories that came from family experiences. The authors share special feelings, events, traditions, and individuals from their heritage. Present a book talk, telling a little about several books such as those listed in the Resources/References section, which represent a variety of cultural backgrounds. Point out elements that are common to all the stories, such as the comfort of shared experiences and traditions or the special meaning a certain article has for family members. Also point out that different families have different traditions and ways of celebrating. Some Chinese families celebrate the lunar New Year with greater festivities than they do Christmas or the calendar new year. Many African Americans celebrate Kwanza instead of or in addition to Christmas. Jewish families celebrate Passover at about the same time that Christians celebrate Easter. Muslim families observe Ramadan and other special days unique to their religion.

SE 1,   IE 4

Teacher: Did any of these stories remind you of your family? Are there special things in your home or in a relative's home that have special meaning for your family? Share a personal story about a family artifact, such as the following. **Teacher: In my sister's home, there is a rocking chair that was used by her husband's grandparents to rock his father, then by his mother to rock him, then by my sister and her husband to rock their children. They will give it to their oldest child to rock his babies. Do you have a family album with old pictures of relatives, perhaps someone who came from another country or another part of the United States?** Allow some time for informal sharing to stimulate students' memories. **Teacher: For our next story-writing project, let's collect stories from people we know. Think about the people you know who are good storytellers. If your grandparents live nearby, they may be the best source of stories because they have lived through many experiences. But you may know other people who always seem to have a good story about what is going on in the neighborhood or what happened in the past. You know teachers and other workers who have been in this school a long time and could tell you about the old days. What about high school students who went to your school? What could they tell you? Remember all the people we talked to when we did the survey for our group story? Some of them told us much more than we could include in that story. They might have really interesting stories that they would be willing to share.**

SE 1,   SE 3,   SE 5,   IE 1,   IE 4

At any point during the introduction, students may volunteer stories and the names of storytellers. Use their ideas instead of or with yours. Compile a list on the board, a chart, or a transparency that students can copy or view. The following could be included:

Family traditions, home or place of worship
Special family traditions for birthdays or other events
Where your family came from and where they originally settled
Something exciting that happened in the neighborhood
An original rap, never published or recorded
A song that only your family sings
A family mystery, still unsolved

Finally, ask students to identify someone they know who they think would be willing to tell a story and to plan to approach that individual to request a story. Remind the students of the preparation they did to make their own stories longer and more interesting. Those who know people and some of their stories should write out the topics of the stories and generate questions to probe and elicit more information. For example,

> Remember when you told me about . . .
> Would you tell me that story about . . . ?
> What did (character, setting) look like?
> Can you tell me more about . . . ?
> How did you feel when . . . ?

Help other children to think of how they might get someone to start telling a story. Use some of the same story starters used by the children when they wrote their personal experience stories and help them draft questions that would elicit adults' recall of early experiences. Role-play the process with the students, letting them ask you questions about your childhood. Point out and write those questions that help to focus on one event that evokes many memories and those that move the story along.

Each student should write down the name and a brief description of the person they will approach to tell a story and should prepare a written list of the questions they will ask. If the children are too young, if you think they will have difficulty in getting the cooperation of an adult, or if you know that some are too shy or otherwise reluctant to approach an adult for the project, arrange in advance for people in the school, community, or a nearby middle or high school to serve as sources for stories. They should be willing to come to the school for the "interview."

Closing

Work with the children to draft a letter to the proposed interviewees, describing the story-writing and story-telling project, enlisting their participation, and asking for their permission to write and retell their stories. An invitation to a community member to come to the class-room to tell a story might be included. Suggest that the students tape-record their conversations if possible. If not, they should take notes. Students can also work in teams to tape-record and write out the interviewees' responses. Discuss with students the importance of making an appointment for the session and of conducting it in a place where there will be no interruptions. Tell them to arrange to take the first draft back to the story-teller so they can check for accuracy and completeness.

Be prepared to arrange for the interview to take place in the school.

Assessment

A 1,   A 3

Make a note of where each child is in the process of preparing to approach someone for a story. Students who wish to get started on their projects immediately should be encouraged to do so if they have done the appropriate preparations. Since this will be a very challenging project for many children, be prepared to reassure them that they can do it and that you will provide support throughout the activity.

Resources/References

Ethnic family stories for book talk:

Arctic Memories. Normee Ekoomiak. The author recalls early memories from an Eskimo childhood. The book is written in Inuktitut and English.

Family Pictures: Cuadros de Familia. Carmen Lornas Garza. A bilingual picture book about a girl who reminisces about growing up. It looks like a family album showing special events in the author's life.

Family Reunion. Marilyn Singer. Members of a large extended family get together to eat, play, and generally have a great time.

The Hundred Penny Box. Sharon Bell Mathis. Michael loves to count the pennies in the box kept by his great-great-aunt Dew, as she tells him the stories behind them.

The Keeping Quilt. Patricia Polacco. A Russian Jewish grandmother makes a quilt to help the family remember their homeland and customs.

The Patchwork Quilt. Valeria Flournoy. An African American grandmother talks about the material she uses for her quilt.

Pueblo Storyteller. Diane Hoyt-Goldsmith. A photo essay in which a Cochiti girl tells of her family heritage.

Totem Pole. Diane Hoyt-Goldsmith. A photo essay story of a half-white, half-Indian boy whose Indian heritage is told through his father's carvings on a totem pole.

When I Was Young in the Mountains. Cynthia Rylant. Memories of growing up in Appalachia.

LESSON 6

At least two days will be devoted to writing up the stories the students have collected and setting up the interview sessions that take place at school. Children do not have to transcribe the interviews or stories they have taped.

Objectives

1. Each student will write the stories they have collected, using the writing process.
2. Each student will read or tell their stories to their classmates.

Material

Taped interview

Instructional Strategies

Opener

IE 4,   SE 2,   SE 4,   SE 5

Students should listen, write down or draw the major events or information they remember, and listen again with a partner who can help fill in.

Body

Model this process once with the entire class, using either a taped interview you have prepared or one that a student has brought in. In the latter case, be sure to preview the tape so you can model effectively. Show how the story you wrote from it is different from the way the information was presented on the tape. Provide time for the students to write and illustrate the stories that emerge from their interviews, using computer software if possible. Remind them to follow the procedures for revising and editing they used for their first stories; review the procedures with the students and refer them to the resources—already introduced—they can use to refine their writing.

Most children will be able to write the story as a third-person narrator. Some may wish to write it as if they were the storyteller, that is, in the first person. In the latter case, a minilesson on point of view would be appropriate. Model part of a story told both ways and allow students to choose the viewpoint they prefer. Avoid suggesting that one way is better than the other.

Closing

If any of the adult participants have volunteered to come to the school to tell a story, they might do so on these days.

Assessment

Students will be finishing stories at different times, so time should be provided for informal oral presentations as they are completed. Completed stories should be available for classmates to read. In addition, students should be encouraged to read the stories that the teacher has collected in the classroom as well as ones they check out from the library.

LESSON 7

Objectives

1. Each student will choose audiences for storytelling.
2. Each student will select stories to tell individually or as part of a small group.

Material

Chart with student names

Instructional Strategies

Opener

SE 1,   SE 4,   IE 2,   IE 4

Teacher: We now have a wonderful collection of stories you have written about yourselves and about people you know. Most of you have told one or both of your stories to your classmates. Now I would like you to think about telling a story to someone else. You could tell one of the

stories you wrote or you could select a folktale or another short story from those you have been reading. First, you'll decide as a class whom you'd like to tell the stories to. Then you will select a story that you think the audience would enjoy. Finally, you will practice your story on your classmates before you tell it to the audience you select.

Body

Discuss possible audiences with the students. One of the most rewarding settings would be a younger class in your school. If multiple classes are working on this project, they may prefer to tell stories to each another. If feasible, also consider audiences beyond the school setting—a nursing home, children in a hospital, a local church group, children in an after-school program, and so on. Depending on the audiences selected, help the children choose stories that would be appropriate.

Some children might wish to tell a published story, since they have already told their original stories informally. This would be a good opportunity to encourage them to consider folktales from their own background. Depending on the ethnic composition of the class, present a book talk on folktales, preferably in picture-book format, that reflects the class. Also have traditional favorites on hand for children who prefer them; they might particularly like to read and tell a variant of a popular tale usually presented in a European version. Avoid traditional tales that are stereotyped with respect to females and minorities. If this type of selection is popular, as it will be with children who have had many such experiences, then you should take time to discuss the negative aspects of those kinds of stories. Students may be encouraged to rewrite their own variant of a traditional tale.

Closing

A story could be selected, prepared, and told by an individual. Or, from two to four students could tell the same story to different audiences, and this would facilitate and simplify their preparation.

Assessment

A 1,   A 2

With the students, prepare a large chart with their names, individually or in pairs, triads, or quads, and fill in the titles of stories for those who have made a decision about which story to tell. Ask the other students to select a story and help you fill in the chart for them. Some might wish to take stories home to read or reread. Go over the chart with the class, completing it with information from students who did not have a story selected the previous day. Assist and encourage those who have not completed this step.

LESSON 8

Objectives

1. Each student will prepare and practice telling their story.
2. Each student will evaluate their own and each other's oral presentations.

Material

Tape recorder

Instructional Strategies

Opener

SE 3,   SE 4,   SE 5,   IE 1

Tell a story to the class. Because you will model how to prepare to tell a story, you might select one that you do not already know well but will have to prepare for this telling.

Body

The following process should be explained to the students. The teacher should read the story aloud several times and identify the major events in the story. Recall with the children how they prepared their personal experience stories to write and tell, jotting down or drawing the main events. Ask them to think about the characters and try to "get into" the behaviors, mannerisms, and especially the voices they suggest. As the teacher, you should model these behaviors as you read the story again. Note phrases that are repeated or are special in some way. You will be telling the story in your own words, but if you are telling a published story, you might want to use some of the language of the original. Suggest a few gestures that are appropriate for the story. Decide whether you would like to use a simple prop, mask, or puppet. Consider displaying a culturally relevant artifact, wearing a costume, or preparing a backdrop reflecting the setting. Consider introducing your story with culturally relevant music or use music during the telling. Children who express themselves best through art might wish their storytelling to take the form of an illustrated talk. Shy children might prefer to use a puppet or mask to tell their stories. Now you should ask the students to practice their story in any or all of the following ways: with others in the class; in front of a mirror at home; with a tape recorder or VCR.

Closing

The students should practice before their classmates and ask for suggestions for improvement.

Assessment

A 1,   A 2,   A 3

Have students summarize the steps they will take to prepare their story and note the progress each child or small group has made. Although telling the story is an objective for all students, some may be so reluctant that they cannot complete the experience without an unduly high level of anxiety or frustration. In order that these children may participate, some alternatives should be available. Some might be willing to tape their stories to be played to the audience. A second

grader who participated in this project would not speak before even his own classmates and would not be videotaped in the classroom. However, he was able to secure a camcorder from a neighbor and had his older sister tape his storytelling. He was delighted to share it in this format. Others might work with a team, assisting or assuming responsibility for illustrations or props or sound effects.

Most children in the primary grades use the language of their home and community primarily or exclusively, especially for oral usage. The culturally sensitive teacher accepts and values whatever language variety students use but is also aware of forms and patterns of usage that may stigmatize young speakers as they broaden the audiences with whom they communicate. Alternate forms considered standard or mainstream should be taught through language play and practice, particularly creative oral activities, role playing, reading aloud, reciting short poems and other pieces, not through public correction. Telling their stories before new audiences provides a realistic motivation for students to use the "school voice" features they have learned, and they should be encouraged to do so.

LESSON 9

SE 4,   A 1,   A 2

Students will prepare and practice their stories by themselves or a partner. Videotape individuals and small groups so that the students can evaluate themselves and each another. Help them to prepare a simple evaluation

form for their audiences. The evaluation form included in this unit or a similar one may be used. Students with little experience with making presentations in front of audiences should be given enough time to practice so they are comfortable with this format.

LESSON 10

SE 1,   A 1

Students will tell their stories to an audience and invite evaluation and feedback. As students return from telling their stories, they should share their experiences with the class. When all have told their stories, they

should engage in an informal evaluation of the unit through discussion or in writing. A highly positive outcome would be the students' expressing the desire to write and tell more stories.

Storytelling Evaluation Form

Name of story:

Name of storyteller:

Did the storyteller have good eye contact with the audience?

Was the storyteller's voice clear and easy to hear?

Did you enjoy the story?

Positive comments about the story and the teller:

Suggestions for the storyteller:

1. Writing and telling stories are important components of nearly every language arts curriculum. How does this unit differ from other curriculum plans? How is it consistent with them?

2. Consider how this unit takes the student out of the classroom and into the community. Why is this important in making curriculum and instruction more culturally responsive than restricting education to the confines of the school?

3. On the surface, this unit may appear highly "unstructured" in terms of prescribing specific activities for students. Look for the overall structure of the unit as a whole and of each lesson. Consider how you can incorporate the objectives that are unique to your students.

SOURCES FOR CULTURE-BASED STORIES

Professional Resource

Bishop, R. S., ed. *Kaleidoscope: A multicultural booklist for Grades K–8.* 1994. Urbana, IL: National Council of Teachers of English.

African and African American

Aardema, Verna
　1989. *Rabbit makes a monkey of lion.* Dial. *PB
　1992. *Traveling to Tondo: A tale of the Nkundo of Zaire.* Knopf. PB
Clifton, Lucille
　1980. *My friend Jacob.* Dutton. PB
Courlander, Harold, and George Herzog
　1988. *The cowtail switch and other West African stories.* Holt. CS
Greenfield, Eloise
　1991. *Night on neighborhood street.* Penguin. PO
Hamilton, Virginia
　1985. *The people could fly: American black folktales.* Knopf. CS
Joseph, Lynn
　1991. *A wave in her pocket: Stories from Trinidad.* Clarion. CS
　1994. *The mermaid's twin sister.* Clarion. CS
Lester, Julius
　1989. *How many spots does a leopard have and other tales.* Scholastic. CS
　1994. *John Henry.* Dial. PB
　1987. *The tales of Uncle Remus.* 1988. *More tales of Uncle Remus.*
　1990. *Further tales of Uncle Remus.* 1994. *The last tales of Uncle Remus.* Dial. CS
McKissack, Patricia
　1988. *Mirandy and brother wind.* Knopf. PB
Mathis, Sharon Bell
　1975. *The hundred penny box.* Viking. PB
Patrick, Denise
　1993. *The car washing street.* Tambourine. PB
Pinckney, Brian
　1994. *Max found two sticks.* Simon & Schuster. PB
Ringgold, Faith
　1991. *Tar beach.* Crown. PB
San Souci, Robert
　1989. *The boy and the ghost.* Simon & Schuster. PB
　1989. *The talking eggs.* Dial. PB

CS = collection of stories; PB = picture book; PO = poetry

Steptoe, John
  1987. *Mufaro's beautiful daughters.* Lothrop. PB

Asian and Asian American

Ishii, Momoko
  1987. *The tongue-cut sparrow.* Dutton. PB
Keller, Holly
  1994. *Grandfather's dream.* Greenwillow. PB
Louie, Ai-Ling
  1990. *Yeh-Shen: A Cinderella story from China.* Philomel. PB
Mahy, Margaret
  1990. *The seven Chinese brothers.* Scholastic. PB
Mochizuki, Ken
  1993. *Baseball saved us.* Lee & Low. PB
Sadler, Catherine E.
  1985. *Heaven's reward: Fairy tales from China.* Atheneum. CS
  1982. *Treasure Mountain: Folktales from Southern China.* Atheneum. CS
Say, Allen
  1991. *Tree of cranes.* Houghton. PB
Yacowitz, Caryn, adapter
  1992. *The jade stone: A Chinese folktale.* Holiday House. PB
Yagawa, Sumiko, reteller
  1981. *The crane wife.* Morrow. PB
Yep, Lawrence
  1989. *The rainbow people.* HarperCollins. CS
  1991. *Tongues of jade.* HarperCollins. CS
Young, Ed
  1989. *Lon Po Po: A Red Riding Hood story from China.* Philomel. PB

Hispanic

Alexander, Ellen
  1989. *Llama and the great flood.* HarperCollins. PB
Altman, Linda, and Sanchez, Enrique
  1993. *Amelia's road.* Lee & Low. PB
Belpre, Pura
  1973. *Once in Puerto Rico.* Warne. PB
Best, Cari
  1994. *Taxi, taxi.* Little, Brown. PB
Bierhorst, John
  1986. *The monkey's haircut and other stories told by the Maya.* Morrow. CS
Bunting, Eve
  1983. *Molly's pilgrim.* Morrow. PB
Carlson, L. M., and C. L. Ventura, eds.
  1990. *Where angels glide at dawn: New stories from Latin America.* Lippincott. CS
Finger, Charles J., ed.
  1965. *Tales from silver lands.* Doubleday. CS
Griego, Margot
  1981. *Tortillas para mama.* Holt. PO
Griego y Maestas, Jose, and R. A. Anaya
  1980. *Cuentos: Tales from the Hispanic Southwest.* Museum of New Mexico. CS
Jagendorf, M. A., and R. S. Boggs
  1960. *The king of the mountains: A treasury of Latin American folk stories.* Vanguard. CS
Martel, Cruz
  1976. *Yagua days.* Dial. PB
Paulsen, Gary
  1995. *The tortilla factory.* Harcourt Brace. PB
Pitre, Felix
  1995. *Paco and the witch: A Puerto Rican folktale.* Lodestar. PB
Soto, Gary
  1990. *Baseball in April and other stories.* Harcourt Brace. CS

Native American

Baylor, Byrd
  1981. *A God on every mountain top: Stories of Southwest Indian mountains.* Scribner. CS
Bierhorst, John, ed.
  1976. *Black rainbow: Legends of the Incas and myths of ancient Peru.* Farrar. CS
  1987. *Doctor coyote: A Native American Aesop's fables.* Macmillan. CS
  1984. *The hungry woman: Myths and legends of the Aztecs.* Morrow. CS
Caduto, Michael, and Joseph Bruchac
  1993. *Keepers of the earth: Native American stories and environmental activities for children.* Fulcrum. CS
Ekoomiak, Normee
  1990. *Arctic memories.* Holt. PB
Goble, Paul
  1989. *Beyond the ridge.* Bradbury. PB
  1992. *Crow chief: A Plains Indian story.* Orchard. PB
  1980. *The gift of the sacred dog.* Bradbury. PB
Harris, Christie
  1980. *The trouble with princesses.* Atheneum. CS
James, Betsy
  1994. *The mud family.* Putnam. PB
McDermott, Gerald
  1993. *Raven: A trickster tale from the Pacific Northwest.* Harcourt Brace. PB
Manitonquat, adapter
  1994. *The children of the morning light: Wampanoag tales.* Macmillan. CS
Miles, Miska
  1971. *Anna and the old one.* Little, Brown. PB
Monroe, Jean Guard, and Ray A. Williamson
  1987. *They dance in the sky.* Houghton. PB

Jewish American

Geras, Adele
  1990. *My grandmother's stories: A collection of Jewish folk tales.* Knopf. CS
Kimmel, Eric, adapter
  1991. *Days of awe: Stories for Rosh Hashanah and Yom Kippur.* Viking. CS
Schwartz, Howard, and Barbara Rush, retellers
  1991. *The diamond tree: Jewish tales from around the world.* HarperCollins. CS
Singer, Isaac Bashevis
  1982. *The golem.* Farrar. PB
  1968. *When Shlemiel went to Warsaw and other stories.* Farrar. CS
  1966. *Zlateh the goat and other stories.* Harper. CS

RESOURCES AND REFERENCES

Story Writing and Storytelling

Barton, B., and D. Booth. 1990. *Stories in the classroom: Storytelling, reading aloud, and role-playing with children.* Portsmouth, NH: Heinemann.

Bauer, C. F. 1993. *New handbook for storytellers: With stories, poems, magic and more.* Chicago: American Library Association.

Benedict, S., and L. Carlisle, eds. 1992. *Beyond words: Picture books for older readers and writers.* Portsmouth, NH: Heinemann.

Harris, V. J., ed. 1993. *Teaching multicultural literature in grades K–8.* Norwood, MA: Christopher-Gordon.

McCabe, A. 1996. *Chameleon readers: Teaching children to appreciate all kinds of good stories.* New York: McGraw-Hill.

Pellowski, A. 1984. *The story vine: A source book of unusual and easy-to-tell stories from around the world.* New York: Macmillan.

Ross, R. R. 1980. *Storyteller.* 2nd ed. Columbus, OH: Merrill.

Trousdale, A. M., A. S. Woestehoff, and M. Schwartz, eds. 1994. *Give a listen: Stories of storytelling in school.* Urbana, IL: National Council of Teachers of English.

Wigginton, E. 1985. *Sometimes a shining moment.* Garden City, NY: Anchor Press/Doubleday.

Craft Patterns and Geometry
A Culturally Responsive Interdisciplinary Unit
Informal Geometry Using Art, Literature, and History
3rd—5th Grades

Goals

1. Students will examine textile patterns used by Africans and Native Americans.
2. Students will learn geometric concepts through their examination of textile patterns.
3. Students will learn aspects of African and Native American culture.
4. Students will experience the universality of textile patterns used by these diverse cultures.

Goals and Objectives

Objectives

1. Students will identify geometric patterns.
2. Students will learn or review the concept of perimeter of geometric shapes.
3. Students will estimate the perimeter of geometric shapes.
4. Students will compare the effectiveness of different units of measure for finding perimeters.
5. Students will find the perimeter of geometric shapes, using a 10×10 grid or centimeter paper.
6. Students will learn or review the concept of area of geometric shapes.
7. Students will estimate the area of geometric shapes.
8. Students will compare the effectiveness of different units of measure for finding area.
9. Students will describe the need for uniform or standard units of measure.
10. Students will measure the areas of geometric shapes, using a 10×10 grid.
11. Students will practice counting large numbers of objects.
12. Students will measure areas of irregular shape.
13. Students will identify squares, rectangles, parallelograms and right, equilateral, and isosceles triangles.
14. Students will measure the perimeters and areas of squares and rectangles, using geoboards and dot paper.
15. Students will measure the areas of parallelograms and triangles, using geoboards, dot paper, and grid paper.
16. Students will explain the concept of similar polygons.
17. Students will be able to recognize similar polygons.
18. Students will explain that all squares are similar but not all rectangles and not all triangles are similar.
19. Students will investigate what changes and what stays the same when a shape is enlarged or shrunken.
20. Students will tessellate polygons in a plane.
21. Students will identify, extend, and create repeating patterns.
22. Students will identify line and rotational symmetry and how to recognize it in African textiles.

Joan Cohen Jones
Eastern Michigan University

with

Diann Ash, Atlanta Public Schools
Priscilla Golley, University of North Georgia
Nancy Schwarzhoff, Eau Claire School District

Introduction

Mathematical knowledge is often seen as a "critical filter for employment and full participation in our society" (National Council of Teachers of Mathematics [NCTM] 1989, p. 4). Yet students from diverse backgrounds are often underrepresented in advanced mathematics and science courses and in careers requiring mathematics and science (National Research Council 1991; Rosser 1995; Secada 1990). When students "tune out" to mathematics, their resulting innumeracy creates a barrier to future success in our technologically oriented society. The National Research Council (1989) warns that if illiteracy and innumeracy are not corrected, our nation will become divided into two groups: a powerful, technologically savvy elite and a "dependent, semiliterate majority, disproportionately Hispanic and Black" (p. 14).

Why does this disparity exist in mathematics achievement? Researchers believe that students from diverse backgrounds may find the mathematics learned in school irrelevant to their lives. According to Davidson and Kramer (1997), "when students experience the mathematics in a classroom as not relating to them or their culture, they may feel invisible and unconnected with the content" (p. 139). Moreover, because the mathematics curriculum is mostly derived from European mathematics, students from non-European backgrounds may believe that only European cultures have worked with and are capable of working with mathematics (Shirley 1995). Compounding this problem is the erroneous idea that mathematics is neutral, gender-free, objective, and beyond the realm of multicultural education (Ladson-Billings 1995). Thus, teachers who strive to make their classrooms equitable may focus on other subjects. Those teachers who do try to add a multicultural emphasis to their mathematics curriculum may be hindered by their own limited and Western-biased mathematics backgrounds.

The textiles produced by a culture serve as excellent vehicles for learning about the culture and the mathematical concepts that are informally used in textile production. In this nine-lesson unit, students will explore informal geometry within the context of geometric patterns found in Navajo rugs and West African textiles. Students will study perimeter and area of polygons, similarity, symmetry, tessellation, and pattern recognition. Two themes tie the unit together: (1) these patterns are universal and reappear in different cultures at different time periods; and (2) virtually all people use mathematics in their everyday life. It should be noted that weaving and textile examples could be drawn from any cultural/regional group to supplement those examples used in this unit.

The unit begins with notes for the teacher that provide background information on the two cultures selected for study. A bibliography at the end of the unit provides reference material for further study. A bibliography of children's literature, folktales, and age-appropriate reference materials has been listed separately for easy access. This bibliography includes books that combine high interest with accurate cultural and historical information about Native Americans and West Africans. Books about American pioneers have also been included for teachers who want to connect Native American weaving and West African textiles with North American crafts such as quilting. We recommend that teachers include readings from the bibliography throughout the unit. Teachers are encouraged to create additional mathematics lessons utilizing the handicrafts and textiles of other cultures in their state and region.

Some of the lessons may take more than one day to complete. Teachers can choose individual activities from the lessons, rather than completing entire lessons. Many of the activities throughout the unit can stand alone, while others make more sense completed sequentially. The activities vary in difficulty. We therefore suggest that teachers read the lessons carefully before deciding which lessons and activities to complete. Five possible paths for completion of the unit are (1) lessons one through nine; (2) lessons one, two, three, four, and nine; (3) lessons one through five and nine; (4) lessons one, five, six, seven, eight, and nine; or (5) lessons one, six, seven, eight, and nine. The content and activities selected are appropriate for students in grades 3 through 5. These lessons can also be adapted for grades 6 through 8.

The first lesson introduces the unit, and the ninth lesson provides closure with a variety of activities and questions for discussion, some of which are interdisciplinary. In lessons two, three, and four, a problem-solving approach involves students in finding perimeter and area of geometric shapes. Through experimentation, students come to realize the need for uniform and appropriately sized units of measure. Students find the perimeters and areas of squares, rectangles, parallelograms, and triangles using a 10×10 grid or dot paper. Lesson five teaches the idea of similarity. Students learn an informal meaning of similarity; that is, two figures are similar if they are the same shape but not necessarily the same size. Lessons six, seven, and eight teach tessellation, pattern recognition, and symmetry. In lesson six, students come to an informal understanding of tessellation by trying to cover or tile paper with a repeating pattern without leaving any gaps or holes. Students learn that mathematics can be creative and artistic. In lesson seven, students learn to recognize, extend, and create repeating patterns. They are asked to use logical reasoning and problem solving to complete the activities. Lesson eight investigates line and rotational symmetry in a global perspective, specifically using African textile designs. Here, too, students learn about the connections between mathematics and art.

The unit lends itself to interdisciplinary exploration, especially the interface of social studies, language arts, and mathematics. For example, the lessons based on Navajo rugs (two, three, four, and five) might be integrated into a unit on the opening of the Santa Fe Trail or the building of the railroad in the American West. The lessons based on African textiles would work well as part of a unit on the history of the Ashanti Kingdom of Ghana or the development of the slave trade along the Ivory Coast. All of the lessons can be integrated with children's literature, music, art, and mythology. The bibliographies provide information in this area.

There is a great deal of information available on the Internet with respect to Navajo rugs and West African textiles, specifically kente cloth. Teachers can print pictures from websites to use as examples for the unit. Specific websites are given in the bibliography. This unit aims to encourage understanding and acceptance of students from diverse cultures as well as appreciation for the mathematics in the world around us.

Background Information for the Teacher

NAVAJO RUGS

The Navajo are the largest Native American tribe in North America (Taylor and Taylor 1993). Their homeland, which they call Dine' Bekayeh, is in Arizona, Utah, Colorado, and New Mexico. The Navajo call themselves Dine' (the people).

The Navajo learned to weave in the seventeenth and eighteenth centuries, probably from their neighbors, the Pueblo Indians. Weaving became women's work because of the structure of Navajo society (Kent 1985). Men were often on the move, while women stayed at home doing craftwork and tending sheep. Weaving became an important part of Navajo life. Each family had access to a loom, which was set up under a tree outside their home or hogan in the summertime and inside the hogan during the winter. The Navajo weavers sat in front of their looms for several hours a day. They created weaving songs to help with the repetitive work and to establish a rhythm to work by. These weaving songs remain an important part of Navajo culture today (Taylor and Taylor 1993). The period from about 1675 to 1863 is known as the classic period in Navajo weaving. The materials were indigenous to the Navajo people, and the designs were simple yet elegant. During the classic period, Navajos mainly wove for their own community usage rather than for trade. The designs during the classic period were open-ended or borderless, with the patterns extending continuously off the actual edge of the fabric to infinity. Thus, in principle, the design would fill all of space (Wetherill 1991).

From 1775, European settlers continued to move westward across the continent, seeking new lands and resources. The Native Peoples, who had long inhabited the land, struggled to maintain their land, resources, and freedom. The Navajo, as well as other Native American groups, thought the settlers were the invaders. The settlers thought the Native Peoples were the attackers. General James Carleton was in command of the military in Arizona and New Mexico in 1862, and he ordered Colonel Kit Carson to protect the settlers by killing or taking prisoner any and all Apaches and Navajos. Carleton's plan was to move the Apaches and Navajos to a reservation and to teach them farming and livestock raising. This was the beginning of the Long Walk to Bosque Redondo where Indian Peoples were held for five years. The Long Walk to Bosque Redondo was almost 400 miles, and many Native Americans died on the walk. Others died while at the Fort because of lack of food, health care, and warmth.

Finally, in 1868, a peace treaty was signed, and the Long Walk Home began. The transition period in Navajo weaving occurred then (1868 to 1895). Navajo weavers began using materials and dyes they obtained from trade and also began to weave mainly for commercial reasons. At the end of this period, a significant stylistic change occurred in weaving: straight-lined borders were used. It has been speculated (Wetherill 1991) that these borders symbolized the boundaries of the reservation. Also, the borders represented the Navajo's acknowledgement of Anglo preferences for self-contained pieces.

At about the same time, commercial dyes were introduced, producing bright colors in woven goods. The Navajo women admired these colors and wove rugs using colorful yarn between 1880 and 1920 (Baldwin 1970; Taylor and Taylor 1993). However, the use of commercial dyes resulted in the deterioration of quality. After 1920, due to efforts of traders and others, old patterns were revived, and vegetable dyes were reintroduced.

Today, Navajo rugs are quite valuable. They are admired for their design and quality. Present-day Navajo rugs are usually woven from French merino yarn (Taylor and Taylor 1993). The Navajo reservation contains thirteen individual weaving regions (Roessel 1995). Each region weaves a particular design and style rug, named for the region where it is woven. For example, the Yei rugs have elongated figures, the same figures used in religious sand paintings. No religious significance is attributed to the rugs, however (Taylor and Taylor 1993).

Weaving remains an integral part of Navajo culture, inhabiting legends, folktales, and custom (Roessel 1995). Each rug tells a story. The Navajo believe that the loom and weaving are divinely inspired. Their stories about weaving name three figures: Spider Woman, Spider Man, and Changing Woman. According to Navajo beliefs, Spider Man told Spider Woman how to construct a loom, and Spider Woman taught Changing Woman to weave. Weaving remains a vehicle for passing traditions and values from one generation to the next.

AFRICAN TEXTILES

Historians have speculated for some time on the origins of weaving in West Africa (Mack 1993). Weavers are skilled at both narrow-strip and wide-strip weaving. The women weave on simple, single-heddle looms, and the men weave on the more complicated double-heddle looms that have foot peddles. The women's looms produce wide strips of fabric, to be used for family clothing. The men's looms produce narrow, four-inch-long strips of material that are sewn together to make rectangular or square cloth and are always produced for sale. Men's weaving is regarded as a professional craft. Many tribes in West Africa practice narrow-strip weaving, but the Ashanti and the Ewe are considered masters of this craft (Adler and Barnard 1995).

The ancient kingdom of Ghana, known as the Ashanti Kingdom, was located about 500 miles northwest of present-day Ghana, in West Africa (Hintz 1987). In the late 1700s, the Ashanti expanded their empire to the area that includes present-day Ghana and consolidated their power (Adler and Barnard 1995). The empire thus created still exists today. A king or Asantahene ruled the Ashanti Empire of the 1700s. The Ashanti court, known at this time for its splendor and luxury, was located in the city of Kumasi (Adler and Barnard 1995). Ashanti weaving styles developed through the needs and demands of the royal court at Kumasi (Mack 1993).

Kente cloth, the woven fabric produced by the Ashanti, is very complex. Narrow strips are woven of silk or cotton in a wide variety of colors and patterns. These strips are later sewn together to produce a checkered pattern. At Bonwire, the Ashanti weaving center, the weavers formed a separate professional guild with their own chief (Mack 1993). In the time of the ancient kingdom, weavers produced cloth of silk only for the Asantahene and royal court. Ashanti kings and queens had their own personal designs. All new patterns invented by the weavers belonged to the Asantahene who either kept them for his own use or gave them to men and women of the court (Mack 1993). During the time of the Ashanti kingdom of the 1700s, textiles were related to the Ashanti political system. Individuals holding certain political or social positions wore particular types of cloth. For example, asasia cloth was made for the king only (Mack 1993). All the patterns woven were named systematically.

In modern Ghana, kente cloth is still woven in Bonwire, but weaving is also done in other towns. Kente cloth is worn for celebrations and religious holidays. In recent years, kente cloth has become a symbol of unity for African Americans and has been incorporated into western dress.

The Ewe began migrating to what is now known as Togo and Ghana somewhere in the sixteenth century (Adler and Barnard 1995). The Ewe were mainly farmers and traders. Unlike the Ashanti, they did not have a king or central ruler but lived in clans. They became well known for their narrow-strip weaving of blue and white cloth. Ewe weaving, unlike Ashanti weaving, did not develop from a central influence but from the desires of the individual customer (Adler and Barnard 1995).

The Ewe began weaving before the sixteenth century. Their looms were portable and were carried with them until they finally settled in their present homeland. The Ewe are known for producing large quantities of cloth for their own use and for trade (Adler and Barnard 1995).

Intricate West African textile patterns are also produced by techniques other than weaving. For example, the Yoruba women of Nigeria make beautiful tie-dyed patterns (Meyer 1995). They also use resist-dying to create adire cloth.

Unit Organization

LESSON 1: INTRODUCTION

Students will

Identify, label, and categorize shapes found in the classroom;

Distinguish between and give examples of shapes, patterns, and symbols;

Describe the shapes and patterns found in examples of ethnic weavings.

LESSON 2: PERIMETER USING NAVAJO RUG DESIGNS

Students will

Discuss the meaning and importance of perimeter;

Estimate and then measure the perimeters of Navajo rug designs, using various manipulatives;

Measure perimeters of designs, using a 10 × 10 grid;

Measure the perimeters of irregular patterns, using a 10 × 10 grid;

Share methods for measuring irregular perimeters;

Measure the perimeter of a room or large object and explain their methods and unit of measure.

LESSON 3: AREA USING NAVAJO RUG DESIGNS

Students will

Estimate and then measure the area of Navajo rug designs, using lima beans, macaroni, and paper clips;

Use the unit square to measure areas of Navajo rug designs;

Measure the areas of irregular patterns, using a 10 × 10 grid;

Share methods for measuring irregular areas;

Create and color their own Navajo designs and measure their perimeter and area.

LESSON 4: AREA AND PERIMETER OF SQUARES, RECTANGLES, TRIANGLES, AND PARALLELOGRAMS

Students will

Measure areas and perimeters of squares and rectangles, using geoboards and dot paper;

Identify and discuss patterns in perimeter and area of squares and rectangles;

Define right triangles and measure their areas, using geoboards and dot paper;

Share their methods for measuring areas of right triangles;

Define parallelograms and measure their areas, using geoboards and dot paper;

Share their methods for measuring areas of parallelograms;

Trace their foot or hand on grid paper, measure its area, and share methods;

Create a design with area and perimeter constraints.

LESSON 5: SIMILARITY OF POLYGONS

Students will

Understand the concept of similarity and examine real-world examples;

Investigate and summarize similarity properties of squares, rectangles, and triangles;

Enlarge and shrink geometric shapes;

Create and enlarge or shrink original designs.

LESSON 6: TESSELLATIONS USING AFRICAN TEXTILES

Students will

Examine patterns in African textiles;

Classify individual patterns as able to cover fabric with or without leaving gaps;

Use one attribute block to create repeating patterns that cover fabric (the plane) without leaving gaps;

Use two different attribute blocks to create repeating patterns that do not leave gaps;

Classify several shapes as being able to cover the plane without gaps (tessellate) or not;

Design and color patterns on grid paper that cover the paper without gaps.

LESSON 7: PATTERN RECOGNITION USING AFRICAN TEXTILES

Students will

Look for repeating patterns in their classroom and on African textiles;

Create and evaluate patterns, using colored tiles;

Establish criteria to determine duplication of patterns;

Design their own repeating patterns.

LESSON 8: SYMMETRY IN AFRICAN TEXTILES

Students will

Examine symmetry in letters of the alphabet and numerals;

Look for symmetry in their partner, using a yardstick;

Recognize line and rotational symmetry in African textiles and patterns;

Create designs with at least one kind of symmetry;

Share their designs and group them according to the type of symmetry.;

Create a line of symmetry and one half of a design, then the mirror image of the design and share with class members.

LESSON 9: CLOSURE

Students will

Become aware of the importance and prevalence of geometry all over the world;

Complete a variety of activities, some of them mathematical and some not, to bring closure to the unit;

Discuss a number of issues related to Navajo culture and African and African American cultures.

The Curriculum and Evaluation Standards for School Mathematics

"Craft Patterns and Geometry," a culturally responsive mathematics unit for third through fifth grades, was developed to reflect and illustrate the *Curriculum and Evaluation Standards for School Mathematics* (1989) published by the National Council of Teachers of Mathematics (NCTM). These Standards, along with the *Professional Standards for Teaching Mathematics* (1991) and the *Assessment Standards for School Mathematics* (1995), represent the collaboration of a team of researchers and teachers interested in presenting a consistent vision of what it means to know and do mathematics in the twenty-first century. These Standards have recently been revised and combined into one document, *Principles and Standards for School Mathematics* (2000), which extends the vision presented here. For more information, contact The National Council of Teachers of Mathematics, 1906 Association Drive, Reston, Virginia, 22091 or visit NCTM online at www.NCTM.org.

The *Curriculum and Evaluation Standards* include distinct sections for each of the three grade-level groupings: K through 4, 5 through 8, and 9 through 12, and a separate section for evaluation. Because "Craft Patterns and Geometry" spans grades 3 through 5, an overview of the *Curriculum Standards* for both grades K through 4 and 5 through 8 is presented. While many of the Standards in both grade-level groupings share the same name and general description, the grades 5 through 8 Standards expect greater depth and breadth. This mathematics unit closely reflects the *Curriculum Standards* for grades K through 4. However, several of the activities and the higher-level questions throughout the unit also reflect several of the Standards for grades 5 through 8.

CURRICULUM STANDARDS FOR GRADES K THROUGH 4

Standard 1: Mathematics as Problem Solving. Problem solving is an integral part of students' mathematics learning and plays a central role in the mathematics curriculum. Students are encouraged to learn mathematical concepts through problem solving by using a variety of strategies and approaches. Many problems originate in students' everyday experiences at school and at home.

Standard 2: Mathematics as Communication. Students have numerous opportunities to communicate about mathematics. They reflect on their thinking and clarify their understanding about mathematics concepts; they discuss, write, and read about mathematics and relate physical objects, diagrams, and pictures to mathematics.

Standard 3: Mathematics as Reasoning. Emphasis is placed on reasoning, explaining, and justifying answers and solution processes rather than just getting the right answer. Students are encouraged to use logical thinking, models, properties of mathematics, and facts to justify their thinking.

Standard 4: Mathematical Connections. Students have the opportunity to connect mathematics to their real lives, other curriculum areas, and other mathematics topics. They are able to transition between conceptual and procedural knowledge.

Standard 5: Estimation. Students understand when it is appropriate to use estimation, learn various estimation strategies, and judge the plausibility of results.

Standard 6: Number Sense and Numeration. Students develop counting skills, understand place value concepts, have experience with how numbers are used in the real world, and develop number sense.

Standard 7: Concepts of Whole Number Operations. Students develop meaning for the four operations of addition, subtraction, multiplication, and division. They learn to use these operations within the context of problem solving.

Standard 8: Whole Number Computation. Students use algorithms, mental mathematics, and estimation for whole number operations.

Standard 9: Geometry and Spatial Sense. Students can describe objects in the physical world that are two and three dimensional. They learn to recognize, classify, draw, describe, and combine shapes. Students learn to identify geometry in the real world while relating geometry concepts to number and measurement concepts.

Standard 10: Measurement. Students come to understand the different characteristics of measurement, including length, mass, area, volume, and time. They relate measurement to problems in everyday life. Students use estimates of measurement where appropriate.

Standard 11: Statistics and Probability. Students collect, organize, display, and interpret data. They create and solve problems that involve the analysis of data.

Standard 12: Fractions and Decimals. Students use physical models to understand fraction and decimal concepts, equivalence of fractions, and operations on fractions and decimals.

Standard 13: Patterns and Relationships. Students identify, describe, continue, and create patterns. Students represent patterns numerically, geometrically, and by the use of variables whenever possible. Students understand the mathematical relationships underlying the patterns they explore.

Matrix of Grades K through 4 Curriculum Standards Referenced to Individual Lessons

	Lesson 1	Lesson 2	Lesson 3	Lesson 4	Lesson 5	Lesson 6	Lesson 7	Lesson 8	Lesson 9
Standard 1	X	X	X	X	X	X	X	X	X
Standard 2	X	X	X	X	X	X	X	X	X
Standard 3	X	X	X	X	X	X	X	X	X
Standard 4	X	X	X	X	X	X	X	X	X
Standard 5		X	X	X					
Standard 6			X	X					
Standard 7									
Standard 8									
Standard 9	X	X	X	X	X	X	X	X	X

Standard 10		X	X	X	X				
Standard 11									X
Standard 12									
Standard 13	X	X	X	X	X	X	X	X	X

CURRICULUM STANDARDS FOR GRADES 5 THROUGH 8

Standard 1: Mathematics as Problem Solving. Students formulate and solve mathematical problems from topics both within and outside of mathematics. Students validate and interpret results and generalize solutions and strategies.

Standard 2: Mathematics as Communication. Students discuss mathematical ideas and make and verify conjectures. Students pattern mathematical situations using a variety of methods, including physical models, oral, written, algebraic, and pictorial techniques. Students use mathematical notation to aid in communicating mathematics.

Standard 3: Mathematics as Reasoning. Students can use deductive, inductive, and spatial reasoning where appropriate. They learn to assess mathematical conjectures or guesses using sound mathematical reasoning.

Standard 4: Mathematical Connections. Students identify connections between different mathematical topics, which enables them to integrate their knowledge of mathematics and strengthen exploration of new topics by building on previous knowledge. Students apply problem-solving techniques and deductive and inductive reasoning to solve problems in other disciplines.

Standard 5: Number and Number Relationships. Students can represent numerical quantities in several equivalent representations (including integer, fraction, decimal, and percent). Students strengthen number sense with regard to whole numbers and develop number sense of fractions, decimals, and percents. They use ratios and proportions in meaningful situations.

Standard 6: Number Systems and Number Theory. Students understand the necessity of extending the whole numbers and understand operations with rational numbers, integers, fractions, and decimals.

Standard 7: Computation and Estimation. Students are able to use computation and estimation strategies for whole numbers, integers, fractions, decimals, and rational numbers; explain and analyze their procedures; use technology to assist in computation; evaluate reasonableness of answers; and solve proportions.

Standard 8: Patterns and Functions. Students identify, describe, continue, analyze, and create patterns. Students understand functional relationships, especially the relationship between variables. Students use tables and graphs to represent relationships and patterns.

Standard 9: Algebra. Students can apply the algebraic concepts of variable, equation, and expression. Students informally investigate nonlinear equations and inequalities.

Standard 10: Statistics. Students collect, display, and analyze data using statistical techniques. Students make and evaluate arguments that are made from statistical methods.

Standard 11: Probability. Students carry out experiments to determine probabilities. They learn to simulate probability experiments by using a sample space. They understand the difference between experimental and theoretical probability.

Standard 12: Geometry. Students can identify, describe, and classify geometric figures using correct mathematical terminology. They can compare the characteristics of different geometric figures. Students investigate transformations, apply the principles of geometry, and appreciate that geometry is an important tool for describing the world around them.

Standard 13: Measurement. Students can make measurements using both estimation and appropriate tools. They extend their understanding of a number of concepts, including perimeter, area, volume, and angle measure. Students develop formulas for solving certain measurement problems.

Matrix of Grades 5 through 8 Curriculum Standards Referenced to Individual Lessons

	Lesson 1	Lesson 2	Lesson 3	Lesson 4	Lesson 5	Lesson 6	Lesson 7	Lesson 8	Lesson 9
Standard 1	X	X	X	X	X	X	X	X	X
Standard 2	X	X	X	X	X	X	X	X	X
Standard 3	X	X	X	X	X	X	X	X	X
Standard 4	X	X	X	X	X	X	X	X	X
Standard 5					X				
Standard 6									
Standard 7		X	X	X	X				
Standard 8		X	X	X	X	X	X	X	
Standard 9									
Standard 10									
Standard 11									
Standard 12	X	X	X	X	X	X	X	X	X
Standard 13	X	X	X	X	X	X	X	X	X

The Content Standards for NCTM and Culturally Responsive Pedagogy

How can mathematics content be altered to address the principles of culturally responsive pedagogy? The NCTM Standards (1989, 1991, 1995) have recommended numerous changes in mathematics content and pedagogy that will result in increased equity in the mathematics classroom. The Standards consist of three documents, the *Curriculum and Evaluation Standards for School Mathematics* (1989), the *Professional Standards for Teaching Mathematics* (1991), and the *Assessment Standards for School Mathematics* (1995).

The *Curriculum and Evaluation Standards for School Mathematics* (NCTM 1989) is based on five goals: Students will (1) learn to value mathematics, (2) become confident in their ability to study mathematics, (3) become mathematical problem solvers, (4) learn to communicate mathematically, and (5) learn to reason mathematically. The first goal explicitly discusses the inclusion of culture in the mathematics classroom. According to NCTM (1989, p. 5),

> Students should have numerous and varied experiences related to the cultural, historical, and scientific evolution of mathematics so that they can appreciate the role of mathematics in the development of our contemporary society . . .

The four remaining goals address behaviors and learning outcomes that will result in increased equity in mathematics classrooms. For example, to accomplish the second goal, NCTM (1989) recommends that students learn that "mathematics is a common human activity" (p. 6). If students become aware of the mathematics in their everyday world and understand its relationship to school mathematics, they will appreciate its relevance. As another example, the fourth goal, that students learn to communicate mathematically, directly applies to how students learn mathematics. This goal emphasizes social interaction in the learning of mathematics, where students build on relationships with each other and rely on interdependence rather than competition. This goal specifically fits with the way some diverse students tend to work best (Malloy 1997).

Several of the standards address culturally responsive pedagogy. Shirley (1995) posits that a natural extension of Standard 4: Mathematical Connections is "to encourage finding examples of mathematics in other cultures" (p. 34). He recommends the inclusion of mathematics such as Chinese numerals and the Chinese version of the Pythagorean theorem. But Shirley also recommends the inclusion of everyday activities that may not look like mathematics to the Western-trained mind but do contain important mathematical relationships, such as "fractal patterns in the layout of traditional Dogon villages in Mali" (p. 36). Thus, Standard 4 supports connecting the mathematics learned in school with students' cultural heritage. As another example, Standard 5: Estimation calls for students to learn about estimation strategies, understand when estimation is appropriate, determine whether results are reasonable, and "apply estimation in working with quantities, measurement, computation, and problem solving" (NCTM 1989, p. 36). The implementation of this standard will encourage the success of some African American students, who tend to "approximate space, numbers, and time rather than use exact calculations" (Malloy 1997, p. 25).

The *Curriculum and Evaluation Standards for School Mathematics* (NCTM 1989) recommends significant changes in content and emphasis in the K through 12 mathematics curriculum. As an example, in grades 5 through 8, NCTM (1989) shifts the emphasis in learning algebra from manipulating symbols and memorizing procedures to "developing an understanding of variables, expressions, and equations" (p. 70) and "using a variety of methods to solve linear equations and informally investigate inequalities and nonlinear equations" (p. 71). Thus, the expectation is that all students can and will learn algebra in a meaningful way. In other words, the Standards support high expectations for all students.

Although the *Curriculum and Evaluation Standards for School Mathematics* (NCTM 1989) has begun to address the principles of culturally responsive pedagogy, more needs to be done. For example, the mathematics curriculum should include more content on the history of mathematics, especially non-Western contributions to the development of mathematics, and informal mathematics. As students learn about their own culture's contributions to mathematics, pride in their culture increases, and they come to understand that mathematics is used in the daily lives of people all over the world. Moreover, as students learn about both formal and informal uses of mathematics, they begin to develop a richer concept of the nature of mathematics and an appreciation for different mathematical worldviews.

A meaningful approach for including multicultural mathematics content is to fully integrate it with what students are learning every day. In other words, multicultural mathematics topics should not be treated as enrichment activities or "rainy day" math. Davidson and Kramer (1997, p. 132) comment

> This approach contrasts with both the mathematics equivalent of Black History Month, in which multicultural mathematics is separate from "regular" mathematics, and with a "tourist curriculum," in which students see this type of mathematics as fun but not as a basis for essential mathematical learning.

Thus, multicultural mathematics topics should become part of the regular mathematics curriculum.

NCTM (1989) advises the use of real-world problems that are meaningful to students and arise out of everyday situations. Unfortunately, NCTM does not specifically recommend mathematics problems that are socially reconstructivist in nature. These kinds of problems can teach the principles of democracy and result in actions that benefit students and their community. It is important for students to learn that mathematical knowledge is empowering and can effect social change. This can be accomplished at all levels. For example, Ladson-Billings (1995) describes a class of Puerto Rican children in New York City who discovered a toxic waste site in their neighborhood. The children documented the illegal dump by collecting data on the number of barrels of waste brought to the dump and the number of people impacted. Then, they contacted the proper authorities. The owner was fined and the dump closed. Not only did the children learn how to effect change in a democracy and work on behalf of their families and community, they learned mathematics as well. This is but one example of how mathematics can be taught in a socially responsible manner. As an introductory exercise, students can survey their class and school with regard to needed computer equipment, changes in safety procedures, or funds for playground improvement. Such an undertaking, while not as dramatic as Ladson-Billings's example, can motivate children to participate actively in mathematics and to see the relevance of mathematics to real problem situations.

Researchers indicate that the way in which mathematics has been taught may be alienating to diverse students. Traditionally, mathematics pedagogy involved whole class instruction where the teacher modeled mathematical thinking while students worked individually. Malloy (1997) and Sleeter (1997) indicate that some ethnically and culturally diverse students perform more effectively in cooperative learning groups. Cooperative learning has also been shown to promote self-esteem for students of color (Croom 1997). Therefore, to make mathematics classrooms equitable for all students, changes are necessary in how mathematics is taught and the way in which students are expected to learn.

The *Professional Standards for Teaching Mathematics* (1991) emphasizes teaching effectiveness, classroom atmosphere, and teacher preparation. NCTM recommends that teachers select "worthwhile mathematical tasks" (1991, p. 25) that engage students in higher-order thinking, focus on conceptual understanding, and correspond to students' diverse interests and backgrounds. Both the teachers' and students' roles in learning mathematics are discussed, with emphasis on classroom discourse, conjecture, questioning, and wait-time. The *Professional Standards for Teaching Mathematics* urges mathematics teachers to develop learning environments that value and respect "students' ideas, ways of thinking, and mathematical dispositions" (NCTM 1991, p. 57). With respect to the preparation and continued training of mathematics teachers, the Standards recommend that teacher education programs help teachers understand "the nature of mathematics, the contributions of different cultures toward the development of mathematics, and the role of mathematics in culture and society" (NCTM 1991, p. 132). If mathematics teachers, school systems, and teacher education programs follow the recommendations in the *Professional Standards for Teaching Mathematics,* mathematics teaching will be consistent with the principles of culturally responsive pedagogy and, therefore, compatible with the needs of students from diverse backgrounds.

The *Assessment Standards for School Mathematics* (1995) emphasizes the importance of equity by making it one of the five assessment standards. NCTM (1995, p. 15) comments

> Assessments have too often ignored differences in students' experience, physical condition, gender, and ethnic, cultural, and social backgrounds in an effort to be fair. This practice has led to assessments that do not take differences among students into account. The experiences each student brings to any classroom and to any assessment are unique.

Thus, NCTM recommends that multiple assessments be utilized, ones that can measure mathematical knowledge in a manner consistent with individual student's strengths.

In summary, changes are necessary in content, pedagogy, and assessment to insure that mathematics classrooms are equitable for all students. The NCTM Standards have begun to address these issues by advocating active learning of mathematics in student-centered classrooms where teachers facilitate students' learning of mathematics and assess students' knowledge equitably. The *Curriculum and Evaluation Standards for School Mathematics* (1989) has revised the content in K through 12 mathematics to focus on conceptual learning, technology, and skills needed for the twenty-first century. However, the Standards have not placed enough emphasis on mathematics curricula based on non-Western contributions to the development of mathematics, informal uses of mathematics, and mathematics as a tool for social action. The *Professional Standards for School Mathematics* (1991) urges sweeping changes in pedagogy, classroom atmosphere, and preservice and in-service teacher education, which, if implemented, will result in mathematics classrooms where all students can achieve academic excellence. The *Assessment Standards for School Mathematics* recommends that assessments be revised to respect individual differences and reflect individual strengths.

"Craft Patterns and Geometry," the nine-lesson unit that follows, effectively incorporates both the Standards and the principles of culturally responsive pedagogy. The content includes measurement, geometry, spatial sense, and pattern recognition—topics given increased emphasis in the Standards. Here, both conceptual understanding and mathematical rigor are emphasized. First, students develop a fundamental understanding of measurement. They get practical experience in recognizing the need for appropriate and then uniform units of measure. They find areas and perimeters of various polygons, at the same time investigating similar and dissimilar characteristics. Students informally investigate the concept of similarity of polygons by enlarging or shrinking shapes. Later in the unit, students learn about various patterns (a precursor to functions and sequences), discover tessellations, and explore line and rotational symmetry. The closing lesson connects the mathematics to social and political issues. Emphasis throughout the unit is placed on discovery, experimentation, conjecture, and communication. Students often collaborate with other students in small groups or pairs, where they problem solve and communicate to refine their ideas about mathematics. The teacher's role is one of facilitator. The teacher creates an exciting atmosphere, motivating students to learn about both the mathematics and the cultural examples. In this unit, students understand the importance and cultural relevance of the subject matter. They are given choices of which tasks to complete, how to complete them, and with whom to work. The teacher uses effective strategies that facilitate students' knowledge through questioning and relevant examples. The tasks selected demonstrate the teacher's high expectations for all students. Mathematical tasks are challenging and based on real-world situations. Art, literature, and history enrich the students' experience. The classroom atmosphere emphasizes cooperation rather than competition. Assessment is ongoing, formative, as well as summative, with attention to special needs.

REFERENCES

Adler, P., and N. Barnard. 1995. *African majesty: The textile art of the Ashanti and Ewe.* London: Thames & Hudson.

Baldwin, G. C. 1970. *Indians of the Southwest.* New York: Capricorn Books.

Croom, L. 1997. Mathematics for all students: Access, excellence, and equity. In *Multicultural and gender equity in the mathematics classroom: The gift of diversity. 1997 yearbook,* eds. J. Trentacosta and M. J. Kenney. Reston, VA: National Council of Teachers of Mathematics.

Davidson, E., and L. Kramer. 1997. Integrating with integrity: Curriculum, instruction, and culture in the mathematics classroom. In *Multicultural and gender equity in the mathematics classroom: The gift of diversity. 1997 yearbook,* eds. J. Trentacosta and M. J. Kenney. Reston, VA: National Council of Teachers of Mathematics.

Hintz, M. 1987. *Enchantment of the world: Ghana.* Chicago: Childrens' Press.

Ladson-Billings, G. 1995. Making mathematics meaningful in multicultural contexts. In *New directions for equity in mathematics education,* eds. W. G. Secada, E. Fennema, and L. B. Adajian. New York: Cambridge University Press.

Mack, J. 1993. Sub-Saharan Africa and the offshore islands. In *Textiles 5000 years,* ed. J. Harris. London: Harry N. Abrams.

Malloy, C. E. 1997. Including African American students in the mathematics community. In *Multicultural and gender equity in the mathematics classroom: The gift of diversity. 1997 yearbook,* eds. J. Trentacosta and M. J. Kenney. Reston, VA: National Council of Teachers of Mathematics.

Meyer, L. 1995. *Art and craft in Africa.* Paris: Bayard Presse.

National Council of Teachers of Mathematics. 1989. *Curriculum and evaluation standards for school mathematics.* Reston, VA: Author.

———. 1991. *Professional standards for teaching mathematics.* Reston, VA: Author.

———. 1995. *Assessment standards for school mathematics.* Reston, VA: Author.

———. 2000. *Principles and standards for school mathematics.* Reston, VA: Author.

National Research Council. 1991. *Moving beyond myths: Revitalizing undergraduate mathematics.* Washington, DC: National Academy Press.

———. 1995. *Everybody counts: A report to the nation on the future of mathematics education.* Washington, DC: National Academy Press.

Peck, K. P. 1985. *Navajo weaving: Three centuries of change.* Santa Fe, NM: School of American Research Press.

Roessel, M. 1995. *Songs from the loom: A Navajo girl learns to weave.* Minneapolis: Lerner.

Rosser, T. 1995. *Teaching the majority: Breaking the gender barrier in science, mathematics, and engineering.* New York: Teachers College Press.

Secada, W. G. 1990. An agenda for equity in mathematics education. *Journal for Research in Mathematics Education* 21 (6): 354–355.

Shirley, L. 1995. Using ethnomathematics to find multicultural connections. In *Connecting mathematics across the curriculum. 1995 yearbook,* eds. P. A. House and A. F. Coxford. Reston, VA: National Council of Teachers of Mathematics.

Sleeter, C. 1997. Mathematics, multicultural education, and professional development. *Journal for Research in Mathematics Education* 28 (6): 680–696.

Taylor, C., and B. Taylor. 1993. Native North America. In *Textiles 5000 years*, ed. J. Harris. London: Harry N. Abrams.

Wetherill, C. 1991. Astronomical imagery in Navajo weaving. *Astronomy Quarterly* 8 (1):1–37.

LESSON 1: Introduction

Objectives

1. Each student will identify and compare symbols and shapes common to their lives.
2. Each student will identify patterns found on textiles from Africa and Native American cultures and will compare the shapes and symbols used in the textiles with those they found in their school and classroom.
3. Each student will identify geographic regions and estimate distance from their home.
4. Each student will ask questions about the patterns and symbols (from cultural and mathematical perspectives).

Materials

Various world maps, yarn, file cards, chartpaper, yardsticks, examples of common symbols and shapes, examples and pictures of African textiles and Navajo rugs, African and Native American children's stories (optional), reading material on the history of weaving in West Africa or the history of Navajo rugs (optional)

Instructional Strategies

Opener

SE 1,   SE 4

Teacher: Shapes, shapes, shapes! They are all around us. How many can you find? For each shape you find, draw its picture, give it a name and see if you can give it a mathematical name. Have students work alone or in teams. Use one file card to record each example. Send teams on a scavenger hunt for shapes in the classroom. For example,

Body

Activity One

IE 4,   SE 4

After students have searched the classroom for shapes, have them reassemble in groups of four to six students. On desk tops, have the teams organize their file cards so shapes that are alike are grouped together. On chart paper, have group members represent each shape found by group members. File cards can be taped to the chart paper. Have students share their collection of shapes with the entire class. Ask each group of students to describe each shape by its properties. Display all charts so the full range of shapes can be seen by all.

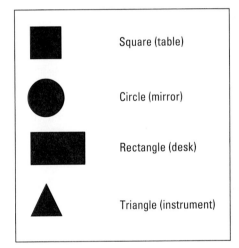

Ask the teams to identify places in the room where individual *shapes* are used to form *patterns*. Have students draw and label examples of these, also.

Examples:

• Rectangular tiles on classroom floor

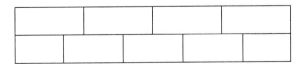

- Triangles inside circles on child's shirt

Teacher: What's the difference between a *shape* **and a** *pattern?* **Where do we see** *patterns?* **Why and how do people use patterns?** (A pattern usually consists of one or more shapes repeated in some manner to form a pleasing image.)

Activity Two

IE 1,   IE 4,   SE 4

Teacher: People often use shapes and patterns in art—on drawings, material, rugs, clothing—because shapes and patterns can be interesting. Look again at the clothing and artwork in the classroom to see examples of shapes and patterns. Have students describe the patterns using mathematical names.

Teacher: People around the world have always used shapes and patterns in their artwork, drawings, and clothing. Let's look at some examples and see if we can describe the shapes and patterns we see. (Show Navajo and Kente cloth examples; each small group of students should have an example of cloth or a drawing to examine and describe.) Have students describe their example to the rest of the class, identifying individual shapes and patterns they see. Keep a class list of any new shapes that surface from these examples.

Teacher: Lots of people have made or woven cloth and rugs using beautiful shapes and patterns. Can you name some of these cultural groups? (Native Americans, Africans, Mexicans, South Americans; all cultural groups, really.) **Teacher: Which group may have designed the fabrics we looked at today? What clues are you using to make an educated guess? Let's learn more about the Native Americans and Africans who made these beautiful patterns.**

Activity Four

IE 4,   SE 2

Provide information to students about the cultural/geographical origins of the cloth sample being used in class. Locate these places on the map, such as the Navajo homelands in Arizona, New Mexico, Colorado, and Utah or Ghana in West Africa. You may use yarn to indicate the distance from hometown to the location of the origin of each cloth (e.g., Atlanta to northern New Mexico for the origin of Navajo rugs). Use the map's scale to estimate the distance between these two locations. The teacher asks questions such as, **How far away is Arizona from (home city)? How far away is Ghana?**

Activity Three

IE 1,   IE 4,   SE 3

Teacher: Sometimes shapes and patterns are used to represent something. Can you find a shape in the room that stands for, or represents something? (Circle on poster that represents the sun; square and triangle on drawing that represent house and roof.) **Teacher: Such shapes are called** *symbols.* **Often, cultural groups use symbols in their art to tell a story or to give a message.**

Closing

A 1

Teacher: Let's review the shapes, patterns, and symbols we found today. What are the mathematical names of each one? What questions do we have about shapes, patterns, and symbols and the ways people use/have used these in their daily lives? (List questions for inquiry during the unit.)

Assessment

A 1

Teacher: (1) Identify a picture or example of a cultural use of shapes or patterns at home tonight. This might be a picture in a book or an example of fabric. If you can, bring this to class tomorrow (or draw a picture of the patterns). Be ready to identify the shapes and patterns to the rest of the class tomorrow. (2) Identify a symbol you see between school and your home. Bring in a drawing of the symbol and an explanation of its meaning.

Navajo Child's Blanket

Navajo Blanket

Navajo Blanket

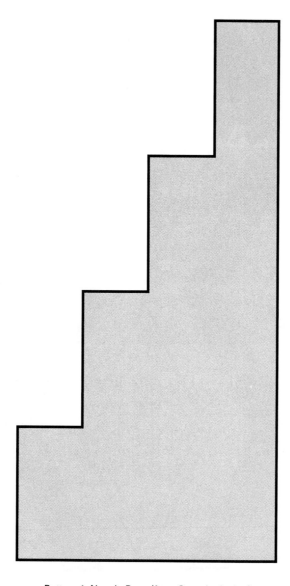

Pattern 1: Navajo Rugs (from Ganado design)

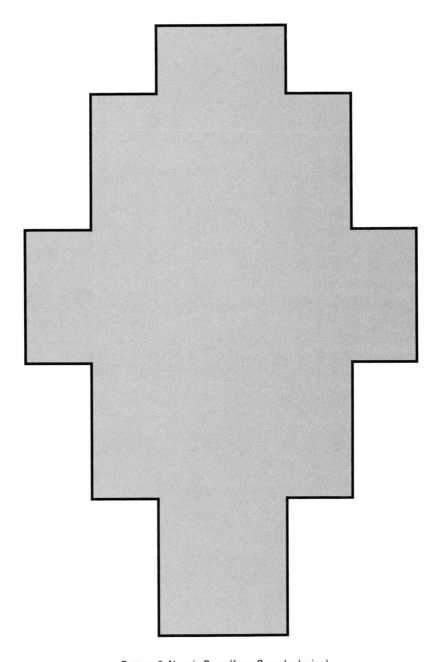

Pattern 2: Navajo Rugs (from Ganado design)

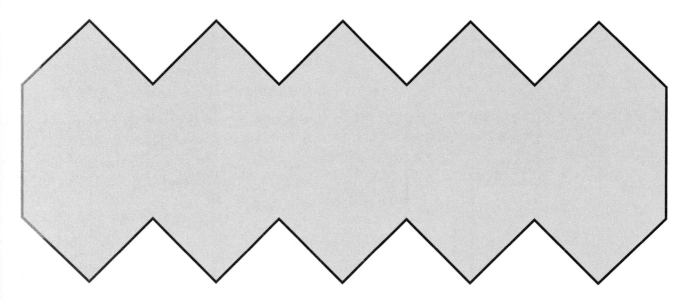

Pattern 3: Navajo Rugs (from Gallop throw rug)

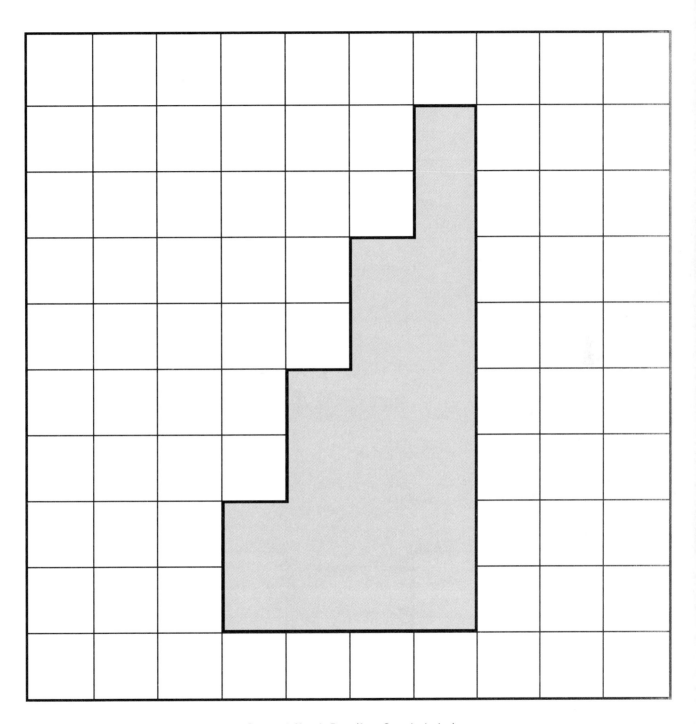

Pattern 1: Navajo Rugs (from Ganado design)

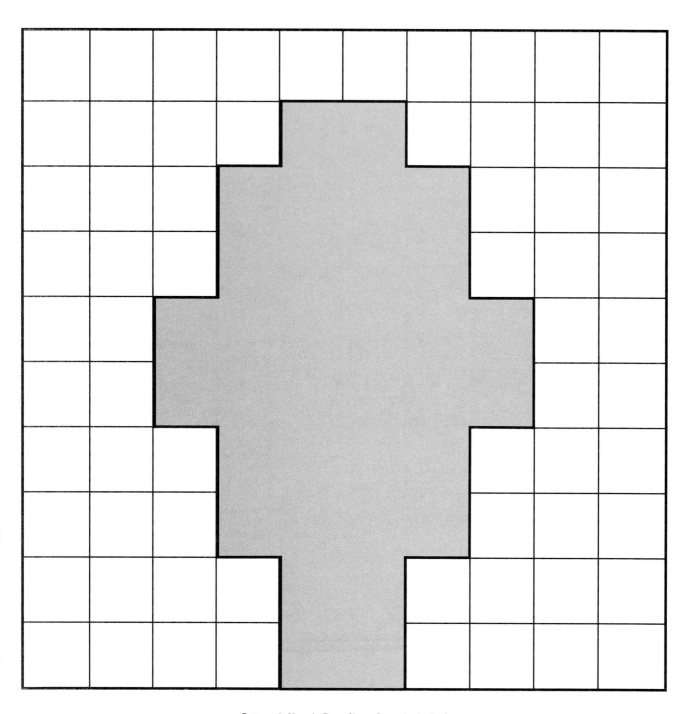

Pattern 2: Navajo Rugs (from Ganado design)

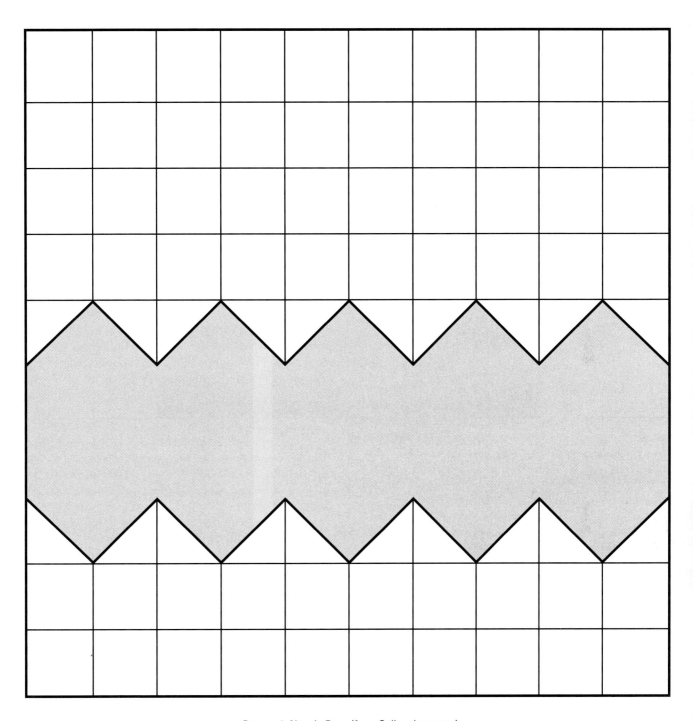

Pattern 3: Navajo Rugs (from Gallop throw rug)

LESSON 2: Finding the Perimeter Using Navajo Rug Designs

Objectives

1. Each student will learn or review the concept of perimeter of geometric shapes.
2. Each student will estimate the perimeter of geometric shapes.
3. Each student will compare the effectiveness of different units of measure for finding perimeters.
4. Each student will find the perimeter of geometric shapes, using a 10×10 grid or centimeter paper.

Materials

10×10-grid paper, centimeter grid paper, coloring pencils or crayons, rulers, examples of Navajo rug patterns on grid paper and plain paper, string, M&Ms®, pattern blocks, centimeter cubes

Instructional Strategies

Opener

IE 4,   SE 1,   A 2

The teacher asks students about the previous assessment. Students were asked to find a pattern at home or in their neighborhood and draw a picture or write a description of the pattern. This may be accomplished in a "show-and-tell" manner as a whole class activity or a "think-pair-share" with partners followed by class discussion. Teacher tapes several of the patterns to the chalkboard. **Teacher: Which of these patterns has the longest boundary? Why?** The class members explore all answers.

Teacher: Sometimes it is important to know how to find a figure's boundary. For example, if I were to put a wallpaper border around this room, what would I need to know before I buy the wallpaper? Teacher shows examples of Navajo rugs. **As you can see from the pictures and examples of Navajo rugs, many of these rugs have borders. Navajo weavers need to estimate how much wool they need to make the boundary or border for a rug before they begin to weave. Does anyone know the mathematical term for the boundary of a figure?** Teacher writes all answers on the chalkboard for later use. If no one volunteers the word *perimeter*, the teacher writes this on the chalkboard.

Note: This is a good place to insert some historical information about the classic and traditional periods in Navajo weaving and how the borders of rugs came to have a special meaning to the Navajo people.

Body

Activity One

IE 1,   SE 3,   SE 4

The teacher shows pictures or fabric swatches of Navajo rugs and blankets. The teacher asks students to examine these designs and discuss what they see. **Teacher: Are these designs similar to anything you have seen? What shapes can you find in each pattern?** Teacher passes out Patterns 1 and 2 (modified Native American designs) on plain paper and explains that these designs were taken from Navajo patterns. **Teacher: If you had to find the distance around each shape, which distance would be longer? Which shape has a larger perimeter?** Teacher allows students to work individually, in pairs, or in small groups to discuss how they might answer these questions.

Activity Two

SE 2,   SE 5,   A 1

Teacher asks students to work in groups of three or four. **Teacher: Estimate which pattern has a larger perimeter.** Students discuss their answers in small group followed by whole class discussion. **Teacher: How can we check our estimates?** Teacher asks each group of students to select one type of manipulative and use it to measure the perimeters of Patterns 1 and 2. Suggested manipulatives include string, M&M's®, pattern blocks, and centimeter cubes. Teacher observes as students use their manipulatives to measure the perimeter. When they are finished, students compare their answers in their groups followed by whole class discussion. **Teacher: Which units of measurement are best to use for the perimeter? Why? Why do different groups get different answers?** Students discuss that some manipulatives are larger and therefore will require fewer of them to go around the perimeter. In other words, the measurement is dependent on the size of the unit of measure. **Teacher: If you were going to measure the perimeter of this room, which units of measurement would you use?** Discussion focuses on the need for larger units, like the length of someone's foot, to measure the perimeter of the room.

Teacher: Use your manipulatives to create three more shapes that have the same perimeter as Pattern 1. Students discuss results in small groups followed by whole class discussion. Teacher observes and provides individual assistance for students who have difficulty with the concepts or with using the manipulatives.

Activity Three

SE 2,   SE 3

Teacher distributes Patterns 1 and 2 on grid paper and asks class members to describe the grid paper in mathematical terms. **Teacher: What shapes are on the grid (squares)? What do you know about squares?** The teacher guides students to use mathematical language as they discuss the characteristics of squares. **Teacher: How many squares are on each sheet of grid paper? Can you think of a way to find the perimeters of the patterns from Activity 2 using the grid paper?** Teacher asks students to discuss in small groups and then as a class. Class members conjecture about how to find perimeter using a square grid (i.e., by defining one unit as the linear length of one side of a square). **Teacher: Do we get the same results using the grid paper?**

Activity Four

SE 1,   SE 5,   A 3

Students continue to work in small groups of three to four. Teacher distributes Pattern 3 on 10 × 10-grid paper. Note that this pattern has several diagonal lines across squares. **Teacher: I have a challenge for you. How does this pattern compare to the other two patterns that you measured? Is the perimeter larger than the perimeters of both patterns? Is it smaller than Pattern 2 but larger than Pattern 1? How can you tell?** Teacher asks students to (1) estimate the perimeter of Pattern 3 and (2) calculate the perimeter of Pattern 3, using the definition of perimeter derived in Activity 3. Students will have to devise a method for counting the length of diagonal lines. After students have completed this task, teacher asks different groups to share both their answers and their methods. Class discusses which methods worked well for counting diagonal distances. The class might vote on their favorite method. **Teacher: Which is longer, a side of one square on the grid or the diagonal of that square?** Teacher provides individual assistance for students who have difficulty estimating the diagonal of the square.

Note: An informal exploration of the concepts from Activity 4 is all that is desired. Clearly, the diagonal of a square is longer than a side of the square, because the diagonal and two sides of the square form a right triangle, with the diagonal as the hypotenuse, the longest side. It is not necessary to discuss the mathematics at this level with third through fifth graders. It is sufficient for them to theorize that the diagonal of the square is longer than the side of the square because it looks that way.

Closing

SE 2,   A 1

Teacher: Who can tell the class the meaning of perimeter in your own words? How do you think you might find the perimeter of larger spaces, like the top of your desk or your bedroom floor? When did the Navajo start using borders in their weaving? Why do you think they changed from an open design to borders?

Assessment

SE 3,   A 2

Teacher: Find the perimeter of a room or large object at home or in your neighborhood and write a paragraph or prepare an oral report describing your unit of measure and the method used. Sketch the shape of the room or object.

An optional exercise is to have the students find the perimeter of the Navajo reservation on a map. Tell the students that the Navajo and Hopi disagree on the location of territorial borders. Have them conduct research to find out more about this disagreement over borders. **Teacher: Are there other examples of border disagreements in the world today?**

LESSON 3: Finding the Area Using Navajo Rug Designs

Objectives

1. Each student will learn or review the concept of area of geometric shapes.
2. Each student will estimate the area of geometric shapes.
3. Each student will compare the effectiveness of different units of measure for finding area.
4. Each student will understand the need for uniform or standard units of measure.
5. Each student will measure the areas of geometric shapes, using a 10 × 10 grid.
6. Each student will practice counting large numbers of objects.
7. Each student will measure areas of irregular shapes.

Materials

10 × 10-grid paper, copies of chart for Lesson 3, coloring pencils or crayons, rulers, examples of Navajo rug patterns on 10 × 10-grid paper and plain paper, macaroni, lima beans, paper clips, small plastic bags

Instructional Strategies

Opener

IE 1,   IE 4

Teacher shows pictures or fabric swatches of Navajo rugs and blankets. Teacher shows Patterns 1 and 2 on grid paper. **Teacher: Last time we learned how to measure the distance around these patterns. We learned a special word for that distance. Who can tell us that word** (perimeter)? Today, we are going to answer another question. If you were to cover each pattern completely with the same material, leaving no gaps, which pattern would require more material?

Body

Activity One

IE 2,   SE 1,   SE 2

Students work in groups of three or four. Teacher distributes copies of Patterns 1 and 2 on plain paper and the chart for Lesson 3. **Teacher: How could you find out which pattern requires more material to cover it?** Teacher distributes three bags to each group, one filled with lima beans, one with macaroni, and one with paper clips. **Teacher: Estimate how many lima beans it will take to cover Pattern 1. Estimate how many lima beans it will take to cover Pattern 2. Repeat using macaroni and then paper clips. Now cover Pattern 1 completely with lima beans. Count the number of lima beans used and compare to your estimate. Do the same with Pattern 2. Repeat with macaroni and paper clips. Record the number of lima beans, macaroni, and paper clips used on your chart.** Teacher observes how students count the manipulatives. (Do they count them one at a time? Do they cover the pattern, remove the manipulatives and separate into groups of 10 before counting?) When all groups finish recording their results, the class discusses them. Different groups may have different answers. **Teacher: Why do we get different answers? Is it important to find a unit of measure that always gives the same answer? What is the problem with using macaroni or beans or paper clips to measure something?**

Activity Two

IE 4,   SE 4,   A 1

Students will continue to work in groups for this activity. Teacher distributes Patterns 1 and 2 on grid paper. **Teacher: Estimate and then count the number of squares it takes to cover each pattern. Record on the chart for Lesson 3.** Teacher observes as children count grid squares and record their answers. **Teacher: Did everyone get the same answer this time? If not, count again. By counting squares, do we have a method that will always give the same answer? Why?** Students discuss in groups and as a class.

Note: The unit square provides a uniform and reliable unit of area in that all the squares are the same size, students are actually filling up the shape, and the squares fit together without gaps. It is very important for chil-

dren to have experience with informal units of measure such as these to understand the need for consistency and uniformity in units of measure and then to transition to standard units (the English or metric system).

Teacher asks students if they know a special name for covering a pattern. If no student volunteers the term *area*, teacher writes this on the overhead or chalkboard. **Teacher: Who can give a definition of area?** Teacher develops this with class and writes the definition on the chalkboard or overhead.

Note: As students become comfortable using square grids, the teacher may want to also include hexagonal or triangular grids for measuring area.

Activity Three

SE 2,   SE 5,   A 3

Students will continue to work in groups for this activity. Teacher distributes Pattern 3 on grid paper. **Teacher: Estimate and then find the area of Pattern 3.** Teacher asks different groups to share their answers and methods for finding the area of Pattern 3, paying special attention to the areas of partial squares. Class members compare and contrast methods used by different groups. Teacher provides individual assistance for students who have difficulty with this concept.

Note: This activity seeks informal reasoning only in order to determine the areas of partial squares. It is sufficient for students to approximate the areas of partial squares; that is, let the area of each partial square equal one-half the area of a square on the grid.

Closing

A 1

Teacher: Why is it important to know how to find area? What have you learned about area? How would you measure the area of our classroom? The playground? The Navajo reservation?

Assessment

SE 3,   A 2,   A 3

Students work individually or with a partner. Teacher distributes grid paper and crayons or colored pencils. **Teacher: Create your own 'Navajo' design on grid paper. Color your pattern in such a way that shapes within the pattern with the same area (based on inspection and estimation only) are colored alike. Determine the perimeter and area of the entire pattern and write a paragraph or prepare an oral report describing your method.**

LESSON 3 CHART

Activities One and Two

	PATTERN 1	PATTERN 2
LIMA BEANS		
MACARONI		
PAPER CLIPS		
GRID SQUARES		

I OBSERVED:

I CONCLUDED:

LESSON 4: Area and Perimeter of Squares, Rectangles, and Triangles

Objectives

1. Each student will identify squares, rectangles, parallelograms and right, equilateral, and isosceles triangles.
2. Each student will measure the perimeters and areas of squares and rectangles, using geoboards and dot paper.
3. Each student will measure the areas of parallelograms and triangles, using geoboards, dot paper, and grid paper.
4. Each student will find areas of irregular shapes.
5. Each student will find areas of geometric shapes found in Navajo rugs and blankets.

Materials

Geoboards, dot paper, grid paper, Lesson 4 chart for Activity 1, Lesson 4 chart for Activity 2, examples or pictures of Navajo rugs, colored rubber bands, Lesson 4 worksheet

Instructional Strategies

Opener

IE 1,   SE 1

Teacher: For the past few days, we have been discussing perimeter and area concepts. Today, we are going to find the perimeter and area of some familiar shapes. Look at some examples of Navajo rugs. Can you find squares, rectangles, and triangles in these shapes? Today, we are going to learn to find the areas of squares, rectangles, and triangles.

Body

Activity One

SE 2,   SE 4,   A 2

Students work in pairs or small groups. Teacher distributes geoboards, dot paper, and the chart for Activity 1 to each pair or group of students. The teacher makes a 4 × 4 square on his or her geoboard. **Teacher: What does it mean to say that the square is 4 × 4? Make a 4 × 4 square on your geoboard. Is there more than one correct answer?** Teacher demonstrates for the students first, if necessary. Students discuss whether or not there is more than one solution and realize that a square, even when rotated or turned upside down is still a square with the same dimensions. **Teacher: Find and record the area and perimeter of the 4 × 4 square. How did you get your answer? Complete the chart for Activity 1.** After students complete the chart, teacher asks students to write a

paragraph describing their methods for finding the areas and perimeters of squares.

Teacher: I am thinking of a square with area 36 and perimeter 24. Make this square on your geoboard and give its dimensions. Teacher asks several more problems of this kind.

Activity Two

IE 2,   A 1

Students work in pairs or small groups. Teacher distributes chart for Activity 2. **Teacher: Now we are going to make some rectangles. What do you know about rectangles?** As class responds, teacher lists the properties of rectangles on the chalkboard or overhead, encouraging students to use mathematically precise language, such as, "rectangles have opposite sides congruent," and "rectangles have four right angles." **Teacher: How is a rectangle different from a square? How is it similar to a square? Make a 2 × 3 rectangle on your geoboard or dot paper.** Teacher demonstrates first if necessary. **Teacher: What does it mean to say that the rectangle is 2 × 3? Find the perimeter and area of the 2 × 3 rectangle. Is there more than one way to make a 2 × 3 rectangle?** Students discuss in pairs, small groups, and then as a class. Some students may suggest that a 3 × 2 rectangle is the same as a 2 × 3. **Teacher: What does a 3 × 2 rectangle look like? Find the perimeter and area of the 3 × 2 rectangle. What do you notice?** Students find that the area of the 2 × 3 rectangle is equal to the area of the 3 × 2 rectangle, which demonstrates the Commutative Law of Multiplication of Whole Numbers (the perimeters of the two rectangles are also equal). In fact, the 3 × 2 rectangle is congruent to the 2 × 3 rectangle and can be obtained by rotating the 2 × 3 rectangle. Teacher asks students to make several more rectangles and asks students to complete the chart for Activity 2. Teacher proceeds as in Activity 1.

Activity Three

SE 2,   A 1

Students work in pairs or small groups of three to four. Teacher shows students several triangles on the geoboard (including some right triangles). Teacher asks students to make these triangles on their own geoboards and reproduce on dot paper. **Teacher: Which of the triangles are right triangles?** As students correctly or incorrectly identify the right triangles, teacher asks for a definition of right triangle. Teacher writes this definition on the chalkboard or overhead. **Teacher: Can a right triangle have two right angles? Why or why not?**

Teacher: Make a right triangle with legs 2 and 3 units on your geoboard. Teacher demonstrates first, if necessary.

Teacher: How can we find the area of the right triangle using the geoboard or dot paper? How does the area of a rectangle or square help? Teacher observes as students experiment with different methods. (One method is to surround the right triangle with the smallest rectangle or square that will fit.) If, after a reasonable length of time, students are unable to find the area of the right triangle, teacher demonstrates this method. Teacher asks students to find the area of the rectangle or square surrounding the right triangle. **Teacher: What part of the rectangle (or square) does the triangle represent (one-half)? How can we find the area of the triangle if we know the area of the rectangle (or square)?** Teacher asks students to complete several more examples with right triangles.

Note: Activities 4 and 5 are more advanced and, therefore, optional. Teacher may choose to go directly to Activity 6.

Activity Four

IE 2,   SE 2,   A 1

Students work in small groups. Teacher distributes lesson 4 worksheet. Teacher makes several triangles on the geoboard and asks students to reproduce on their geoboards and dot paper. **Teacher: Identify all triangles that have two equal legs (or sides). Does anyone know the name of such a triangle (isosceles)?** Teacher elicits from students an informal definition of isosceles triangle and writes definition on the chalkboard or overhead. Teacher completes a similar activity to define equilateral triangles. **Teacher: Draw an isosceles or equilateral triangle on dot paper or create one on your geoboards. Find the area of the triangle, using your own methods.** Teacher observes as students find the area of the isosceles or equilateral triangle they created. Teacher asks each group to share their methods with the class. **Teacher: Now find the area of the triangle by surrounding it with the smallest rectangle or square that will fit. Which method do you like best? Why?**

If students do not come to this conclusion on their own, teacher explains that once the triangle is surrounded with a rectangle, the remainder of the rectangle consists of two right triangles. **Teacher: We can use what we learned in Activity 3 to find the area of these two right triangles and subtract from the area of the rectangle to find the area of the original triangle.** Teacher may suggest that students color different triangles in different colors to help them understand this.

Activity Five

SE 2,   SE 5

Students work in pairs or small groups. Teacher makes several examples of parallelograms on the geoboard and asks students to reproduce on their geoboards and dot paper. **Teacher: Can anyone tell us what this shape is called (parallelogram)? What do you notice about paral-** lelograms? How are parallelograms similar to rectangles? How are they different? Teacher creates a new parallelogram on the geoboard. **Teacher: How can we use the area of a square or rectangle to find the area of this parallelogram?** Students who need more direction can be asked how to make their parallelogram into a square or rectangle by subtracting and adding parts of it. (Here, the teacher may want to suggest that students cut out a paper parallelogram, cut off one corner and glue it to the other side, or model this on the geoboard.) Teacher encourages student participation and experimentation. After students determine how to find the area of a parallelogram from the area of a rectangle, teacher recommends that students make several different parallelograms on their geoboards, record on dot paper, and find areas.

Activity Six

IE 4,   SE 3,   A 3

Students work in pairs or small groups. Teacher distributes centimeter paper. **Teacher: Draw the outline of your foot (shoe on for best results) or hand on centimeter paper. Find the area of each outlined foot or hand. How will you find the areas of partial squares?** Teacher asks students to describe their methods orally or in writing.

Two methods for finding the area of an irregular shape, such as a foot or hand, are described as follows:

1. Add up all the whole and partial squares inside the foot (or hand) outline. Determine that the area of the foot (or hand) is greater than the number of whole squares and less than the sum of whole and partial squares inside the outline of the foot (or hand).

2. Draw the smallest rectangle surrounding the foot (or hand). Find the areas of the shapes outside the foot (or hand) but inside the rectangle. Let each partial square equal one-half full square. Subtract the area outside the foot (or hand) outline from the area of the rectangle.

Note: Because this activity deals with parts of the body, it is important to be sensitive to students whose special needs may prevent them from completing this activity or who may feel uncomfortable in doing so.

Closing

A 1

Teacher shows students examples of Navajo patterns that are geometric but irregular. Asks students how they would find areas of these shapes.

Assessment

SE 5,   A 2

Teacher: Use grid paper to design a figure that has an area of 40 square units and a perimeter between 35 and 75 lengths of one side of a square.

Activity One

PERIMETER AND AREA OF A SQUARE

SIZE	PERIMETER	AREA
1 × 1		
2 × 2		
3 × 3		
4 × 4		
5 × 5		
6 × 6		
10 × 10		

Activity Two

PERIMETER AND AREA OF A RECTANGLE

SIZE	LENGTH	WIDTH	PERIMETER	AREA
2 × 3				

LESSON 4 WORKSHEET

Activity three

Activity four

Activity five

LESSON 5: SIMILARITY OF POLYGONS

Objectives

1. Each student will understand the concept of similar polygons.
2. Each student will be able to recognize similar polygons.
3. Each student will understand that all squares are similar but not all rectangles and not all triangles are similar.
4. Each student will investigate what changes and what stays the same when a shape is blown up or shrunken.

Materials

Dot paper (several sheets for each student), geoboards, pictures or photos of Navajo rugs or African textiles

Instructional Strategies

Opener

IE 1,   IE 4,   SE 1

Teacher shows photographs or pictures of Navajo rugs or African textiles. **Teacher: We have seen lots of photographs and pictures of Navajo rugs (or African textiles). Are the pictures the same size as the actual rugs (or textiles)?** Students discuss how pictures are smaller than original rugs (or textiles). **Teacher: Are the photographs and pictures the same shape as the rugs (or textiles)? There is a special word for two objects that have the same shape but are not necessarily the same size. Does anyone know that word?** Students volunteer terms as teacher writes the different names on the chalkboard or overhead. If no one guesses the term *similar*, the teacher writes this on the chalkboard or overhead. **Teacher: What are some other examples of similar shapes?** Students think-pair-share and then discuss as a class. Teacher writes all examples on chalkboard or overhead. Students decide as a class whether each example satisfies the definition of similar. Possible answers include pairs of the same style jeans in different sizes; shoes of the same style in different sizes; copy machines reducing or enlarging images; photo enlargement; different-sized, same-brand chocolate bars; or different-sized, same-brand bags of chips.

    Teacher: Today, we are going to learn about similar polygons, like the squares and rectangles we studied earlier.

Body

Activity One

SE 3,   A 1

Students work in pairs for this activity. Teacher distributes several sheets of dot paper to each pair of students. **Teacher: With your partner, make a 4 × 4 square on dot paper. Now make an 8 × 8 square on dot paper. Compare the two squares. Are these squares similar? Why?** Teacher asks students to focus on what is the same about the squares (angles, shape) and what is different (size, perimeter, area). **Teacher: How many of the small squares can fit in the large square? Do you think that all squares are similar? Why or why not?** Students discuss in pairs and then as a class. Teacher writes student answers on chalkboard or overhead. Student answers will probably be informal, but teacher strives for mathematical reasoning, such as, "all squares have the same shape," and "all squares have four right angles."

Activity Two

IE 2,   A 2

Students continue to work in pairs. **Teacher: Make a 2 × 3 rectangle on dot paper. Now, double the dimensions. What are the new dimensions (4 × 6)? Make a 4 × 6 rectangle on dot paper. Compare these rectangles. What is the same, and what is different? Are these two rectangles similar? Why or why not? How many of the smaller rectangles can fit in the larger rectangle?** Students discuss their answers in pairs and then as a whole class. The teacher aims for specific but informal answers, such as, "the bigger rectangle is twice as long and twice as wide but still the same shape." Students will recognize that four of the smaller rectangles can fit in the larger rectangle. In other words, by doubling the dimensions, we have quadrupled the area.

    Teacher: Remember, last time we made a 3 × 2 rectangle? Please make that again on dot paper. Compare the 3 × 2 rectangle to the 4 × 6 rectangle. What do you notice? As students discuss this in pairs and as a class, the question will probably arise as to whether a rotated rectangle, like the 3 × 2, is similar to the 4 × 6. The answer is yes, but this is not obvious and can generate interesting discussion among students. **Teacher: Are all rectangles similar? Why or why not?** If students have difficulty understanding that all rectangles are not similar, the teacher asks them to make a 3 × 4 rectangle and a 2 × 8 rectangle on dot paper. Clearly, these rectangles have different shapes. Teacher asks students to describe the shapes of each of the rectangles.

Activity Three

SE 2,   SE 4

Students work in pairs. **Teacher: We have been blowing up shapes by doubling their dimensions. Now let's see if we can shrink shapes, too. Make a large rectangle on dot paper. Then shrink it by using dimensions one-half of the original. What do you notice? Are the two rectangles similar?**

Activity Four

SE 3,   SE 4,   A 1

Students work in pairs. Teacher asks one person from each pair to make a triangle on dot paper and the other member of the pair to make a triangle similar to their partner's triangle, but not the same size, on another piece of dot paper. Teacher walks around and observes student work. Pairs compare their triangles and decide whether or not they are similar, then write or orally report their reasoning.

Closing

IE 4,   A 1

Teacher: What did you learn about similar figures today? What kinds of shapes did we find that were similar? Can you look around the classroom and find figures that are similar?

Assessment

SE 5,   A 2

Teacher: For homework, draw an irregular shape on dot paper or grid paper. Then, enlarge the shape, making all the dimensions twice as large, or shrink the shape, making all the dimensions one-half of the original. Find the perimeter and area of the original shape and the perimeter and area of the transformed shape. Write a paragraph or be prepared to give an oral explanation describing your methods and what you observe when you compare the perimeter and area of the original shape to the transformed shape.

Ashanti Cloth

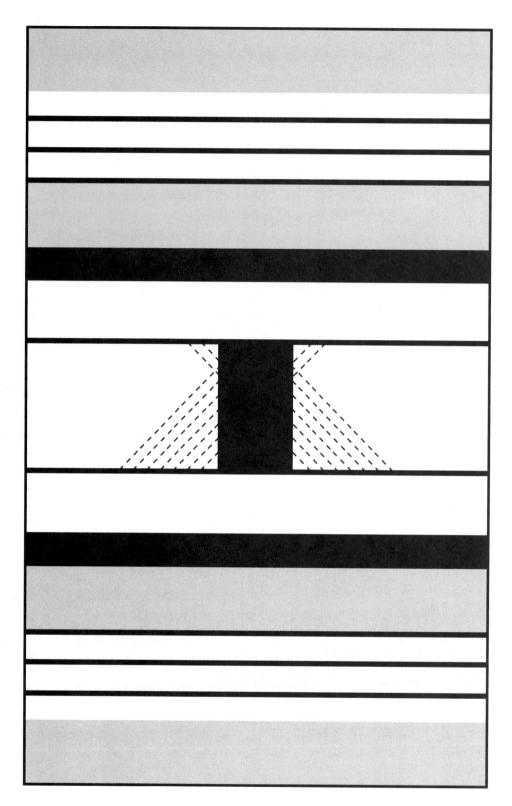

Ashanti Cloth

Ashanti Cloth

Ewe Cloth

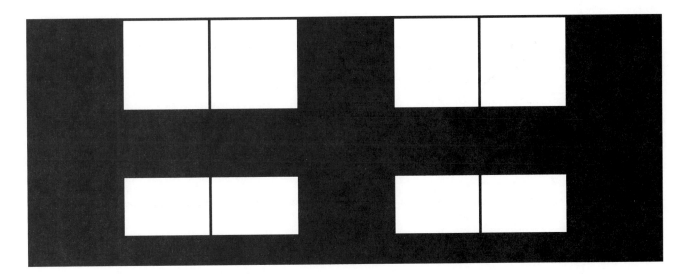

Ewe Cloth

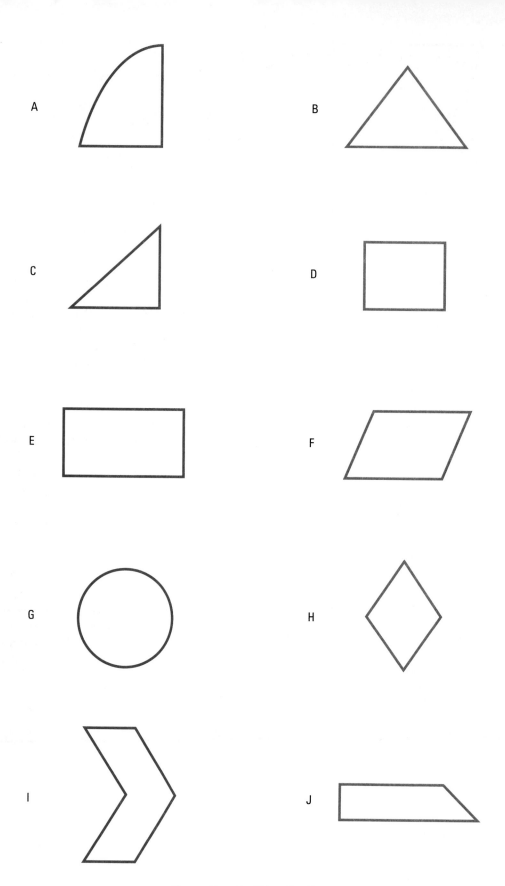

Shapes Found in African Textiles

LESSON 6: Tessellations Using African Textiles

Objective

1. Each student will tessellate polygons in a plane.

Materials

Samples of African designs and prints (pictorial or actual swatches), attribute blocks (a complete set for each group) or pattern blocks, large pieces of paper, "Shapes Found in African Textiles" worksheet, construction paper or posterboard cutouts of shapes from worksheet

Instructional Strategies

Opener

IE 1,   IE 2,   SE 1

Teacher shows several examples of West African textile designs. Some designs contain patterns that completely cover the plane without leaving gaps or holes. Other patterns do not completely cover the plane. Teacher asks students to discuss similarities and differences of the various designs in small groups, followed by whole class discussion. Teacher makes a list on the chalkboard or overhead of student responses. Some of the students' responses might not include covering the plane (in their own terminology). **Teacher: If I had a very large piece of white fabric and painted this pattern on it, would the pattern cover the entire fabric, or would there be gaps where the white fabric showed through?** Teacher draws students' attention to floor tiles, ceiling tiles, and so on, and asks them to comment on those designs. Most floor and ceiling tiles are squares, with edges parallel to the walls. **Teacher: We have seen some very interesting designs. We are going to make some of our own designs today by creating designs that cover an entire sheet of paper, leaving no gaps.**

Body

Activity One

IE 4,   SE 2,   A 2

Students work in cooperative groups for this activity. Each group should have a set of attribute blocks or pattern blocks and large pieces of paper. Teacher asks each student to choose one block and one piece of paper. **Teacher: Trace the attribute (or pattern) block on paper, repeating the pattern across the paper in a horizontal row. Next, expand your design and attempt to cover the entire paper by tracing the block repeatedly to cre-** ate a pattern. Share your designs with your group members. Does your design cover the whole piece of paper without leaving gaps? Why or why not?

Note: Students may ask about what happens if the design goes off the edge of the paper. This is a very reasonable concern. Since the paper represents an infinite plane that has no edges, the design cannot really go off the edge. Perhaps the best way to handle this is to let students know that it is fine if the design goes off the edge of the paper. We are concerned with gaps between tracings of the pattern.

Teacher: Will each group hold up designs that covered the paper, leaving no gaps? What shapes did you use? Teacher writes the names on the chalkboard or overhead of the shapes that successfully covered the paper. **Teacher: Now let's have each group hold up the designs that covered the paper but left gaps.** Teacher writes the names of these shapes in a separate column on the chalkboard or overhead. Class members discuss and resolve disagreements in a whole class discussion. **Teacher: What might you conclude about the different shapes? Why do some shapes leave gaps while others do not?**

Note: In mathematical terms, we are trying to tile the plane. Certain shapes, such as a square, equilateral triangle, and regular hexagon (all edges the same length and all angles the same measure) will tile, or cover, the plane without leaving gaps.

Activity Two

IE 2,   SE 4,   A 1

The students again work in cooperative groups. **Teacher: Choose two attribute or pattern blocks that you think will together cover the entire piece of paper, leaving no holes or gaps. Make a repeating pattern by tracing the blocks.** Activity proceeds as in Activity 1, with in-group and whole class discussion. Teacher walks around and observes students' written work. Teacher asks students to color their designs after discussion.

Note: Some combinations of shapes (such as trapezoids and triangles) can be used to tile the plane successfully. Other combinations will not work.

Activity Three

SE 3,   A 1

Teacher shows class a transparency of the "Shapes Found in African Textiles" worksheet and distributes cutouts of these shapes for student use. Teacher asks each student to select one of the shapes and determine whether that shape will cover the plane without leaving gaps. Through small group and whole class discussion, students classify each shape as being able to cover the plane without gaps or not.

Closing

IE 4,   A 1

Teacher holds up the African patterns used at the beginning of the lesson. **Teacher: Let's look at these patterns again. If I took each pattern and repeated it all over a piece of fabric, would it cover the fabric leaving no gaps? Let's answer this for each pattern.** Teacher guides students to use mathematical language in their discussion and to base their responses on the shapes used in the patterns and their previous findings using blocks. At this stage, it is not necessary for students or teacher to use the terms *plane* or *tessellation*.

Assessment

SE 3,   SE 5,   A 2

Teacher distributes grid paper. **Teacher: I have a challenge for you. Try to 'tile,' or cover, the whole page without leaving gaps, using two shapes of your choice in a repeating pattern. Don't be concerned if your design goes off the edge of the page. When you are finished, color your completed page. Write a paragraph describing your pattern and why you think it covers the page without leaving gaps.**

LESSON 7: Pattern Recognition Using African Textiles

Objective

1. Each student will identify, extend, and create repeating patterns.

Materials

Square tiles (24 or more squares in red, blue, and green for each two-person team)

Instructional Strategies

Opener

IE 1,   SE 1,   SE 3

Teacher: We can find patterns everywhere. For example, the days of the week form a pattern. Calendars always show the week beginning on Sunday and ending on Saturday. A baseball lineup is a pattern that tells us the batting position of each player. What are some other patterns that you know of? Students discuss patterns in their everyday life. Teacher makes a list on the chalkboard or overhead of the patterns mentioned by students. **Teacher: Mathematicians are very interested in investigating patterns. Today, we are going to learn about shape patterns that repeat. Can you find some in our classroom? Remember to look at patterns on clothing, book covers, wallpaper, and pictures.** Next, teacher shows several examples of African patterns and encourages students to examine them closely for patterns that repeat. **Teacher: Describe all that you see (first with partners and then in a whole class discussion). Today, we are going to make some repeating patterns ourselves.**

Body

Activity One

IE 2,   SE 2,   A 1

Students work in partners for this activity. Teacher distributes a set of square tiles to each pair of students. **Teacher: Each team should select three blue and three green tiles and lay them out in a horizontal row with the green tiles to the right of the blue tiles.** Teacher writes BBBGGG on the chalkboard or overhead to represent this arrangement. **Teacher: If we had placed three green tiles first and followed them by three blue tiles, like GGGBBB, would this be the same arrangement?** Students discuss with partners and then with the class. **Teacher: Now continue the arrangement across your desktop. What do you think now? Is BBBGGG the same as GGGBBB? Why or why not?**

   Note: There may be considerable disagreement over whether BBBGGG is the same pattern as GGGBBB. Some students will recognize that both patterns can be viewed as parts of the same, larger pattern. But many students will not agree with this. Both responses are correct.

Activity Two

IE 2,   SE 3,   A 1

Teacher: See how many additional patterns you can find using three blue and three green tiles. Teacher observes as students create patterns across their desktop. After teams have completed the task, teacher asks each team to write all of their patterns on the chalkboard. The class decides which of the patterns listed on the chalkboard are duplicates. As students discuss this issue, they will have to resolve whether order is important in determining a distinct pattern. For example, they will have to decide whether BGBGBG is the same as GBGBGB, bringing up the same issue that was discussed in Activity 1. The teacher might ask students to vote on whether changing the order creates a different pattern.

Teacher: Now, each team select three red tiles. Develop patterns with three blue, three green, and three red tiles. Record, just as we did earlier, and check for duplication. What helps you know if your pattern is really new or like one you have already made? How can we change the directions to limit the number of different patterns? Students consider these questions orally with the class, in a think-pair-share with their partner, or by writing their response.

Closing

IE 4,   SE 4,   A 1

Teacher shows students examples of African textiles that use patterns. **Teacher: Think-pair-share with your partner and describe the patterns. Pay attention to what repeats and how many times it repeats in each pattern.**

Assessment

SE 5,   A 2

Teacher: For homework, (1) on grid paper, design a pattern that has two or more different designs or shapes repeating in some fashion, or (2) find a design that has two or more different patterns repeating. Bring the design to class.

LESSON 8: Symmetry in African Textiles

Objective

1. Each student will understand and identify line and rotational symmetry and how to recognize it in African textiles.

Materials

Mirrors, yardsticks, overhead projector, centimeter graph paper, learning centers with objects that display symmetry, "Shapes Found in African Textiles" worksheet.

Instructional Strategies

Opener

IE 4,   SE 1

Teacher distributes mirrors to students. **Teacher: What do you see when you look in the mirror? What do identical twins see when they look at each other? When you look in the mirror or when twins look at each other, they see a 'mirror' image of themselves. We have been studying patterns for several days. Did you know that some patterns have identical, or matching, images within them? Even some letters of the alphabet have identical images. For example, let's look at an uppercase letter B.** Teacher shows students the letter B, covers either the top or bottom half of the letter and then reveals the half covered. **Teacher: What do you notice? Do you know a term for this (symmetry)?** Teacher writes the word *symmetry* on the overhead or chalkboard. Teacher repeats the activity with another symmetrical letter, perhaps A. Teacher then asks students to think-pair-share to find other letters or numbers that have symmetry (e.g., X, Y, E, 8, 0, 3). **Teacher: Can you define symmetry?** Teacher and students develop a class def-inition and teacher writes this on the chalkboard or overhead. **Teacher: Today we are going to learn about symmetry in African textiles.**

Body

Activity One

SE 2,   SE 4   A 3

Students work in pairs for this activity. Teacher distributes a yardstick or meter stick to each pair of students. **Teacher: Before we find symmetry in African textiles, we are going to find symmetry in ourselves. How can you place this yardstick so that you divide your partner into two halves that look exactly the same?** (Students should place the yardstick vertically down the center of their partner's body.) **The yardstick is called the *line of symmetry*. When a pattern or design has two identical parts that are mirror images, separated by a real or imaginary line, we say that the design has line symmetry. This line helps us find out what kind of line symmetry the design has. For example, for the letter B, where is the line of symmetry? What do we call this kind of line (horizontal)? Therefore, the letter B has horizontal line symmetry. Where is the line of symmetry for the letter A? What do we call this kind of line (vertical)? Therefore, the letter A has vertical line symmetry.**

Note: In this and any activity that utilizes an individual's physical attributes, teachers should take care to modify the activity as necessary.

Teacher: Now let's look around the classroom for examples of symmetry. Teacher sets up different learning centers around the classroom that demonstrate symmetry in the world. Some examples to include are orange halves, some leaves, certain flowers, shells, African and Native American masks, and pictures or photographs of buildings and other objects that display symmetry.

Activity Two

IE 1,   SE 2,   A 1

Teacher: Now we are ready to discuss symmetry in African textiles. Teacher holds up several examples of African textiles or shows transparencies on the overhead. Teacher asks students to determine if there is symmetry. **Teacher: Can you find patterns that have two identical parts? Can you draw a line of symmetry to separate the two identical parts of the figure?** Teacher asks students to come to the chalkboard or overhead to show the identical parts and line of symmetry. **Teacher: Can I turn any of these pictures of African textiles so that it still looks the same? How many turns will it take? This is called** *rotational symmetry.* Some shapes have more than one type of symmetry. Teacher shows the "Shapes Found in African Textiles" worksheet. **Teacher: Which of these shapes have symmetry? What kind of symmetry do they have?**

Activity Three

SE 3,   SE 5,   A 1

Teacher distributes centimeter grid paper. **Teacher: We are going to do something fun. I would like you to draw a line on your grid paper. You decide if the line is vertical (straight up and down), horizontal (left to right), or slanted. Then draw a design on one side of the line, making sure that the design touches the line at least twice, where you begin and end the design. Your line is a line of symmetry and you have drawn one-half of a design. Now complete the design by drawing its mirror im-** age on the other side of the line. Teacher walks around and observes student work. Students complete the activity individually and share their designs with others in their group, explaining their designs and the type(s) of symmetry displayed, in their own words. Some students may prefer to write their explanation.

Activity Four

IE 1,   IE 4,   A 1

Teacher: Create a design on centimeter paper that has at least one type of symmetry. Teacher plays show-and-tell with the class by asking students to show their designs and explain the symmetry. Class members group designs that have the same type of symmetry.

Closing

A 1

Teacher: Think-pair-share with your partner to describe the meaning of symmetry. What are the different types of symmetry that we learned about? Give some examples.

Assessment

SE 3,   SE 5,   A 2

Teacher: For homework, find something in your home or neighborhood that has symmetry. Either bring the object to class tomorrow or draw a picture of it and bring that to class.

LESSON 9: Closing Lesson

Rather than including a fixed set of activities, the closing lesson includes several suggestions for the teacher. The class activities suggested here may be presented in a separate lesson, to provide closure for the unit, or may be included as part of any of the previous eight lessons. The discussion questions are designed to give students opportunities to discuss fair pay, the role of women, and other social issues at the elementary level. Teachers should include these questions where they fit best, based on use of the unit.

The goals of this lesson are to bring unity and closure to the unit. Students will become aware that many of the patterns used are universal and found in many different cultures. They will become aware of the importance and relevance of patterns and geometry in society.

Suggested Activities

IE 1,   IE 3,   IE 4,   SE 1,   SE 2,   SE 3, SE 4,   SE 5,   A 1

- Students draw their favorite pattern on poster board or construction paper and color the pattern. Next, each student shares their pattern by holding it in front of the class, identifying the pattern, and telling something about it, both culturally and mathematically. Students should be prepared to answer questions such as (1) Is this a Navajo pattern, an African pattern, or a new kind of pattern? (2) Does the pattern have symmetry? (3) If yes, what type of symmetry? (4) What is the perimeter of the pattern? How did you get your answer? (5) What is the area of the pattern? Explain how you got your answer. (Some students may prefer to write their explanation rather than present it to the class orally.)

- Students learn to potato-print muslin with one of the patterns they learned about in class. Students make potato print cards or T-shirts. Students observe whether their patterns cover the T-shirt without leaving gaps.

- Students make construction paper models of their patterns and put these together to form a quilt. Student groups estimate the perimeter and area of the quilt, write their estimates on a piece of paper, and hand it to the teacher. The class decides which group's estimate is closest.

- Students collect data on their construction paper patterns. For example, students might count how many patterns of each color are created and graph this on a bar graph. Or, students might count how many patterns with line symmetry, rotational symmetry, and two kinds of symmetry are created and graph this.

- Students take a field trip to a local museum or gallery to see fabric, crafts, art, or furniture that have geometric patterns.

- Students use cameras or video cameras to record patterns found in their school, home, neighborhood, or city (e.g., the facades of buildings, tiles, and gardens).

- Students listen to a storyteller or craftsperson knowledgeable in Native American or African crafts or culture who has been invited to speak to the class.

- Students read folktales about the Navajo or West Africans to motivate discussion about what life was like for Navajo children in the 1800s or African children in the ancient kingdom of Ghana.

- Students plan and develop an exhibit at their school that highlights the crafts, culture, and history of their community.

Suggested Questions for Discussion and Interdisciplinary Projects

IE 1,   IE 2,   IE 3,   SE 1,   SE 2,   A 1

- Historically, Navajo women have been paid very little for the rugs they weave. For example, in 1973, a typical price was thirty cents per hour for a rug that took more than five hundred hours to complete. Why do you think that Navajo women have been paid so little for their rugs? Why did they continue to weave, despite the low price? Why are some people paid so much less for their work than other people?

- African Americans sometimes wear kente cloth as a sign of unity and cultural pride. Kente cloth provides a link to their African ancestry. Interview your parents and grandparents. What can they tell you about your own family's history? Where did they come from? Are there any mementos that have been handed down in your family, such as photographs, jewelry, or clothing? What do these mementos mean to your family? What do they represent?

- In Ghana, men weave kente cloth. The weavers are part of a professional guild and weaving is considered a full-time job. But, in Nigeria, weaving is done by women and has traditionally been considered part of their domestic duties. Why do you think that happens?

- In 1863, more than 8,000 Navajos were rounded up and imprisoned at the Bosque Redondo reservation near Fort Sumner. The United States Army killed their sheep and destroyed their farms, making the Navajo completely dependent on the army for their survival. The United States Army felt that their actions were justified because the Navajo were raiding Anglo-American settlements. At the same time, Anglo-Americans were trying to obtain Navajo land. Imagine that you are a Navajo child, living at this time. How would you feel if you were forcibly moved by the army and your most valuable possession (sheep) was taken from you? Imagine that you are a pioneer child recently come to the American West with your family. How would you feel if you were at risk of Navajo raids? Would you think that the actions taken by the army were justified?

- Navajo and West African patterns seem to have a lot in common. What are some similarities between Navajo and West African weaving? What are some differences? How do you think two groups of people who lived thousands of miles apart produced textiles with these similarities?

RESOURCES AND REFERENCES: CHILDREN'S LITERATURE

Aardema, V. 1981. *Bringing the rain to Kapiti plain.* New York: Dial.

Aardema, V. 1985. *Bimwili and the Zimwi.* New York: Dial.

Applah, P. 1967. *Tales of an Ashanti father.* London: Deutsch.

Baldwin, G. C. 1970. *Indians of the Southwest.* New York: Capricorn.

Bascom, W. R. 1992. *African folktales in the New World.* Bloomington: Indiana University Press.

Blood, C. L., and M. Link. 1990. *The goat in the rug.* New York: Macmillan.

Bonvillain, N. 1995. *The Navajo.* Brookfield, CT: Millbrook Press.

Castaneda, O. S. 1993. *Abuela's weave.* New York: Lee & Low.

Cobb, M. 1995. *The quilt-block history of pioneer days.* Brookfield, CT: Millbrook Press.

Cohlene, T. 1990. *Little Firefly. An Algonquian legend.* Vero Beach, FL: Watermill Press.

Chocolate, D. N. 1993. *Talk, talk: An Ashanti legend.* Troll.

Doherty, C. A., and K. M. Doherty. 1989. *The Apaches and Navajos.* New York: Franklin Watts.

Driving Hawk Sneve, V. 1993. *The Navajos. A first Americans book.* New York: Holiday House.

Duncan, L. 1996. *The magic of Spider Woman.* New York: Scholastic.

Engel, L. 1970. *Among the Plains Indians.* Minneapolis: Lerner.

Erdoes, R. 1972. *The sun dance people.* New York: Knopf.

Feelings, M. 1972. *Moja means one: Swahili counting book.* New York: Dial.

Ford, J. G. 1996. *A kente dress for Kenya.* New York: Scholastic.

Grossman, V. 1991. *Ten little rabbits.* San Francisco: Chronicle.

Hintz, M. 1987. *Enchantment of the world: Ghana.* Chicago: Children's Press.

Iverson, P. 1990. *Indians of North America: The Navajos.* New York: Chelsea House.

Katz, L., and P. A. Franklin. 1993. *Proudly red and black: Stories of Africans and Native Americans.* New York: Atheneum.

Kroll, V. 1992. *Wood-hoopoe Willie.* Watertown, MA: Charlesbridge.

Lerner Publications. 1988. *Ghana in pictures.* Minneapolis: Author.

Lerner Publications. 1988. *Nigeria in pictures.* Minneapolis: Author.

Martin, R. 1992. *The rough-face girl.* New York: Putnam.

Mendez, P. 1989. *The black snowman.* New York: Scholastic.

Mobley, C., and A. Mobley. 1994. *Navajo rugs and blankets: A coloring book.* Tuscon: Treasure Chest.

P'Bitek, O. 1978. *Hare and Hornbill.* London: Heinemann.

Roessel, M. 1995. *Songs from the loom. A Navajo girl learns to weave.* Minneapolis: Lerner.

Rosen, M., ed. 1992. *The Oxfam book of children's stories: South and north, east and west.* Cambridge, MA: Candlewick.

Ross, G. 1994. *How rabbit tricked otter and other Cherokee trickster stories.* New York: HarperCollins.

Smucker, B. 1995. *Selina and the bear paw quilt.* New York: Crown.

Swentzell, R. 1992. *Children of clay. A family of Pueblo potters.* Minneapolis: Lerner.

REFERENCES FOR TEACHERS

Bradley, C. 1992. The four directions Indian beadwork design with Logo. *Arithmetic Teacher* 39 (9): 46–49.

Bradley, C. 1993. Making a Navajo blanket design with Logo. *Arithmetic Teacher* 40 (9): 520–523.

Callahan, W. 1994. Teaching middle school students with diverse cultural backgrounds. *Mathematics Teacher* 87 (2): 122–126.

Gadanidis, G. 1994. Deconstructing constructivism. *Mathematics Teacher* 87 (2): 91–94.

Zaslavsky, C. 1994. *Multicultural math: Hands-on activities from around the world.* New York: Scholastic.

Zaslavsky, C. 1999. *Africa counts: Number and pattern in African cultures.* 3rd ed. Chicago: Lawrence Hill.

Internet Sites

http://navajorugs.spma.org/
The *Navajo Rugs of the Hubbell Trading Post* is a National Historic site that contains pictures of the different types of Navajo rugs and information about each rug style.

http://www/artsednet.getty.edu/ArtsEdNet/LACN/worlds/Navajo/index.htm/
Navajo Art: A Way of Life, maintained by the Getty Education Institute for the Arts, provides K–12 curriculum suggestions for integrating Navajo art into the classroom as well as pictures of Navajo rugs that can be downloaded and printed. The site also has information on the origin of Navajo weaving, including the legend of Spider Woman.

http://www.si.edu/cgi-bin/nav.cgi
This site is maintained by the Smithsonian Institution's National Museum of the American Indian. It has a picture of a Navajo blanket but also has information on other Native American groups.

http://www.philaK12.pa.us/schools/lowell/KENTE.CLOTH. HTML
This site was developed by a third grade class. It includes a third grade lesson. One can see and download pictures of kente cloth and the lesson plan. There is also information on the origins of kente cloth.

http://www.ontheline.org.uk/explore/journey/ghana/kentecr.htm
This site shows photographs of kente cloth and has a little information on the weaving of kente cloth.

http:www.middlebury.edu/~atherton/AR325/textiles/kente_cloth.html
This site, maintained by Middlebury College, shows pictures of kente cloth and information about the weaving of the cloth.

http:www.equity.enc.org
This site, *Making Schools Work for Every Child*, is maintained by the Eisenhower National Clearinghouse. It contains mathematics and science materials that address equity.

Weather
A Culturally Responsive Science Unit

Goals and Objectives

Goals

The goal in designing the weather unit is to develop a curriculum that meets the needs of a changing educational environment.

1. Students will build upon their personal experiences and cultural background.
2. Students will appreciate the universality of weather as well as the uniqueness of weather.
3. Students will extend their understanding of weather and weather forecasting by exploring the major phenomena that affect weather (temperature, water vapor, air pressure, and wind).
4. Students will extend their understanding of selected severe weather phenomena.

Objectives

1. Students will be able to demonstrate that heat moves from warmer objects to cooler ones and how this concept relates to weather.
2. Students will be able to define and use the following terms: temperature, wind directions, wind speed, and precipitation.
3. Students will be able to explain cloud formation and how clouds affect weather.
4. Students will be able to explain selected severe weather types.
5. Students will be able to demonstrate how temperature, water vapor, air pressure, and wind affect weather.

Molly Weinburgh

Georgia State University

with

Julie Turner, Atlanta Public Schools
Sean Blass, Atlanta Public Schools
Michael Hughes, Georgia Southern University

Introduction   The purpose of this unit is to help the students build on their previous knowledge of weather in order to understand the four factors that most influence the atmosphere. To accomplish this purpose, the unit is organized into five topics: temperature, winds, air pressure, precipitation, and severe weather. Each topic is covered over a series of lessons, using hands-on, inquiry experiences, which provide microlevel experiences to help the students visualize what is happening on the macrolevel when weather changes occur. In addition, each lesson has suggestions for optional activities for the students who wish to explore this topic further. The students are also encouraged to use the Internet to find additional information about weather.

The content and activities were selected to meet the National Science Education Standards for content in grades 4 through 6. The lessons assume the students have general background knowledge about weather, climate, and research processes. The topic of weather is generally included in sixth grade curriculum guides and standards.

It is everywhere; it happens all the time. "It" is the weather, and the weather is constantly changing. The clothes people wear and the activities people do depend on the weather. Violent weather may cause damage and harm to people and to property. Severe weather often causes major disruptions in the lives of people in the community. At such times, people in other communities often rally to provide supplies and help to those who were in harm's way. Because weather plays such a big part in our lives, people from all cultures have observed patterns in the weather, created explanations of the weather, and tried to predict the weather. Some of these explanations have taken the form of stories, myths, legends, and old sayings that have been passed from generation to generation. These stories are interesting, having their origins in people's understanding of natural events, and help us understand the people who created and used them. Because weather prediction prior to modern technology was based on local patterns, some interesting stories are included in this unit that can be used to help demonstrate the differences and similarities found in different regions. You are encouraged to find more and have your students find more.

Background Information for the Teacher

Most students realize that weather can be calm and peaceful or very violent. Rain may be gentle or frozen; winds soft or twisting; and temperatures mild or sweltering. Even if students have not personally experienced the extremes, they have seen and heard about the results of severe weather on the TV news and in popular movies.

The men and women who have been trained to investigate the atmosphere are called **meteorologists.** They collect weather data, using instruments such as thermometers, barometers, anemometers, wind vanes, and rain gauges. The scientific study of weather is called **meteorology.** Due to weather satellites and radar, meteorologists are able to predict weather with much better accuracy than before, but they are still not always correct. This is because so many factors must be taken into account when trying to predict the weather.

Being able to predict the weather allows people to plan and can prevent loss of property and lives. We can predict weather patterns by knowing more about the four important factors that influence the state of the atmosphere. These are (1) the effects of the sun **(temperature),** (2) water vapor **(precipitation),** (3) atmosphere **(air pressure),** and (4) air currents **(wind).** This unit concentrates on these four components and how they combine to produce local weather.

Temperatures vary throughout the day, from season to season, and at different latitudes. The sun is the source of almost all of the earth's heat. Sunlight hits the earth at different angles. The equator is hot because the sun shines almost directly overhead so the rays hit the earth at a right angle. The poles are much cooler because the rays from the sun hit the earth at a smaller angle. The smaller the angle, the less energy and less heat. The angle at which sunlight hits the earth changes during the day and during the year. The number of daylight hours also affects the temperature. Also affecting temperature is the type of material on which the sun's rays fall. Water, soil, snow, and concrete heat and cool at different rates.

Water vapor in the air is another factor that helps to determine the weather. The amount of water vapor varies greatly from location to location, as well as throughout the day for any given location, because the amount of water vapor is dependent on the temperature and volume of the air observed. Warm air will hold more water vapor than cool air. When referring to the water vapor in the air, meteorologists use the term **humidity.** Humidity is usually given as a percent because we compare the actual amount of water vapor to the largest amount the air can hold at that temperature. A 20 percent humidity means the air is holding 20 percent of what is possible at that temperature. If the temperature decreases, the humidity will increase, and precipitation is more likely. Where humidity is high, evaporation occurs slowly because the air already contains a high percentage of moisture.

The **water cycle,** consisting of evaporation, water vapor, condensation, and precipitation, describes how water changes its form and moves around the world. This cycle helps us understand why some air currents contain moisture and others do not. This is a very important concept for children to understand. Clouds must be present for any type of precipitation to occur. The type of cloud seen in the sky helps us know what type of precipitation to expect. The temperature of the air where the precipitation develops helps determine the type of precipitation: rain, snow, or sleet. A meteorologist must determine the temperature where the clouds and precipitation will develop in order to forecast rain or snow. For example, while there might be freezing temperatures on the ground, the temperature in the clouds where the precipitation develops might be 36 degrees. Thus, the prediction will be for rain, not snow.

Air pressure is a third factor. Air exerts pressure all the time because air, which is matter, has mass. Gravity pulls on the mass, causing pressure. The pressure on earth's surface is 1 kilogram per square centimeter (or 14.7 pounds per square inch) at sea level. The pressure decreases as altitude increases. An instrument used to measure changes in air pressure is the barometer. Changes in the level of mercury in the barometer mean changes in the air pressure. When air is warmed, the molecules move farther apart, the gases become less dense, and the air pressure lowers. An area of lower pressure is called a **low** and an area of high pressure is called a **high.** The change in air pressure is used to help predict weather changes. A falling barometer often means that rain and storm conditions are coming because low-pressure areas often have clouds and precipitation. A rising barometer often means that good weather is on its way because high-pressure areas often have fair weather.

Wind is the movement of air and is the fourth factor influencing weather. It is caused by differences in air pressure. Uneven heating of the earth causes the difference in pressure. Wind can be very localized or global. Air moves from cold areas (where air molecules are close together, or more concentrated) to hot areas (where air molecules are further apart, or less concentrated). Locally, the area with the most dense air also has the highest pressure. Air moves away from a high pressure center toward a lower pressure center. So wind moves from high to low pressure areas. These large, constantly moving air masses play a part in local weather.

HOW TO OPEN THIS UNIT AND BUILD ON YOUR STUDENTS' PRIOR KNOWLEDGE

The following unit opener is suggested as a vehicle for assessing your students' prior knowledge about weather.

Teacher: Raise your hand if you or someone in your family has ever asked, "What will the weather be like tomorrow?" or "What are the chances school will be closed because of snow?" or "I wonder if I should carry an umbrella?" Looks like a lot of us are concerned about the weather. Think about workers who are concerned about the weather. Can you name one and explain why this type of worker is concerned about the weather? (An example might be farmers who depend on the weather for preparing the ground, planting, growing, and harvesting the crops.) **In teams, identify as many jobs/workers as you can who are particularly concerned about the weather. Give the reason they think about the weather. Fill in the Data Retrieval Chart as you and your partner complete your thinking.** Other examples could include: transportation/pilots/need clear weather for take off and landing and overall safety; fishing/fishermen/need clear weather for safety; weather and traffic report helicopters/helicopter pilots/need clear weather for safety.

Data Retrieval Chart

Jobs	Workers	Relationship with Weather

Teacher: We have seen that the weather is of great concern to many people. What do we know about the weather? Let's do some brainstorming to review what we already know.

The teacher gives each student post-it notes and asks each student to write everything they know about weather (one idea per note). The teacher explains that this exercise will help direct the upcoming lessons so that they build upon, but do not repeat, what is known. After an appropriate length of time, the teacher arranges the students into groups of four. Each group has a piece of butcher paper. The group assignment is to sort the individual comments (found on each student's post-it notes) into categories. The groups create a graphic organizer to represent what they believe they now know about weather. Each student records in their journal the groups' ideas with individualized notes to increase personal understanding.

The teacher collects the graphic organizers in order to have an idea about the range of the students' understanding. The graphic organizers should be posted around the room and used throughout the unit; that is, as students learn new information about the weather, they can reorganize the knowledge on these graphic organizers. This is a good way to help students have a concrete image of the knowledge they are developing about any given topic.

The teacher will then hang a large map of the school district or town on the wall. Next, the teacher will divide a poster board into three columns and list the students' names in the first column, their address in the second, and leave the third column blank for the student to record the temperature. Each student will find their address on the map and mark the address with their initials. A star of the same color will then be put beside the student's name to help match them later. The students will complete the third column of this chart, "Temperature," during Lesson 3 of this unit.

Poster Board Example

Name	Address	Temperature
Teacher's Name		
Student 1		
Student 2		
Student 3		
Student 4		

REFERENCES

Internet sites
http://www.cnn.com/WEATHER/index.html
http://headlines.yahoo.com/weather
http://weather.lycos.com/
http://www.whnt19.com/kidwx/
http://162.127.88.3/shyviews
http://www.windandweather.com/

Related literature for students
Aardema, V. 1981. *Bring the rain to Kapiti Plain*. Dial. Cary: NC.
This is a rhythmic African folktale in which Ki-pat shoots an arrow into large clouds, causing rain to fall and ending the drought.

Bennett, D. 1988. *Rain.* Bantam. New York: New York.

This simple text is good for slower readers. Bold illustrations follow a drop of rain through the water cycle and explain storms, thunder, and lightning.

Branley, F. M. 1985. *Flash, crash, rumble, and roll.* Harper. New York: New York.

This nonfiction book clearly explains lightning and thunder.

Branley, F. M. 1987. *It's raining cats and dogs: All kinds of weather and why we have it.* Houghton Mifflin. Boston: MA.

This entertaining and informative book explains wind, precipitation, tornadoes, dust devils, and other related phenomena.

DePaola, T. 1975. *The cloud book.* Holiday House. New York: New York.

Clouds are identified by both their common and scientific names and are compared to familiar objects. This is for slow readers.

Dorros, A. 1990. *Feel the wind.* Harper. New York: New York.

The author uses simple terms to explain air currents, define the weather terms for wind, and describe uses of wind.

Gibbons, G. 1987. *Weather forecasting.* Four Winds. Salem: Oregon.

The author explains why weather is studied, defines the terms used to describe weather, and discusses the people and equipment needed for tracking and gauging weather's constant changes.

Gibbons, G. 1990. *Weather words and what they mean.* Holiday House. New York: New York.

This book clearly defines the factors that influence weather. Good for all readers.

Lloyd, D. 1982. *Air.* Dial. Cary: NC.

This book discusses the position uses of air, its destructive potential, and the problems of dirty air.

Martin, B., Jr., and J. Archambault. 1988. *Listen to the rain.* Holt, Rinehard, & Winston. Orlando: FL.

This book of poetry introduces the sights and sounds of rain, using very descriptive words and lovely illustrations.

Polacco, P. 1990. *Thunder cake.* Putnam. New York: New York.

This book for K–4 depicts the story of a grandmother helping her granddaughter overcome her fear of thunder by counting and making a cake.

Simon, S. 1989. *Storms.* William Morrow. New York: New York.

This book describes the atmospheric conditions that create storms and discusses the value and importance of storms in maintaining the world's climate.

Williams, T., and T. Major. 1984. *The secret language of snow.* Pantheon. New York: New York.

The Kobuk Eskimos have ten different words for snow. Each chapter starts with one of these words and then discusses the meteorological conditions that produce the particular type of snow and the interactions of the animals with it.

Unit Organization

LESSON 1

Students will

Define temperature, heat, and conduction and state the relationship of each to weather;

Explain that heat (not cold) is transferred during conduction;

Explain that much of the weather we experience is the result of transporting heat;

Identify questions about heat and temperature for further research.

LESSON 2

Students will

Determine why the air is cooler at the poles;

Determine why the air is cooler in the winter;

Define radiation and identify the sun as the major source of earth's energy;
Recognize that different materials reflect the solar energy in different amounts.

LESSON 3

Students will

Recognize that temperature is not the same in a given region;
Draw some conclusions as to why temperature may vary in a given region.

LESSON 4

Students will

Determine the effect of temperature on air movement;
Describe why warm air rises;
Define convection.

LESSON 5

Students will

Determine the causes of land and sea breezes;
Name and describe the characteristics of the six major winds in the United States;
Explain the Beaufort wind scale.

LESSON 6

Students will

Define front;
Describe the weather associated with fronts;
Draw and explain the symbol for warm fronts and cold fronts on the weather map.

LESSON 7

Students will

Determine that air has weight;
Demonstrate the strength of air;
Identify air pressure and how it affects objects.

LESSON 8

Students will

Describe the movement of air in areas of high and low pressure;
Use knowledge of high and low pressure to predict weather.

LESSON 9

Students will

Describe how the terms humidity and relative humidity are related;
Name the instrument used to measure relative humidity.

LESSON 10

Students will

Explain (verbally, pictorially, etc.) how precipitation occurs.

Students will

- Decide the best way to collect needed data/information on severe weather;
- Decide the best way to report data/information;
- Suggest an appropriate research methodology;
- Select appropriate research tools for finding out more about severe weather;
- Demonstrate how temperature, wind, water vapor, and air pressure combine to produce the conditions needed for severe weather.

LESSON 14

Students will

- Explain any edits made to the graphic organizer;
- Make a connection between their own understanding and general understanding as seen in myths and sayings;
- Recognize the value of old sayings about weather.

The Content Standards: The National Science Standards

Soon after the publication of the National Mathematics Standards, the scientific community led by the National Research Council developed national standards for science education in six areas. These include standards for science teaching, assessment, and content. The National Science Education Standards (NRC 1996), or Standards, were never intended to be a curriculum but rather to provide criteria for judging progress toward a national vision of teaching and learning science. As such, the Standards can be used by curriculum writers to guide and shape materials. The influence of the Standards can be seen throughout the weather unit.

A theme found in all sections of the Standards is that science is for all students. The overview of the Standards states, "Everyone needs to be able to engage intelligently in public discourse and debate about important issues that involve science and technology. And everyone deserves to share in the excitement and personal fulfillment that can come from understanding and learning about the natural world." The document specifies that standards are for *all* students and includes excellence as well as equity. The Standards use phrases such as ". . . apply to all students, regardless of age, gender, cultural or ethnic background, disabilities, aspirations, or interest and motivation in science." In addition, the Standards encourage teachers to become aware of the cultural and experiential background of students and the effects these cultural experiences have on learning. There can be little doubt that a unit with an emphasis on culturally relevant pedagogy would be consistent with all aspects of science standards.

In addition to statements about who should be learning science, the Standards state the *content* that should be taught by the end of the fourth, eighth, and twelfth grades. Weather was selected as the topic for the unit because teachers in the early middle grades teach the concept. An examination of the grades 5 through 8 content standards reveals that this is not a topic that is addressed directly. Therefore, this unit builds on the grades K through 4 standard that states "Weather changes from day to day and over the seasons. Weather can be described by measurable quantities, such as temperature, wind directions and speed, and precipitation."

In middle school, students are expected to develop their abilities to do scientific inquiry as seen in Content Standard A (Science as Inquiry). Content Standard B (Physical Science) concepts are also taught as a part of this unit on weather. The students understand that heat moves in predictable ways, flowing from warmer objects to cooler ones, until both reach the same temperature. Students also explore earth/space science concepts (Content Standard D) about the water cycle. Examples of this standard can be seen in Lessons 7 and 8. Many of the Science in Personal and Social Perspectives standards (Content Standard F) are covered in the weather unit. Students learn that internal and external processes of the earth system cause natural hazards, events that change or destroy human and wildlife habitats, damage property, and harm or kill humans. Students understand the risks associated with natural hazards.

The Standards also address *science teaching*, which focuses on the behaviors, beliefs, and attitudes of teachers of science; these standards are highlighted in this unit. Teachers understand how to (1) recognize and respond to student diversity and encourage all students to participate fully in science learning, (2) orchestrate discourse among students about science ideas, (3) use multiple methods to gather data on student understanding, (4) engage students in designing the learning environment, (5) display and demand respect for the diverse ideas, skills, and experiences of all students, and (6) nurture collaboration among students.

How, when, and why children should be *assessed* is included in the Standards. The Assessment Standard recognizes that students who are not part of the majority culture need to have their knowledge and understanding examined and expressed in nontraditional ways.

National Research Council. 1996. *National science education standards.* Washington, DC: National Academy Press.

LIST OF THE CONTENT STANDARDS IN SCIENCE

Content Standard A: Science as Inquiry

- Students demonstrate abilities necessary to do scientific inquiry. (K–4 and 5–8)
- Students understand about scientific inquiry. (K–4 and 5–8)

Content Standard B: Physical Science

- Heat moves in predictable ways, flowing from warmer objects to cooler ones, until both reach the same temperature. (5–8)
- The sun is a major source of energy for changes on the earth's surface. (5–8)

Content Standard D: Earth/Space Science

- Weather changes from day to day and over the seasons. Weather can be described by measurable quantities, such as temperature, wind direction and speed, and precipitation. (K–4)
- Water, which covers the majority of the earth's surface, circulates through the crust, oceans, and atmosphere in what is known as the "water cycle." (5–8)
- Clouds, formed by the condensation of water vapor, affect weather and climate. (5–8)
- Global patterns of atmospheric movement influence local weather. (5–8)

Content Standard F: Science in Personal and Social Perspectives

- Internal and external processes of the earth system cause natural hazards, events that change or destroy human and wildlife habitats, damage property, and harm or kill humans. (5–8)
- Science and technology have advanced through contributions of many different people, in different cultures, at different times in history. (5–8)

Content Standard G: History and Nature of Science

- Women and men of various social and ethnic backgrounds—and with diverse interests, talents, qualities, and motivations—engage in the activities of science, engineering, and related fields. (5–8)
- Many individuals have contributed to the traditions of science. (5–8)

Matrix of Standards Referenced to Individual Lessons

	Lesson 1	Lesson 2	Lesson 3	Lesson 4	Lesson 5	Lesson 6	Lesson 7	Lesson 8	Lesson 9	Lesson 10	Lesson 11–13	Lesson 14
Standard A	X	X	X	X	X	X	X	X	X	X	X	X
Standard B	X	X	X	X	X	X	X	X	X			X
Standard D		X	X		X	X		X	X	X		X
Standard F			X		X		X	X	X	X	X	X
Standard G	X	X		X		X	X				X	X

LESSON 1: Temperature—Are You Hot? I'm Cold.

Objectives

1. Each student will define temperature, heat, and conduction and state the relationship of each to weather.

2. Each student will explain that heat (not cold) is transferred during conduction.

3. Each student will explain that much of the weather we experience is the result of transporting heat.

4. Each student will identify questions about heat and temperature for further research.

Materials

Station 1:	networked computer
Station 2:	three bowls of water (one hot, one cold, and one lukewarm)
Station 3:	bowls of hot and cold water, wooden and metal spoons

Instructional Strategies

Opener

SE 1

Have a volunteer student pretend that she or he is the director of the National Oceanic and Atmospheric Administration (NOAA). The director is making a radio announcement. Have the rest of the class listen to the radio report and be ready to ask the director questions about the report:

Director: "The winter of 1999–2000 was the warmest winter in the United States since the government began keeping records some 105 years ago. This was the third year in a row that record warmth was recorded in the United States during the winter months" (NOAA report, posted on 13 March 2000).

Body

SE 1,   SE 3,   SE 4,   IE 2,   A 1

Teacher: What questions do you have for the director of NOAA? Have students record questions on a chart. Questions might include, What are the causes of the warmer winters? Is this a world-wide pattern? What effects do the warmer winters have on people's lives, their jobs, and their communities? Is this part of global warming? What is global warming? How do we measure the temperature, and are these measurements the same now as they were 100 years ago? What does temperature have to do with the weather?

Teacher: Let's spend some time today thinking about and investigating these questions about temperature, heat, and the weather. We have three learning centers set up in the room. (Have the class already divided into three groups prior to this point in the lesson. The three groups could either rotate every ten to fifteen minutes to each of the three centers, or the students could select two of the centers to work in for twenty minutes each. Make decisions here in the context of your class and student needs.) As students work at the various science stations, the teacher should assist and ask questions of students so that they are focusing on key ideas.

The stations:

Station 1:	computer work
Station 2:	temperature
Station 3:	heat transfer

Closing

A 1,   A 2

Teacher: What were the major ideas covered today? (Look for the answers heat and temperature.) **What did Station 2 help you discover about how well your body can determine actual temperature?** (Look for answers such as "not very well," and reinforce this response by discussing what happened when the cold and warm hand was put into the water that was at room temperature.) **What did Station 3 help you discover about heat?** (Heat moves through some substances better than others do.) **What does the fact that heat moves differently have to do with the topic of weather?** (Different earth materials will transfer heat differently.) **What did Station 1 help you discover?** (Look for a variety of answers about El Niño and global warming.) **What questions from the radio broadcast were you able to answer?** (Varied answers.)

Assessment

A 1,   A 2

During the lesson, the teacher will move among the stations, listening and looking for evidence that students are discovering that heat is transferred, heat and temperature are not the same, and that much of weather is the result of transporting heat. The teacher will use probing questions at the stations to help establish these ideas.

Lesson Preparation

Set up three learning stations in the room.

Station 1 will be a networked computer station so students can locate predetermined websites about the weather, La Niña, El Niño, and global warming/ocean heat. A few websites that are helpful include

http://www.suntimes.com/output/news/warm24.html;

http://space.com/science/planetearth/warm_winter_000313_wg.html

JOURNAL QUESTIONS:

Are the oceans warmer? How do we know? What are the possible causes? What effects are being predicted? What does global warming mean? What effect does La Niña have on the warming of the oceans and on land temperatures? What about El Niño?

Station 2 will be a wet table. Place these questions on a worksheet at the center of the table: Do you always feel comfortable (temperature) in the same room as members of your family? Do all your friends wear the same amount of clothing each day? Is your most comfortable room temperature the same as your best friend's? Next place the three bowls on the table. The bowl on the left contains very warm water, the middle bowl contains water at room temperature, and the bowl on the right contains cold water.

JOURNAL QUESTIONS:

Students should make an educated guess. Will you be able to tell accurately the temperature of the water in the middle bowl? The procedure is as follows: Taking turns with your partner, place your left hand in the bowl on the left; place your right hand in the bowl on the right. Guess the temperature of the water in each bowl. Take your hands out of the water and wait for one minute. Put both hands in the middle bowl. After you have completed this task, answer these questions in your journal: How did your hands feel when you put them in the bowls of water? What temperature is the water in each bowl? How can you tell? How accurate do you think you are?

Station 3 contains another science experiment. Set bowls of hot and cold water on a table with wooden and metal spoons.

JOURNAL QUESTIONS:

Students should make an educated guess. What will happen to the wooden and metal spoons when placed in the hot water? In the cold water? Why? What would happen if we used different objects? What does the experiment have to do with heat transport and the weather?

LESSON 2: How Is the Sun Related to Temperature?

Objectives

1. Each student will determine why the air is cooler at the poles.
2. Each student will determine why the air is cooler in the winter.
3. Each student will define radiation and identify the sun as the major source of earth's energy.
4. Each student will recognize that different materials reflect the solar energy in different amounts.

Materials

Flashlight (one per student); smooth ball; white board; globe; transparency "How Much Solar Energy Is Reflected into Space?"; thermometer (one per child)

Instructional Strategies

Opener and Body

SE 1,   SE 2,   SE 3

The teacher gives each pair of students a flashlight, a large smooth ball, and a piece of white cardboard. **Teacher: Spend one minute observing as much as possible about the interaction of the light from the flashlight and the ball and recording all data observed. Spend an additional minute observing the interaction of the light from the flashlight and the cardboard and recording all data.** The teacher will have pairs join into groups of four to compare data and draw a conclusion.

SE 2,   A 1,   A 2

Ask groups to share. As the students describe observations that are relevant to the study of the sun's rays hitting the earth, write them on the board. Examples are "the circle was larger at the pole and less bright"; "the circle was larger and less bright when the paper was at a slant." Hold up a globe and ask the students to think of the flashlight as the sun. **Teacher: What do you think will be happening at the poles? At the equator?** (A minilecture is appropriate here to help with this idea if the students are having trouble. The sun is the source of almost all of the earth's energy. Like the light from the flashlight, the energy is radiant energy, or energy transferred by wave motion. When the sun's rays strike the earth perpendicular [at a right angle] to the surface as happens at the equator, they are more direct and hotter than those that hit the earth with a smaller angle. This is because the same amount of energy is concentrated in a small area as happened with the flashlight and ball/cardboard. This accounts for why the equator is hotter than the poles.)

SE 2

Teacher: Why does North America have warmer summers and cooler winters if the sun's radiant energy always hits it at the same angle? Students should remember from previous lessons that the earth is tilted on its axis. (With probing questions from the teacher, the students should be able to explain that the earth's axis stays tilted in the same direction all the time. This means that as the earth orbits the sun, the United States is tilted toward the sun in the summer and away from it in the winter.)

Teacher: Use the cardboard and flashlight to demonstrate the position of the sun and earth for maximum intensity and demonstrate the position of the sun and earth for minimum intensity. (Watch for inaccurate representations and further clarify the concepts.)

SE 3

Teacher: Does anything besides the angle of the radiant energy make a difference in the temperature at any given location? Ask the students to brainstorm and record all thoughts in their science journal (which will be used throughout the unit).

Show the transparency "How Much Solar Energy Is Reflected Back into Space?" Ask the students to explain this table. (If more energy is reflected, it will warm the air more and make it feel warmer. If a similar idea is not on the brainstorm list, it will need to be added.)

Closing

A 1,   A 2

Teacher: Explain why the northern United States is cooler than the southern United States, using today's lesson as evidence. (Look for answers such as the slant of the sun's rays.) **Why is it cooler in the winter?** (Position of the earth relative to the sun.) **How did the transparency "How Much Solar Energy Is Reflected Back into Space?" relate to yesterday's lesson?** (Look for answers that reflect the idea that heat is conducted differently by different substances.)

What do you think the temperature will be tonight? (Look for reasonable answers.) **Why?** (Students should base their answers on temperatures they heard on the news.) **Do you think the temperature will be the same across the entire school district? Let's collect some data to help answer this question.** (Teacher will give out thermometers and explain the homework assignment.)

Assessment

A 1,   A 2

The teacher should move around the class, observe students' work with the ball and flashlight, and listen for misconceptions. The teacher should use probing questions to help students develop scientific concepts. Use the minilecture opportunity to fill in and extend and develop students' knowledge.

Homework

Have each student take a thermometer home and record the temperature outside their home at eight o'clock. The students should record the temperature and bring the readings to school the next day.

Optional Activities

1. Students may want to make their own thermometer. Some websites that may help are

   http://www.windandweather.com/js/res temp-thermo.htm

   http://k12science.ati.stevens-tech.edu/sciencelink/worshops/instrumentpics.html

2. The *Old Farmer's Almanac* was first published in 1792. (Who was President of the United States in 1792?) The *Almanac* was really popular; the editors predicted the weather, the tides, sunrise, and sunset. (Who needs that kind of information?) The great thing was that the *Old Farmer's Almanac* was right about 80 percent of the time. In 1936, a new editor decided to drop the weather predictions from the *Almanac*. What do you think happened to the *Almanac*? Conduct a short investigation to find out.

3. There are many sayings people in different parts of the country have about the weather. Here are a few:

   - If animals have an especially thick coat of fur, expect a hard winter.
   - When squirrels bury their nuts early, it will be a cold winter.
   - Hornets' nests built in the top of trees indicate a mild winter, and nests close to the ground indicate a hard winter.

Can you think of other sayings like these? Who uses these sayings? How do you think each one developed? Do you think there's any truth to these sayings?

How Much Solar Energy Is Reflected into Space?

Thick Clouds	**75–95 Percent**
Fresh Snow	**75–90 Percent**
Thin Clouds	**30–50 Percent**
Sand	**15–45 Percent**
Grassy Field	**10–30 Percent**
Water	**10 Percent**
Forest	**3–10 Percent**

LESSON 3: What Is the "Local" Temperature?

Note to teacher:

Prior to Lesson 3, the teacher will help the students fill in the third column of the temperature chart found in the "Background Information for Teachers" section.

Objectives

1. Each student will recognize that temperature is not the same in a given region.
2. Each student will draw some conclusions as to why temperature may vary in a given region.

Materials

Wall maps, calculator (optional), colored dots or markers, fact cards

Instructional Strategies

Opener

SE 1,   SE 2,   SE 3

The teacher assesses the accuracy of the map and recorded temperature chart. **Teacher: There appears to be an error. I listened to the weather report last night and heard that the temperature in (your city/district) was (fill in appropriate temperature); however, there are several different temperatures recorded on the chart. Why are there several different temperatures on the chart? Share your ideas with a partner.** The teacher writes the students' ideas on the board or butcher paper.

Body

SE 2

Teacher: How can we find the range of temperatures in the district? (To do this, the highest and lowest temperatures must be found.) Ask a pair of students to go to the chart and find the highest (maximum) and lowest (minimum) temperatures; mark these high and low readings on the chart and write them on the board. Explain that the difference in maximum and minimum temperatures is the *range* of *air temperatures* for the district.

IE 4,   A 1,   A 2,   SE 2,   SE 4

Teacher: Having the chart is a good idea, but let's think of a way to more quickly locate the range. What visual tool might be appropriate? (A graph). What should we place on the x-axis and the y-axis? Why? The teacher draws a large graph template on the board with air temperature labeled on the vertical axis (y-axis) and students' names on the horizontal axis (x-axis). **Teacher: Place your home temperature at the appropriate place above your name.** Each student should then mark the appropriate position on the graph with a large X. Discuss the difference in this visual and the chart.

SE 2,   SE 3

Teacher: Now I see the range, but I want to know more. On a piece of paper, calculate the average temperature. Approach the graph and draw a line across it at the average temperature. Ask the students to examine the graph and tell a partner what they now can determine from it. (Some temperatures are above and some below the average. Some might fall on the line, but none may fall on the line.) **Whose air temperature is the farthest away from the line? How far is it? Is it warmer or colder than the line? Whose is the farthest away in the opposite direction? What can we tell from comparing these two distances?** (Look for range.)

SE 4

Teacher: There are two piles of dots (or red and blue markers) next to the map. Get a red dot if your temperature is above the line and a blue dot if your temperature is below the line. Go to the map and place the dot over the star that marks your address. (Model this for the students with your own address.)

When all the students have marked their address, ask the class to look at the map and try to determine if there are any areas that have more red than blue and any areas with more blue than red. Ask a student to tell which area of the town/district is warmer and which is colder. Ask if anyone can think of a reason for this. Remind students of physical characteristics to watch for:

- changes in elevation
- high concentration of buildings and sidewalks
- bodies of water
- manufacturing areas

SE 5

Teacher: From the information we see on the map and from what you have told us, what can we say about temperature? Suggest other experiments that might prove/disprove the theory. (For example, if there is a body of water near the school that influences the temperature, the class can test the hypothesis that the body of water makes a difference. Even if the theory is suspect, allow the students to design and conduct an experiment, keeping in mind that fostering scientific inquiry, designing and conducting theory, and refining one's hypotheses is the process to reinforce.

Closing

A 1

Review the three ways of examining temperature data: chart, graph, and map. Remind the students that all three methods reveal the same thing. Ask a student to explain what the class has learned about local temperature. (Not the same everywhere, has some patterns, may be caused by physical conditions and different rates of heat transport.)

Assessment

A 1,   A 2

The teacher will listen to students' answers to the question about why the temperature is not the same at all locations in the school district. Use the suggestions to help guide the students' understanding of why physical characteristics of a location make a difference in the temperature.

Optional Activities

Place the following fact cards in a learning center or as part of an interactive bulletin board. Have students read the fact cards and demonstrate their understanding of the fact as well as the ways the problem might be avoided or minimized.

Heat Cramps: Exercising in hot weather can produce muscle cramps because of brief imbalances in body salts. Cramps become less frequent as a person becomes used to the heat.

Heat Syncope, or Fainting: People who are not used to exercising in the heat can have a quick drop in blood pressure that can lead to fainting. Recovery is generally quick.

Heat Exhaustion: Losing fluid and salts through perspiration can lead to dizziness and overall weakness and an elevated body temperature. Heat exhaustion is more likely after several days of hot weather.

Heatstroke: The body temperature may get as high as 105°F. This elevated temperature is very serious, and medical help is needed because it can result in death.

Hypothermia: When exposed to very cold weather, the body's core temperature may drop below 95°F. A person in hypothermia will first experience severe shivering, but as the temperature falls, shivering decreases. This drastic drop in body temperature can result in death.

Frostbite: The skin can actually freeze if it becomes cold enough. The ears, nose, hands, and feet are the most apt to freeze.

Airplane Takes Off: As the temperatures rise, the distance that is needed for an airplane to get off the ground increases. A typical 727 needs 7,600 feet at 59°F and 10,600 feet at 120°F.

LESSON 4: Air Movement—What Is Wind?

Objectives

1. Each student will determine the effect of temperature on air movement.
2. Each student will describe why warm air rises.
3. Each student will define convection.

Materials

Journal, aquarium, clamp light, bowl of ice, plastic wrap, matches, punk, candles (one per every two students), matches, tissue paper, feather

Instructional Strategies

Opener

SE 3

Teacher: Write in your journal as many statements as possible about the wind. After an appropriate length of time, ask the students to watch as you do a demonstration. Remind them to think about their statements about wind and what has been studied for the last three days.

Body

SE 1,   SE 2,   IE 4

Attach a clamp lamp with a 100-watt bulb to one end of an aquarium. Be sure the light shines down on one end. Place a bowl of ice at the other end of the aquarium and cover the aquarium with plastic wrap. Light the end of a punk, blow out the flame, and insert the smoking punk through the plastic wrap near the bowl of ice.

Teacher: Describe in any way (verbal, drawing, mime) to your partner what happens to the smoke. (The smoke should sink over the ice and begin to rise near the lamp because warm air rises.) Give each pair of students a heat source (lamp or candle) and sheet of tissue paper. Have the students cut a 2-inch diameter spiral from the tissue paper. Cut a piece of thread 6 inches long and tape one end to the center of the paper spiral. Hold the free end of the string and observe. Turn on (or light) the heat source. Hold the paper spiral over the heat source and observe. Ask the students to describe what they observe. Using the data from the demonstration and from the students' experiments, ask the students to make a statement about wind. (Heat makes the air rise).

Collect more data by having the students move around the room dropping a small feather. Have students observe the movement of the feather at different places in the room.

Closing

A 1,   SE 2

Teacher: Think of places in your community and in your outside school activities where you have observed the movement of air. Some examples: The "ripples" that can be seen coming from a street on a hot day, hot-air balloons, the second floor being hotter than the first floor.

Assessment

A 1

Discuss the activities with the students and help the students synthesize the information. As air warms, the molecules spread out, making the air lighter (less dense). This process, in turn, allows the warm air to rise. As air cools, the molecules move together, making it denser, and it drops. The differential heating of the earth's surface and the resulting convection (the transfer of heat by actual movement of the heated materials) is what causes winds.

Optional Activity

An exciting activity in many parts of the world is kite flying. In some cultures, flying a kite is purely recreational, but in other cultures, flying a kite can be part of religious ceremonies. Have the students research kite flying in various cultures.

LESSON 5: From Where Do Winds Come?

Objectives

1. Each student will determine the causes of land and sea breezes.
2. Each student will name and describe the characteristics of the six major winds in the United States.
3. Each student will explain the Beaufort wind scale.

Materials

Beaufort scale, two beakers, soil, water, two thermometers, clock, heat source

Instructional Strategies

Opener

SE 1

Teacher: Sometimes big winds can create a real mess in people's lives. In 1999, there were four major weather disasters in the United States that caused billions of dollars worth of damage each. In addition, each of these disasters caused many deaths. Three of the four involved big winds: Hurricane Floyd (September 1999), the tornadoes in Oklahoma and Kansas (May 1999), and the tornadoes in Arkansas and Tennessee (January 1999). How could winds create so much damage?

Body

SE 2

Teacher: How big are the winds of a tornado or hurricane? Rate the wind on a 1 to 12 scale with 1 being the mildest and 12 being the strongest. Write or draw a description of the strongest wind you have experienced. After an appropriate length of time, hand out a copy of the Beaufort wind scale (at the end of the lesson) so that students can check how accurate they were by just using their own judgment. Explain that the scale gives us a standard and a way to compare winds.

SE 4,   SE 5

Have the students work in groups of four. Ask the students to build on yesterday's lesson on convection currents by collecting more data about winds. **Teacher: Let's find out**

Does land or water heat up faster?

Does land or water cool down faster?

Do land and water hold heat the same amount of time?

The teacher gives each group of students two beakers, soil, water, two thermometers, a clock, and a heat source. Ask the students to design and carry out an experiment to answer the questions. (The teacher circulates around the room to help the students when problems arise.)

SE 2

Have students describe what happened in this activity. (The soil heated and cooled more quickly than the water.) The difference in the time that it takes land and water to change temperature influences the movement of air above it. During the day, the land heats more quickly than the water. Hot air above the land rises, and cooler air above the water moves in to take the place of the ris-

ing warm air. This air movement is called a *sea breeze,* and it moves from water to land. At night, the land cools faster than the water. The hotter air above the water rises, and the cooler air above the land moves in to take the place of the rising warm air. This is called a *land breeze,* and it moves from the land to the water.

Show the students a map of the United States and ask them to think about where major wind currents might enter. Remind them to think about temperature variations and the activity that has just been completed. Help the students to realize that the winds must originate over land or water. If they originate over land, they are called *continental winds,* and if they originate over water, they are called *maritime winds.* If they come from the north, they are *polar,* and from the south, they are *tropical.* The four combinations are (1) polar maritime, (2) polar continental, (3) tropical maritime and (4) tropical continental. Looking at the map, help the students to see that six wind currents are produced.

Closing

A 1,   IE 2

Teacher: Can someone remind the class of what you learned from your own experiment? (Land heats and cools faster than water.) **What does this answer tell us about how land breezes are created?** (Night winds occur because the wind is moving from the land to the water.) **What does this answer tell us about how sea breezes are created?** (Day winds occur because the wind is moving from the water to the land.) **Can anyone think of a saying about wind? If so, what scientific phenomena might help explain the saying.**

Assessment

A 1,   A 2

The teacher will give the students a map of the United States and ask the students to label the six major winds.

Optional Activities

1. Students may want to make an anemometer. If so, direct them to the websites listed on the Beaufort scale.

2. Students can conduct a research study tracing the evolution of hurricane names. Ask them to find out some interesting things about the names of hurricanes, such as how were hurricanes named in 1953? In 1979? Why were male names added in 1979? Why are multicultural names used today? The students can plan a presentation for class.

Beaufort Number	Speed (mph)	Wind Name	Sea Indication	Land Indication
0	<1	Calm	Sea is like a mirror	Smoke rises vertically
1	1–3	Light air	Ripples	Smoke drifts
2	4–7	Light breeze	Small wavelets	Leaves rustle
3	8–12	Gentle breeze	Large wavelets; crest	Small twigs move
4	13–18	Moderate breeze	Small waves	Small branches move
5	19–24	Fresh breeze	Moderate waves	Small trees sway
6	25–31	Strong breeze	Whitecaps	Large branches move
7	32–38	Moderate gale	Sea heaps up	Whole trees move
8	39–46	Fresh gale	Foam blown in streaks	Twigs break off trees
9	47–54	Strong gale	Sea rolls	Branches break
10	55–63	Whole gale	Very high waves	Some trees uprooted
11	64–73	Storm	Exceptionally high waves	Widespread damage
12	74	Hurricane	Sea completely white	Severe destruction

websites:

http://www.windandweather.com/js/res windgauge.htm
http:/k12science.ati.stevens-tech.edu/sciencelink/workshops/instrumentpics.html

LESSON 6: What Are Fronts?

Objectives

1. Each student will define front.
2. Each student will describe the weather associated with fronts.
3. Each student will draw and explain the symbol for warm fronts and cold fronts on the weather map.

Materials

Divider, aquarium, dense liquid (water, salt, blue coloring), less dense liquid (oil, red coloring), index cards

Instructional Strategies

Opener

IE 4,   SE 1,   SE 3

Teacher: I am pouring a dense liquid in this side and a less dense liquid in this other side. Watch what happens. Place a small glass aquarium so that the students can see it. Use an easily removable partition to divide the aquarium in half. Pour a dense liquid, representing cold, heavy air, into one side. (Use water mixed with salt and blue food coloring for the dense liquid.) Pour a *less* dense liquid, representing warm, light air, into the other side. (Use cooking oil and red food coloring for the less dense liquid.) This represents where warm air meets cool air. The partition is the "front." Remove the partition quickly. The cold, heavy (blue) liquid pushes below the lighter (red) liquid. Very little mixing occurs. Ask the students to discuss (in pairs) what they see.

Body

SE 5,   A 2,   A 3

The teacher instructs the students to remember the demonstration as they continue the lesson. Distribute an index card to each group of students. The cards will have written on them the name of one of the four front types (cold front, warm front, occluded front, and stationary front). Allow the students to use any method they wish (the Internet, books, computer programs, etc.) to find out as much as they can about their front type. Students must include the symbol for the front, type of weather the symbol is most associated with it, and how the front develops. After about twenty minutes, the students can report to the class about their front.

Closing

A 1

The teacher or a student reviews the four front types. Ask the students to explain how the demonstration at the beginning of the class relates to fronts. (Students should be encouraged to use methods of reporting that accommodate special needs of the group members.)

Assessment

A 1,   A 2,   A 3

The teacher will grade the students' reports on fronts using any method. This is also a time when the teacher may want to give the students a more standard assessment about their knowledge of temperature and air movements.

SE 5

Optional Activity

Have the students collect the weather page from the local paper for several days. Use the U.S. map to explain the weather and fronts.

LESSON 7: How Does Air Pressure Affect the Weather?

Objectives

1. Each student will determine that air has weight.
2. Each student will demonstrate the strength of air.
3. Each student will identify air pressure and how it affects objects.

Materials

(See list of materials for each station that follows this lesson.)

Instructional Strategies

Opener

IE 2,   IE 3,   SE 1

Begin the lesson with several folk sayings related to air pressures. Stress that similar sayings are common in many cultures. Examples are "Smoke that curls downward and lingers means a nearing storm"; "If all the cows are lying down, it will rain"; "Roosting birds indicate a storm, because thinning air is harder to fly in."

Body

SE 4,   SE 2

After reading several folk sayings, move from station to station to obtain data that will help the students determine why these sayings were and are used by people to predict weather.

Station 1:   egg in a bottle
Station 2:   moving newspaper
Station 3:   drilling with a straw
Station 4:   altitude

The teacher assigns stations for fifteen minutes. Have students record observations and results in their journal.

A 1

Students return to their seats to debrief about the activities by having them explain what they think each station demonstrated. If necessary assist students with the concepts covered in the centers.

Activity 1 demonstrates that air exerts pressure. As the air in the bottle is heated, it expands and moves out of the bottle. As the air begins to cool, it contracts. There is less air in the bottle, which causes greater pressure on the outside to "push" the egg into the bottle. The egg can be "pushed" out again by blowing into the bottle (increasing the pressure inside) and allowing the egg to seal the hole.

Activity 2 also demonstrates that air has weight. The paper does not move because the air pressure is exerted downward. Since the paper is flat against the board and table, no air is beneath the paper to counteract the pressure from above.

Activity 3 demonstrates the strength of air. The trapped air inside the straw (with the finger on the end) makes the straw strong enough to break the skin of the potato. Air pushing on the inside of the straw prevents it from bending.

Activity 4 demonstrates that the amount of pressure decreases with height. The lowest ball of clay will be much flatter than the upper ball of clay due to the increased pressure exerted on it.

Air pressure helps determine weather. When air pressure is high, it presses down and pushes the air down.

This pressure usually prevents warm, moist air from rising, so clouds do not form. High pressure usually means fair weather, but there are some exceptions. The reverse is true when air pressure is low. Low pressure usually means cloudy weather.

Closing

A 1,   A 2

Teacher: Now that you have completed the four experiments, explain how air has weight. (Students should refer to Activity 2.) **What do you know about air pressure?** (Students should refer to Activities 1 and 4.) **How do these experiments help us understand weather better?** (High pressure usually means fair weather; low pressure usually means cloudy weather.) **How else does air pressure affect us?** (Possible answers: Ears "pop" in planes; it is harder to breathe on mountains; divers experience the bends.) **Did you know that animals change their behavior when there is a sudden drop in air pressure?** (Possible comments: Cows and horses that are generally very even tempered might become unruly. Dogs and cats become restless.) **Can anyone think of an old saying that might capture this idea that animals react to a drop in air pressure?** (One answer is that anglers say that fish bite better just before a storm.)

Assessment

A 1,   A 2

The teacher will move around the class observing students' work for signs of misunderstanding. Using the students' comments and questions, the teacher should assist the students.

Station 1
Materials:
Gatorade bottle
hot water
medium hard-boiled egg

1. Peel the hard-boiled egg.
2. Place the egg on the mouth of the Gatorade bottle. Observe. Remove the egg.
3. Pour heated water into the bottle and immediately pour it back out. Quickly place the egg back on the mouth of the bottle. Observe.
4. Hold the bottle upside down with the small end of the egg in the bottle neck.
5. Tilt the bottle down until there is a small opening between the neck of the bottle and the egg.
6. Blow into the bottle, making a closed seal with your mouth. Before you remove your mouth, tilt the bottle so that the egg closes the hold. Observe.

Station 2

Materials:

thin board

counter edge

newspaper

1. Place one end of the thin board on a table with slightly less than half of the board hanging off the edge.
2. Lay a sheet of newspaper over the part of the board on the table.
3. Strike the protruding board as hard as you can. Observe.

Station 3

Materials:

two plastic drinking straws

raw potato

1. Put the potato on the table.
2. Hold one of the straws near the top, leaving the top open.

3. Raise the straw about 4 inches above the potato and quickly push the straw into the potato. Observe.
4. Repeat with the second straw but use your thumb to close off the upper end of the straw. Observe.

Station 4

Materials:

five books

clay or Play-Doh

wax paper

1. From the clay, make five balls that are equal in size.
2. Place wax paper on the table and put the first clay ball on it. Add another sheet of wax paper above the ball of clay.
3. Place one of the books on the wax paper.
4. Repeat until you have paper, ball, paper, book, paper, ball, paper, book, etc. Observe.

LESSON 8: What Are Highs and Lows?

Objectives

1. Each student will describe the movement of air in areas of high and low pressure.
2. Each student will use knowledge of high and low pressure to predict weather.

Materials

U.S. weather map, strips of papers, blank U.S. maps, weather map from newspaper for the past two days

Instructional Strategies

Opener

Ask the students to share their knowledge of air pressure with a partner. (This should be a review of Lesson 7.) Share some of the ideas with the class.

Body

A 1,   A 2

Teacher: If air has pressure, is it the same over the entire earth? Clear up any misconceptions. Show the students a weather map of the United States. Explain the *H* and *L* on the map.

SE 1,   SE 2

Ask the students to cut (or rip) two strips of paper about an inch wide. Hold one strip in each hand in front of your face (students' hands should be just above their heads). The paper strips should be about 3 to 5 inches apart. Have the students tell a neighbor what they think will happen if they blow between the strips of paper. Now blow steadily between the two sheets of paper.

Ask the students to share with a neighbor what they observed and what they think this means. In a class discussion, help the students to see that they are removing some of the air between the strips of paper when they blow. This action causes an area of low pressure between the strips. As a result, the outer air forces the strips of paper together.

SE 2

Teacher: From what you have just seen, what directions will the wind blow in an area of low pressure? The correct response is that as the strips move inward, the wind in an area of low pressure also moves inward. On the board write a large *L* with arrows pointing toward the *L*. Explain that in addition to moving into the area, the air moves upward. This upward flow of air often causes clouds and precipitation to form. Consequently, lows are associated with rain (snow, etc.). **Teacher: What do you think will happen to the wind pattern where there is an area of high pressure?** Students should be able to tell that the wind will move away from the high pressure. On the board, write a large *H* with arrows pointing away from the *H*. Ask the students what kind of weather is associated with high pressure. The answer is that fair weather is associated with highs. As winds blow out of a high, the air spreads creating conditions that are not conducive to cloud formation.

SE 5,   A 1,   A 3

Have the students either (1) electronically or (2) manually create a weather map. For the electronic form, have the students go to http://athena.wednet.edu, click on Weather, then on Weather Charting, and complete the activity on creating a weather map. For the manual form, give the students a blank map of the United States and a weather map of the United States from the local newspaper for the last two days. Students will have the first two days of a four-day forecast sequence. Have them predict and draw the sequence of forecast images for the next two days using the information they now have on high and low pressure areas.

Closing

A 1,   A 2

Have the students share their weather maps and tell why they made the predictions they did.

Assessment

A 1,   A 2

As students present their maps, listen for accurate descriptions of the movement of air in areas of high and low pressure and for correct predictions.

Optional Activity

There have been some interesting stories of how weather has affected human history. For example, historians think that drizzly, overcast weather aided the allies during the invasion of Normandy. Have the students find other examples to share with the class.

LESSON 9: Water Vapor—Humidity

Objectives

1. Each student will describe how the terms humidity and relative humidity are related.
2. Each student will name the instrument used to measure relative humidity.

Materials

Glue, marker, large glass jar, pencil, tape, flat toothpick

Instructional Strategies

Opener

IE 1,   SE 1

Teacher: How does the weather affect your hair? The teacher explains that various ethnic groups have different hair texture. **What makes this difference that we see?**

Body

If students refers to *humidity*, ask why they think the humidity would have anything to do with changes in hair texture.

SE 3

Have the students in groups of four set up a "wet air station." Put the directions on the overhead.

1. Secure one end of a strand of hair to the center of the toothpick with the tape.
2. Color the pointed end of the toothpick with the marker.
3. Tape the free end of the hair to the center of the pencil.
4. Place the pencil across the mouth of the jar with the toothpick hanging inside the jar. (The jar just gives it a place to hang and keeps the wind from moving it.)
5. Place the jar where it will be safe.

6. Observe the directions that the toothpick points for one week.

(The instrument that has just been made is a hair hygrometer. Hygrometers are used to measure humidity. The hair stretches when the humidity increases. This is why straight hair gets straighter and curly hair gets curlier. The stretching and shrinking of the hair pulls on the toothpick, causing it to move.)

IE 4

Teacher: We will not know anything about hair for a few days. In the meantime, do you know of any other everyday ways of telling if the humidity is high? Examples: Salt will clump when the humidity is high and will be hard to pour. Static electricity in your hair and clothing is more pronounced on dry days.

Closing

A 1

Teacher: Is there a difference in humidity and relative humidity? Assist the students in understanding that any water vapor in the air is humidity and that what most people really want to know is the *relative humidity*. Relative humidity is the percent of moisture the air holds relative to the amount it could hold at a given temperature.

Assessment

A 1,   A 2

The teacher will listen as the students participate in the closing discussion, particularly noting students' understanding of the distinction between humidity and relative humidity.

LESSON 10: Precipitation

Objective

1. Using different learning preferences, each student will explain how precipitation occurs.

Materials

Rain stick (one per group), 1-quart glass jar with lid, hot water, ice cubes

Instructional Strategies

Opener

IE 1,   IE 3,   SE 1

Teacher: Students, close your eyes. The teacher slowly inverts the rain stick. **What do you hear?** Invert the rain stick with more energy. **What do you hear now?** Have a student explain why they thought of rain when the rain sticks moved. (The teacher explains the origin of the rain stick. The stick is made in a very dry part of Chile and is used in ceremonial dances to help bring rain. In addition, rain sticks are easy to make. See the directions for making a rain stick at the end of this unit. This is an opportunity to work with the art teacher on a project.)

Body

SE 3

Teacher: What conditions are necessary for rain to occur? Write the answers in your journals. Have the students do the following activity in groups of four.

IE 4,   SE 5

Precipitation Activity

1. Each group should examine a 1-quart glass jar to be sure that there is no moisture on it or the lid.

2. Pour enough hot water into the jar to cover the bottom (about 1/4 inch).

3. Turn the metal lid upside down over the mouth of the jar and put three to four ice cubes on the lid. (Any melting water will be caught by the sides of the lid.)

4. Observe the underside of the lid for about ten minutes. Record what you observe in any way you wish.

Ask the students to work in their groups and compare what they thought was needed to form rain and what they did in the activity. After an appropriate amount of time, ask the students to share.

The students should be able to express that some of the liquid water in the bottom of the jar evaporates. The lid is cold because of the ice on its top. The water vapor condenses and then changes back to a liquid when it hits the cold underside of the lid. As the amount of liquid increases, drops form on the underside of the lid. In nature, liquid water evaporates from the earth, rises, and condenses as it hits the cooler upper air. Clouds are made of tiny drops of liquid water suspended in the air. Water drops in the clouds range in size from .000079 to .0039 inches in diameter. The tiny water drops join together, forming drops that are too big to stay suspended in the air. Falling raindrops range in size from .24 to .79 inches.

Closing

Teacher: Sometimes it rains too much. Rivers swell and flow over their banks. Flooding can be a serious problem. What happens to property and people in floods?

In 1999, the oldest all-Black town in the United States was devastated by floods. That town is Princeville, North Carolina. When that happened, many people wanted to help. Students from Atlanta, Georgia Public Schools decided to help and organized a community service project. They went to Princeville, bringing supplies and help for the towns' citizens.

Can you find examples of other weather disasters? How do people help out in times of weather disaster? How could you help?

Ask the students to draw a picture to represent what happens to cause rain. Ask them to label it as it is in nature and as it was represented by the activity. Have one student come to the front of the class and draw his/her picture on the board. Have a second student explain the picture.

Assessment

A 1,   A 2,   A 3

The teacher will ask students to describe the cycle that produces rain.

RAIN STICK DIRECTIONS:

You can make a rain stick from any cardboard cylinder. Wrapping-paper rolls or paper-towel rolls are very good. Cover one end of the cylinder with tape. Stick toothpicks into the cylinder so that most of the toothpick is inside the cylinder. You will want to put one into the tube about every 2 inches. In order to secure the toothpick, you may want to fold back the end that is sticking out and tape it to the side of the cylinder. When you have enough toothpicks sticking in the cylinder, pour a little rice into it. Cover the second end with tape. You should be able to turn the cylinder back and forth and let the rice filter down, hitting the toothpicks. As the rice hits the toothpicks, it makes the sound of rain.

LESSONS 11–13: Severe Weather Research

Objectives

1. Each student will decide the best way to collect needed data/information on severe weather.
2. Each student will decide the best way to report data/information.
3. Each student will suggest an appropriate research methodology.
4. Each student will select appropriate research tools for finding out more about severe weather.
5. Each student will demonstrate how temperature, wind, water vapor, and air pressure combine to produce the conditions needed for severe weather.

Materials

Video clip of severe weather, Group Research Plan, Evaluation Form, Report Form

Instructional Strategies

Opening

SE 1,   IE 1

Show a video of several types of severe weather. Ask the students why we need to know about weather conditions that are unusually violent. Allow time for a discussion.

Body

SE 5,   SE 1,   SE 4,   A 1,   A 3

Allow each group to decide the type of weather they are interested in investigating. Guide the students in deciding how to research their topic. If the students have never created a research plan, instruct them on how to do so at this time. The plan and your expectations will determine the quality and rigor of the research. This re-

search should lead the students to an in-depth understanding of some types of severe weather.

A 1,   IE 4

Help the student groups develop a research plan by writing questions they want to ask about the weather. Use the Group Research Plan (at the end of the lesson plan) to help guide the work. The students should formulate the questions, decide which student is responsible for finding the answer, choose the strategy to find the answers, and plan how they will present the findings to the class. Provide books, Internet, CD databases, laser disc, and so on for the students to use. Move among the groups and help guide the "discovery."

IE 2,   IE 1,   SE 2,   SE 5

After the students have researched their topic, have them "publish" a scientific journal. Have all the student groups present their research. Each student will grade their own performance and the performance of the group. In addition, all students will help evaluate each group report.

Closing

SE 2

Have the students list the types of weather presented in class. Mark the weather systems that are most common in your area. Ask the students to share stories about their experiences with these types of weather systems.

Assessment

A 1,   A 2,   A 3

For Lesson 11, check the Group Research Plan to see if students understand the assignment. For Lesson 13, collect the Evaluation Form and the Report Evaluation Form from the groups and solicit student input to assess the performance and assign a grade to each group.

Topic: _____

Student Names: _____

1.   We would like to answer the following questions:

2.   We believe that we can find the answers by using the following sources:

3.   The best way for us to inform others about what we have learned is to:

4.   We will distribute the tasks in the following way:

Evaluation Form

COOPERATIVE ACTIVITY

Name: _____

I.   Student self-evaluation

My role in this group was _____

Here is a list of the ways I helped my group complete the task.

I give my own performance in the group a grade of _____ because

II. Student group-evaluation

I give _____ a grade of _____ because

I give _____ a grade of _____ because

I give _____ a grade of _____ because

III. For teacher use only

Group grade _____

Individual grade _____

Comments:

Report Evaluation Form

Student Names _____

Topic: _____

Total points possible: 100   Total points earned: _____

1. Effort (10 points)

   Comments:

2. Organization (10 points)

   Comments:

3. Content (60 points)

   Comments:

4. Presentation (10 points)

   Comments:

5. Quality of responses to peer questions (10 points)

   Comments:

LESSON 14: Closing/Reconstructing Knowledge

Objectives

1. Each student will explain any edits made to the graphic organizer.
2. Each student will make a connection between their own understanding and general understanding as seen in myths and sayings.
3. Each student will recognize the value of old sayings about weather.

Materials

Graphic organizer from the unit opener, colored markers

Instructional Strategies

Opener

IE 1

Teacher: Let's listen to a story from Mexico about the sun.

The Aztec Indians in Mexico knew that the sun was very important in making the crops grow. The sun was so important that they believed the sun was a god and gave him the name Huitzilopochti. They believed that Huitzilopochti was a warrior who fought against the power of night so that the sun could be reborn every morning. He had to be kept strong, and people were sacrificed to provide him with human hearts and blood, which were thought to be his favorite foods.

Teacher: Have you wondered about the thunder? Maybe this story will explain about thunder. Thor was the Norse god of thunder. He was thought to be very strong and to have wild red hair and a beard. Thor raced across the sky in a chariot pulled by two giant goats and brewed up storms by blowing through his beard. He lived in a great hall called Bilskirnir, which means lighting.

Teacher: Have you ever wondered what causes a rainbow? Let's listen to what the Kabi people from Queensland in Australia think. The Kabi people worship a god called Dhakhan who is half fish and half snake. Dhakhan lives in deep water holes in the ground. He appears as a rainbow in the sky when he moves from one hole to the next. He is most often seen after a rain.

The teacher asks several students to tell the class their favorite folk saying about weather.

Body

IE 4,   SE 4,   SE 2

Ask the students why people over the ages have developed sayings such as the ones shared. Have the students share their ideas with a partner.

After sharing with a partner, ask the students to share some of the reasons with the whole class. Record the answers on the board for all to see. As time permits, develop a rich discussion about the reasons for sayings. Probe for the connection between the type of stories told and certain types of climates or locations. (Example: Stories about heavy rain and flooding will not come from desert areas. But there are many stories from around the world about heavy rains.) Begin to bring in the idea that the sayings are used to help people explain or predict things that happen in their lives. **Note:** This would be a good time to use map skills. Students could locate on the map the origin of the sayings.

Teacher: Do any of you ever use a saying to guide your own actions? (Perhaps give an example, such as, "When I see a red sky in the morning, I bring a raincoat with me. Why would I do this?") **Are these sayings always correct? Are they correct some of the time? Can someone tell me more about the accuracy of some of the sayings?**

After a good discussion of the accuracy of the sayings, give each group their graphic organizer from the first day. Ask the students to use a new color marker to edit the graphic organizer. After an appropriate amount of time, have each group explain to the class what they changed and why. Use any opportunity to reinforce the concepts learned during the unit.

Closing

A 1,   A 3

Have each student write a "new" weather saying based on what they now know about weather.

Assessment

A 1,   A 2

The teacher may wish to administer a standard written exam. In addition, other assessment techniques can be implemented. Students can write an article for the magazine *Science Today* that explains the importance of temperature, air pressure, air movement, or water vapor in the creation of weather.

The Constitution: Voting Rights
Culturally Responsive Social Studies Lessons
Civics/United States History
6th–8th Grades

Goals and Objectives

Goals

1. Students will understand that enfranchisement is a fluid process that has led to the expansion and contraction of the electorate throughout U.S. history.
2. Students will explore the impact of changes in the composition of the electorate on those elected to political office.
3. Students will appreciate the importance of voting in a republican form of government.

Objectives

1. Each student will take on a role and participate in a series of mock presidential elections.
2. Each student, as part of a group, will analyze and evaluate documents relating to the expansion and contraction of the right to vote throughout U.S. history.
3. Each student, as part of a group, will form generalizations regarding changes in voting requirements.
4. Each student will analyze the impact of demographic changes in the electorate on persons elected to political office.
5. Each student will help design and implement an analysis of neighborhood voting patterns.
6. Each student, either individually or as part of a group, will create and present a contribution to a class voter education project.

Virginia E. Causey
Columbus State University

with
George Mills, Marietta Middle School
Benjamin Ridgeway, DeKalb County School System

Introduction

The National Council for the Social Studies identifies the primary purpose of teaching social studies as helping young people "to develop the ability to make informed and reasoned decisions for the public good as citizens of a culturally diverse, democratic society in an interdependent world." Unfortunately, recent national tests and surveys have revealed students' poor performance and lack of interest in social studies, and the deficiency in performance and engagement is greater for children of color and those at lower socioeconomic levels. Not surprisingly, adults with those same characteristics tend to be much less active participants in civic life. Thomas Jefferson, among others, pointed out the critical need for educated, active participants in a healthy democracy. Consequently, the social studies classroom must live up to its calling and create an intellectual and values-based climate that fosters the development of critical thinkers who understand and act upon their responsibilities as citizens.

The growing diversity of student populations has forced educators to take a look at their own attitudes, curriculum, and pedagogy. Culturally responsive pedagogy is an important approach for engaging *all* students in a meaningful and challenging exploration of social studies. One of the ten themes in the NCSS national standards for social studies is the study of culture and cultural diversity. Social studies should serve as a vehicle for an equitable approach to issues of diversity. Two related overriding principles should guide the teaching of social studies: (1) **multiple interpretations** and (2) **education for citizenship.** First, consider the concept of **multiple interpretations.** Much of the study of history and social science is someone's interpretation, a "best guess." For years, there was a "standard history" written by the European-background middle- and upper-class white men who dominated the field. By the 1960s, with the emergence of a more diverse population of historians and social scientists, the questions they asked about the past changed; therefore, the answers they uncovered often changed. Historians and social scientists began to look at data previously ignored and at social classes and ethnic groups and women who had received little attention in the traditional curriculum. The message for social studies teachers is to help their students' see the world from many points of view. The national standards in social studies and in history stress the importance of students thoughtfully examining controversial and values-laden issues, recognizing opposing points of view, and developing sensitivity to similarities and differences.

Students need to learn that the existence of cultural and philosophical differences are not "problems" to be solved; rather, they are healthy and desirable qualities of democratic community life. Students see more interconnections and more relevance in their study of history and the social studies when they are exposed to various viewpoints, when they become the active interpreters of data, and when they apply their knowledge in real-life settings. The key for teachers is to view the dialogue between present and past as ongoing, not set in stone.

The national standards in social studies, history, and civics emphasize the teaching of critical thinking and decision-making skills. Pedagogy that encourages looking at history from multiple viewpoints can lead to higher-order thinking, a critical mind-set. This approach of acknowledging multiple viewpoints frightens some Americans. One newspaper editorial took issue with the National History Standards' emphasis on multiculturalism and multiple perspectives by quoting codirector Gary Nash: "We're trying to let children out of the prison of facts, the prison of names and dates and places, and make them active learners, inquiring citizens, and people who don't passively absorb the words on the page." Most teachers work very hard to create opportunities for students to be active learners, inquiring citizens, and critical thinkers. Multiple viewpoint teaching approaches can lead to a feeling of inclusion on the part of the learner that should result in higher levels of engagement and a sense that the classroom has a significant connection to real life.

The second major principle for teaching social studies is **education for citizenship,** the traditional purpose for including social studies in the school curriculum. Social studies should help enlighten public discourse because students will possess the knowledge, intellectual skills, and attitudes necessary to confront, discuss, and consider action on important issues. Attention to diversity issues plays a critical role in that endeavor. Teachers and students must pay attention to diversity in order to promote four key elements of citizenship: (1) inclusion, (2) mutual understanding, (3) common values, and (4) social action. The first important element is **inclusion.** Attention to diversity helps students feel as if they are a vital part of the nation, not outsiders, and can help in the assimilation process for new immigrants. This inclusion also can help raise self-esteem when students see themselves and their ancestors in the curriculum.

A second element crucial in citizenship transmission is **mutual understanding.** Each person experiences life in an individual way, responding to the world from a personal perspective. People also share common perspectives as members of groups, communities, and nations. Valuing diversity within the classroom setting can lessen conflict and help build a sense of unity. Personal and pluralist perspectives developed within the framework of civic responsibility are a hallmark of our democratic national culture committed both to individual liberty and the common good. Attention to multiculturalism will not divide or "Balkanize" the nation as some critics assert. On the other hand, it can help bring a deeply divided nation together by heightening our understanding and appreciation of each other.

The third characteristic related to citizenship education is promoting **common values.** American society has been built upon the foundation principles of justice, equality of opportunity, and liberty. Schools have traditionally been the conduit through which the common values have passed to generations of young people. These ideals form the "unum" underlying the reality of the "pluribus." The core values have not always been a reality in the experience of every individual or group in American history, but our Constitutional system has most often been the tool groups have used to gain and expand their rights. By highlighting the experiences of diverse groups, teachers can help students internalize these democratic principles. The students can understand American core values as relevant and real, not as abstract principles that apply to someone else.

The final critical element in citizenship education is **social action.** The national standards emphasize that the mission of social studies is not just to facilitate learning a body of knowledge, but also how to think about that knowledge and how to be flexible in using many resources to resolve civic issues. Students should explore a variety of issues in a thorough, fair-minded manner. As they examine each position and analyze the strongest points in favor of it, the strongest points in opposition to it, and the consequences that would follow from a specific course of action, students become better able to confront persistent issues and dilemmas. They are prepared to participate with others in making decisions and acting upon those decisions. Students who possess knowledge, skills, and values are prepared to take appropriate action for civic improvement. The social studies classroom should provide real opportunities for social action within the school and community. This is especially important for poorer students and students of color who are often marginalized in our system. They feel empowered when they see the effects of their civic action. Individual and group action designed to support both individual dignity and the common good bring our nation's ideals and practices closer together and promote more significant engagement for social studies students.

Diversity in American education is not an option; it is a reality. The challenge for educators is to deal with diversity positively, to embrace it as a resource that will enrich the learning experiences of students. Culturally responsive pedagogy is a critical element in creating classroom environments that facilitate significant learning experiences for *all* students. The lessons included in this chapter apply the principles of culturally responsive pedagogy in numerous ways.

Social studies classes offer the ideal laboratory where students can investigate and analyze issues related to diversity and then take informed action based upon their learning experiences. Consideration of multiple perspectives both in history and in contemporary life helps students become critical thinkers. Education for citizenship facilitates student feelings of inclusion, a better understanding of other cultures, internalization of core democratic values, and thoughtful civic action. As teachers apply the principles of culturally responsive pedagogy in social studies classrooms, students should see the world through a less distorted lens and should become better equipped to fulfill their roles as active citizens in a global society.

Background Information for the Teacher

The materials and strategies in this unit were selected for use in a sixth through eighth grade civics/U.S. history class. However, the topic of voting rights would be suitable for younger students and could be used in fifth grade with minor modifications. Moreover, the topic would be highly relevant to high school civics, government, and/or U.S. history classes, and the lessons could be used with few changes.

The unit is divided into a series of lessons. A lesson does not necessarily correspond to a class period. Many activities will vary in length according to student responses. The teacher will most likely want to allow frequent discussion of content and issues raised in studying changing requirements for voting. The scripting of the lessons is intended only as a guide. Each teacher will want to adapt the lessons to fit their particular instructional situation. In addition, each teacher should make appropriate adjustments for the ability and experience levels of their students.

There are two options for how the ten lessons in this unit may be implemented in the classroom. The teacher may choose to teach the lessons sequentially, following the initial study of the Constitution. However, if the unit is used in U.S. history, we strongly recommend an approach that would incorporate the lessons throughout the course, teaching each lesson where it would naturally fall in the chronology. For example, if the teacher chooses to use the second option, the voter education project (Lessons 4, 8, 9, and 10) could expand to cover a longer portion of the school year, if desired.

Voting in 1800—just after initial study of the Constitution;

Voting in 1832—during the study of Jacksonian Democracy;

Voting in 1872—during the study of Reconstruction;

Voting in 1908—during the study of the Progressive Era;

Voting in 1932—at the beginning of the study of the Great Depression;

Voting in 1972—during the study of the civil rights movement or of Nixon's presidency.

THE HISTORY OF SUFFRAGE IN THE UNITED STATES

The history of suffrage in the United States is a story of a gradually expanding (and sometimes contracting) franchise. The British colonists brought with them the concepts of English common law that formed the legal basis for suffrage during the colonial period. Generally, only white male property owners twenty-one years and older, about 4 percent of the population, had the right to vote. Native Americans, African American slaves, and free blacks were not citizens. There were, however, rare instances in the colonial era when women voted. One example is Margaret Brent of Maryland, a wealthy landowner who in 1648 took advantage of a suffrage law that did not specify gender. The Maryland legislature quickly remedied the oversight and disfranchised "Mistress Brent." English common law viewed a wife as the property of her husband. His vote represented them both. Women were considered mentally incapable of making the informed decisions necessary for good government. During the American Revolution, John Adams found it humorous when his wife Abigail (who had been running the family farm at a profit during his absence) requested the creators of the new American government to "remember the ladies" when writing the new code of laws.

The writers of the U.S. Constitution did not specify requirements for voting, leaving each of the new states to set its own criteria. Each of the new state constitutions maintained the racial, gender, and age qualifications of English common law. The first change in suffrage prerequisites was the property requirement. As Americans spread into western territories, land became more generally available, and the property requirement came to be viewed as undemocratic. None of the states that entered the Union after the original thirteen included property requirements in their constitutions. In the 1820s and 1830s, with the rise of popular democracy, most of the original thirteen states eliminated the property requirement as well. Virginia and North Carolina were the last states to let it go in the 1850s.

The end of the Civil War brought a change in racial requirements for voting. The Military Reconstruction Act of 1867 took the right to vote away from former Confederates, and, as a result, the number of white voters in the South plummeted. The Radical Republican Congress then responded to efforts by conservative white southern Democrats to disfranchise the freedmen with the passage of the Fifteenth Amendment. It was ratified and became law in 1870. For the first time, the U.S. Constitution overrode state and local suffrage laws. The Fifteenth Amendment proclaimed that "race, color, or previous condition of servitude" could not be used as a condition for voting. With the end of Reconstruction in 1877, however, white southern Democrats regained political control and soon found ways to deny the vote to African American men. The Ku Klux Klan, other organized groups, and white individuals used violence throughout the late nineteenth and early twentieth centuries to effectively discourage black voting. In addition, literacy tests, poll taxes, grandfather clauses, and the White Democratic primary combined to virtually eliminate black political participation by the turn of the century. The federal government turned away from its earlier commitment to African American voting rights. The Supreme Court upheld the Southern suffrage laws, noting that none overtly used race as a disqualifying condition for voting.

During the Progressive Era, reformers were concerned about vote fraud. In 1888, the Australian, or secret ballot, was introduced in the United States. Most states adopted its use by the early 1900s. Prior to its adoption, voters used colored ballots to represent different candidates or parties. Vote buying was prevalent with hired "poll watchers" who made sure the votes that had been bought were actually delivered. With the use of the secret ballot, political bosses could never be sure a bought vote actually went for the designated candidate.

Progressive reformers also supported woman suffrage. The Seneca Falls Convention in upstate New York in 1848 had initiated the woman suffrage movement. Suffragists had hoped the Fourteenth Amendment could be interpreted as giving women the vote, but Susan B. Anthony was arrested and convicted trying to vote under its auspices. The movement was strongest in the West where Wyoming became the first state to grant women the right to vote in 1890. In the early years of the twentieth century, suffragists and male Progressives joined in an intense campaign for the enfranchisement of women. Women's economic contributions to the war effort in World War I and the endorsement of President Woodrow Wilson finally led to the passage of the Nineteenth Amendment in 1920. One of the arguments in favor of woman suffrage had been that women's influence would clean up politics. However, the first president elected with women's votes was Warren G. Harding, who presided over one of the most corrupt administrations in U.S. history!

Native Americans had historically been members of sovereign nations within the borders of the United States. At the turn of the century, most Native Americans were confined to reservations or other land allotment systems under the control of the federal government. The official government policy toward Native Americans in the early years of the twentieth century was "acculturation": Native Americans should give up their way of life and fully assimilate into "American" culture. On reservations and in Native American schools, native languages, dress, customs, and religion were outlawed. In the spirit of acculturation, in 1924, Congress passed the Indian Citizenship Act, which granted suffrage to Native Americans in national elections. Many states, however, declined to extend the right to vote in state and local elections until years later.

By the 1940s, the barriers to African American voting slowly began to fall. The Supreme Court threw out the white Democratic primary in 1944. The first federal civil rights act passed in 1957. The Twenty-Fourth Amendment in 1964 outlawed the poll tax. Black Americans finally gained full suffrage with the Voting Rights Act in 1965. This 1965 act ended literacy tests and gave the federal government the power to intervene in local voting districts when necessary. As a result, the number of African Americans voting and holding office soared.

The final addition to the franchise has been 18-year-olds. Georgia was the first state to grant suffrage to 18-year-olds in its 1945 constitution. The persuasive argument was that if American young men could fight the Germans and the Japanese, then they ought to be able to vote. The identical case was made in the 1970s when a national amendment for the 18-year-old vote was proposed during the Vietnam War. The Twenty-Sixth Amendment passed Congress and was ratified in record time. Despite strong national support for their right to vote, 18- to 20-year-olds have consistently voted less frequently than any other group in the United States.

From the founding of the nation, the right of suffrage has generally expanded. But if the health of a republican form of government is measured by the percentage of people who vote, the United States is not well. Throughout the twentieth century, the percentage of eligible voters who actually go to the polls has hovered at about 50 percent. The U.S. turnout is the lowest of any democracy in the industrialized world. The future course of the nation lies in the hands of young people who must be more committed to meaningful political action.

Unit Organization

LESSON 1

Students will

Take on a role and participate in a mock presidential election;

Analyze and evaluate documents relating to the right to vote in 1800;

Form generalizations regarding changes in voting requirements;

Understand that enfranchisement is a fluid process that has led to the expansion and contraction of the electorate throughout U.S. history;

Appreciate the importance of voting in a republican form of government.

LESSON 2

Students will

Take on a role and participate in a mock presidential election;

Analyze and evaluate documents relating to the right to vote in 1832;

Form generalizations regarding changes in voting requirements;

Design and implement an analysis of neighborhood voting patterns;

Understand that enfranchisement is a fluid process that has led to the expansion and contraction of the electorate throughout U.S history;

Appreciate the importance of voting in a republican form of government.

LESSON 3

Students will

Take on a role and participate in a mock presidential election;

Analyze and evaluate documents relating to the right to vote in 1872;

Form generalizations regarding changes in voting requirements;

Understand that enfranchisement is a fluid process that has led to the expansion and contraction of the electorate throughout U.S. history;

Appreciate the importance of voting in a republican form of government.

LESSON 4

Students will

Help design and implement an analysis of neighborhood voting patterns;

Create and present an analysis of neighborhood voting patterns;

Discuss the importance of voting in a republican form of government.

LESSONS 5, 6, 7

Students will

Take on a role and participate in a mock presidential election;

Analyze and evaluate documents relating to the right to vote in 1908 (Lesson 5), 1932 (Lesson 6), and 1972 (Lesson 7);

Form generalizations regarding changes in voting requirements;

Understand that enfranchisement is a fluid process that has led to the expansion and contraction of the electorate throughout U.S. history;

Discuss the importance of voting in a republican form of government.

LESSON 8

Students will

Analyze the impact of demographic changes in the electorate on persons elected to political office;

Design and implement an analysis of neighborhood voting patterns;

Create and present a contribution to a class voter education project;

Appreciate the importance of voting in a republican form of government.

LESSON 9

Students will

Design and implement an analysis of neighborhood voting patterns;

Create and present a contribution to a class voter education project;

Appreciate the importance of voting in a republican form of government.

LESSON 10

Students will

Create and present a contribution to a class voter education project;

Appreciate the importance of voting in a republican form of government.

The Content Standards: NCSS Standards

The social studies unit developed to illustrate the principles of culturally responsive pedagogy is also consistent with the National Council for the Social Studies standards. These standards were developed by classroom teachers, university and college teacher educators, and school district social studies coordinators from across the country. They address overall curriculum design and are organized to incorporate learning experiences from the disciplines that comprise the social studies. The ten themes that form the framework of the social studies standards follow:

1. **Culture:** Students examine the characteristics of different cultures. They analyze belief systems and how cultures change to accommodate different beliefs and ideals. This theme typically appears in units dealing with geography, history, sociology, and anthropology.

2. **Time, Continuity, and Change:** Students read about and reconstruct the past, developing a historical perspective and looking at how they are connected to the past, how the world has changed, and how it might change in the future. This theme is central to units in history.

3. **People, Places, and Environments:** Students create spatial views and geographic perspectives as they study location and why things are located

where they are, what are "regions," and human-environmental interactions. Geography units typically focus on this theme.

4. **Individual Development and Identity:** Students examine how personal identify is shaped by one's culture, by groups, and by institutional influences. They study human growth and development and the roots of human behavior. Psychology and anthropology units typically address this theme.

5. **Individuals, Groups, and Institutions:** Students study how institutions are formed, what controls and influences them, how they influence individuals and culture, and how they are maintained or changed. This theme often appears in units dealing with sociology, anthropology, psychology, political science, and history.

6. **Power, Governance, and Authority:** Students explore the historical development of structures of power, authority, and governance and their evolving functions in contemporary U.S. society and other parts of the world. Units in government, political science, and history usually incorporate this theme.

7. **Production, Distribution, and Consumption:** Students analyze factors related to what is produced, how production is organized, how goods and services are distributed, and the effective allocation of land, labor, capital, and management. This theme forms the core of economics units.

8. **Science, Technology, and Society:** Drawing upon the natural and physical sciences, social sciences, and humanities, students evaluate the influence of technology on societies past and present, looking at changes resulting from technological innovation and the benefits and costs that arise from technology. This theme appears in units in history, geography, economics, civics, and government.

9. **Global Connections:** Students study the global connections among world societies, past and present, and the frequent tensions between national interests and global priorities over issues such as health care, human rights, the environment, ethnic diversity, political/military alliances, and trade. Geography, anthropology, history, and economics units often include this theme.

10. **Civic Ideals and Practices:** Students confront questions related to personal civic participation, the balance between rights and responsibilities, and the role of the citizen in the community, nation, and the world. Units in history, civics, political science, and anthropology typically address this theme.

The unit "The Constitution: Voting Rights" addresses the NCSS themes of (1) Culture; (2) Time, Continuity, and Change; (5) Individuals, Groups, and Institutions; (6) Power, Governance, and Authority; and (10) Civic Ideals and Practices.

Expectations of Excellence: Standards for Social Studies may be ordered from the NCSS Internet site (www.socialstudies.org), toll free at 800-683-0812, or by fax at 301-843-0159.

Matrix of Standards Referenced to Individual Lessons

	Lesson 1	Lesson 2	Lesson 3	Lesson 4	Lesson 5	Lesson 6	Lesson 7	Lesson 8	Lesson 9	Lesson 10
Standard 1	x	x	x		x	x	x	x		
Standard 2	x	x	x	x	x	x	x	x	x	x
Standard 5	x	x	x	x	x	x	x	x	x	x
Standard 6	x	x	x	x	x	x	x	x	x	x
Standard 10	x	x	x	x	x	x	x	x	x	x

	Unit Lessons									
	1	2	3	4	5	6	7	8	9	10
Simulating presidential elections	x	x	x		x	x	x			
Analyzing and evaluating documents; Inquiry	x	x	x		x	x	x			
Forming generalizations regarding suffrage changes	x	x	x		x	x	x	x		
Designing and implementing voter education project				x					x	
Presenting voter education project										x

LESSON 1: What Is Democracy? Analysis of Voting Rights in the Election of 1800

(**Note to the teacher:** Prior to this lesson, students should have studied the Articles of Confederation and the writing and ratification of the Constitution.)

Objectives

1. Each student will take on a role and participate in a mock presidential election. (psychomotor)
2. Each student will analyze and evaluate documents relating to the right to vote in 1800. (cognitive)
3. Each student will form generalizations regarding changes in voting requirements. (cognitive)
4. Each student will understand that enfranchisement is a fluid process that has led to the expansion and contraction of the electorate throughout U.S. history. (affective)
5. Each student will appreciate the importance of voting in a republican form of government. (affective)

Materials

Music for lesson opener,

a tape/CD player, ballots for "Best Musician" election,

characteristic tokens for students to draw (put each set of tokens in a separate envelope),

a ballot box with a sign marked "1800,"

the 1800 ballot for each student,

a packet of documents on 1800 for each group of three to four students.

The packet includes

- Two copies of the "Voting Rights in 1800" graphic organizer;
- One copy of "Analysis of the Election of 1832";

- Documents related to the election of 1800.
  Follow "Guidelines for the Use of the Documents."
  Copy "Presidential Information" charts for each student.
  Copy "Voting Requirements Changes" handout for each student.
  Create an overhead or laminated poster of the graphic organizer.
  Copy "Evaluation Sheet" for each student.
  Make a transparency of the quotation by Franklin Roosevelt.

Instructional Strategies

Opener

SE 1,   SE 2,   SE 3

Teacher: We're going to hold an election in class today for best American musician. In the background, the teacher is playing a recording by a musician the students would be certain not to like, such as Frank Sinatra, Tom Jones, Ethel Merman, Julio Iglecias, Leonard Bernstein, or Tammy Wynette. The teacher hands out ballots to each student. On the ballot is one candidate, the name of the musician the teacher is playing. The teacher tells students they must vote for the person listed on the ballot. Write-in candidates are not allowed.

After the students vote or protest, the teacher takes up the ballots and throws them away. **TEACHER:**

- **What was wrong with this election?**
- **Was this a democratic election?**
- **How can we define *democracy?***

The teacher solicits responses from students until a consensus definition is formed. The teacher writes the definition on the board, then asks a series of questions:

- **What characteristics do democratic elections have?**
- **What was so bad about making a decision the way we did?**
- **Are there any places in the world either now or in the past where this is the kind of "democracy" practiced?**
- **What are some problems that you think might arise from such a system?**
- **How is the United States' political system similar to and different from our classroom election today?**

The teacher reads the following quotation: **A woman named India Edwards wrote, "Voting is the most basic essential of citizenship and I think that any man or woman in this country who fails to avail himself or herself of that right should hide in shame. I truly wish there were some sort of badge of dishonor that a non-voter would have to wear." What did Ms. Edwards mean? Do you think that people in the U.S. should *have* to vote in every election?**

Body

IE 3,   SE 1

The teacher asks students to imagine they are traveling back in time in order to investigate the history of voting in the United States. Each student will assume a role in this time travel. Each student will take one token (or card) from each of the six envelopes.

The following categories should be represented by different colored tokens or by colored cards with the characteristic printed upon it. (The number in parentheses would be how many tokens or cards would be needed for a class of 24 students.)

Gender:	50% MALE (12)	50% FEMALE (12)
Ethnicity:	60% CAUCASIAN (14)	20% AFRICAN AMERICAN (5)
	10% NATIVE AMERICAN (3)	10% RECENT IMMIGRANT (2)
Age:	20% 18-YEAR-OLD (5)	10% 13-YEAR-OLD (2)
	20% 85-YEAR-OLD (5)	50% 40-YEAR-OLD (12)
Literacy:	70% I CAN READ (17)	30% I CANNOT READ (7)
Region:	60% I LIVE IN THE NORTH (15)	40% I LIVE IN THE SOUTH (9)
Socio-economic status:	30% I OWN PROPERTY (7)	70% I OWN NO PROPERTY (17)

Ask students to create a name tag with their characteristics listed on it. The students will pin or tape the name tag on their shirt where everyone can see what their characteristics are.

SE 4,   SE 5

The teacher asks students to form groups of three to four. Students should join a group that shares at least one of their characteristics. Students will group themselves according to whatever characteristic(s) they choose, but they can join only one other group.

SE 2,   SE 3,   A 1

The teacher explains that students will participate in a series of mock presidential elections beginning in 1800 and continuing to the present. The teacher asks students to calculate the time span between the present and 1800. He/she reviews student prior knowledge about events in U.S. history prior to 1800, particularly government under the Articles of Confederation and the writing of the Constitution. The teacher asks students how life in 1800 was different from their lives. **Teacher: Let's see if the way people voted and the types of people elected president were different then.**

At a table or the teacher's desk, he/she places a sign with "1800" written on it. The teacher also has copies of ballots for each student.

SE 1,   SE 2

The teacher passes out ballots and tells students to mark their choice, then tear off the top half of the ballot and keep it in their notebook. Students should form a line in front of the ballot box to deposit their ballots. The teacher stands by the ballot box. However, the only ballots accepted are from students with these characteristics:

male	Caucasian
40 or 85 years old	can read or not
from the North or South	own property

All others will be turned away with no explanation. The teacher directs the students who got to vote to line up on one side of the room. The students who were turned away are sent to the other side of the room.

IE 1,   IE 2,   SE 2,   SE 3

The teacher asks students to compare the number of people who got to vote in 1800 to the number who did not. Out of a class of 24 students, there would be only seven property owners, and some of those would likely be female, or disqualified by ethnicity or age. So the number of voters would be very small. The teacher asks what it felt like for those who didn't get to vote. **Teacher: What problems might arise from an election like this?** Students should make guesses about why so few people were allowed to vote and who would have wanted voting requirements to remain as they were in 1800. The teacher writes the student hypotheses on the board. He/she leads the discussion so students understand Caucasian men of property controlled the law-making process.

SE 1,   SE 4,   SE 5

The teacher tells students they will analyze evidence to find out more about voting in 1800. The teacher places students in original groups. Within the groups, the teacher either assigns roles for students or allows students to choose their roles: *facilitator*—organizes and distributes the documents to be read, makes certain everyone participates (manages time limits if there are only three members for the group); *archivist*—records information on the graphic organizer to be turned in; *reporter*—shares the group's findings in the debriefing; *manager* (if there are four members)—manages time limits and helps keep group on task. *All group members are researchers and document analysts.*

The teacher passes out packets with documents to the facilitator in each group. Each packet is marked "1800." The teacher also passes out Handout 1, "Voting Rights in 1800," to each student.

IE 1,   IE 2,   IE 3,   IE 4,   SE 1,   SE 2,
SE 4,   A 1,   A 2

The teacher tells students that the packets contain documents related to voting requirements around 1800. The facilitators will pull all of them out and divide them among the group. One at a time, each group member will read one of their documents to the group. After each document is read, the group will create a one-sentence summary and analyze what the document says about voting. The archivist will use the organizer in the packet to record the group's findings. After all documents are read and analyzed, the group should make generalizations about who could and could not vote in 1800 and complete page 2 of Handout 1, "Analysis of the Election of 1800."

Before the groups begin, analyze one of the documents together. The teacher asks the facilitators to take out the document titled "English Common Law." The teacher calls on a student to read the document aloud. Students then write down the document title in the first block of Handout 1. Next, agree upon a one-sentence summary of the document. Finally, the teacher works with students to figure out what the document says about voting. The teacher gives the groups thirty minutes to analyze the rest of the documents and complete the "Analysis of the Election of 1800."

The teacher circulates to provide feedback, to keep groups on task, and to provide formative assessment. Before groups begin, the teacher may want to have the class define vocabulary words students may not be familiar with, such as *suffrage, franchise,* and others.

IE 1,   IE 2,   IE 3,   IE 4,   SE 2,   SE 3,
A 1,   A 2

Debriefing: The teacher has the reporter from Group 1 analyze one document for the class, asking,

- **Who wrote this?**
- **What does the document have to do with voting?**
- **What group or groups would be affected by this? How?**

The teacher repeats the process with all groups until all documents are discussed.

IE 1,   IE 2,   IE 3,   IE 4,   SE 2,   SE 3,
A 1

The groups then share the generalizations about voting they made on "Analysis of the Election of 1800." The teacher uses questioning to bring students to generalize that not very many of the American people could vote in 1800. **Teacher:**

- **What groups were not allowed to vote?**
- **Why do you think so few people were allowed to vote?**
- **What were the general attitudes about these groups not allowed to vote?**

Give students a chance to identify each disfranchised group: women, African Americans, Native Americans, and poor people, and to discuss attitudes prevalent in 1800. The teacher asks if people today still have some of these ideas about who should and should not vote. The teacher asks students to make a prediction: do they believe the percentage of people who are allowed to vote will go up or down as we time travel up to the present? The teacher tells students they will investigate this question in their mock elections coming up.

The teacher then tabulates the results of the mock election for 1800. He/she points out that in 1800, Thomas Jefferson won the election. He/she asks students to turn to a picture of Jefferson in their textbook so they will have a visual image, then leads students in organizing information on the presidents. The teacher passes out Handout 2, "Presidential Information," to each student. Students take the top half of their ballot and write down the important information about Thomas Jefferson onto the chart. They can use their texts to supplement this information. When students finish their charts, the teacher leads a debriefing to be certain all information is correct.

SE 2,   SE 3,   A 1,   A 2

The teacher reminds students that they discovered only Caucasian men with property could vote in 1800.

Teacher: Was the president elected similar to the people who voted or different from them?

Students should see similarities. The teachers asks students to make one more prediction:

Teacher: If more people were able to vote, do you think the type of person elected president would change? How? Why?

The teacher tells students to keep the "Presidential Information" chart in their notebooks. He/she asks the facilitators to place the documents back in the envelopes and pass them to the front. He/she also takes up the group written work for assessment. He/she also takes up student characteristics name tags to use in the next lesson (optional—students may draw new characteristics in the next lesson, if the teacher chooses).

The teacher passes out Handout 3, "Voting Requirement Changes," for students to keep track of changes in suffrage requirements. The teacher also has an overhead transparency or poster board or butcher paper representation of the same chart large enough for all students to see.

IE 4,   SE 2,   SE 3,   A 1,   A 2

As a large group, the teacher leads the class in filling out the cells of the chart. He/she tells students to keep their chart in their notebooks because they will use it to see if voting requirements change over the years.

A 1,   A 2

The teacher passes out Handout 4, "Evaluation Sheet," for self- and peer evaluation of group work performance. (The use of this evaluation form is recommended for all cooperative work in the unit.)

Closing

SE 1,   SE 2,   SE 4,   IE 1,   IE 2,   IE 3,
IE 4,   A 1,   A 2

The teacher discusses the homework assignment: the students will write a journal entry about how they felt when they either got to vote or were turned away from voting. Students should pretend they are a person who had all the characteristics they drew, living in 1800. How would they feel if they were one of the few who got to vote or one of the many who could not? (Another approach would be a teacher response journal—the teacher writes the first entry and makes a copy for each student. Students then respond to the teacher's entry and turn in their journals for the teacher to read.)

The teacher closes with a quotation from President Franklin Roosevelt about the importance of voting in a democratic government (Transparency 1). Ask students to think about the importance of voting as they write their journal entries and as they continue to investigate who could and could not vote.

Assessment

Student understanding will be assessed through teacher observation of group work and class discussion, through group written work, through the journal entries, and through participation in the voter education project.

CANDIDATES

JOHN ADAMS—John Adams was born in 1735. He was a member of the Federalist party, one of the two major political parties in 1800. He had served as vice president under George Washington's presidency and as president from 1796 to 1800. He also helped write the Declaration of Independence in 1776 and provided strong leadership during the American Revolution and the creation of the United States. Adams was a wealthy lawyer from Massachusetts.

THOMAS JEFFERSON—Thomas Jefferson was born in 1743. He was the founder of the Democratic Republican party (now called the Democratic party). He had served as vice president under John Adams from 1796 to 1800. He was the principal writer of the Declaration of Independence, U.S. ambassador to France, and secretary of state under George Washington's presidency. Jefferson was a wealthy plantation owner from Virginia.

Ballot—Election of 1800

Mark your choice for ONE of the following:

_____ JOHN ADAMS

_____ THOMAS JEFFERSON

Group _____   _____

Members: _____   _____

VOTING RIGHTS IN 1800		
Document Title	**One-Sentence Summary of the Document**	**What Does It Say About Voting Requirements?**

Based upon your analysis of the documents, answer the following:

1.   What groups of people were allowed to vote in 1800?

2.   List at least three groups of people who were not allowed to vote in 1800.

3.   Why do you think these groups were not allowed to vote in 1800? What were the general attitudes many people held toward these groups at that time?

4.   What contributions were these groups making to the United States even though they couldn't vote?

Name _____

PRESIDENTIAL INFORMATION				
President	Political Party	Age When Elected	Leadership Experience	Social/Economic Status

VOTING REQUIREMENT CHANGES	Name_____		
Election Year	What Groups of People Were Allowed to Vote?	List at Least 3 Groups Not Allowed to Vote	What Changed Since the Last Election? List the document titles, the groups affected, and how voting requirements changed.
1800			Not Applicable
1832			
1872			
1908			
1932			
1972			

NAME _____

Student Evaluation: My role in this group was _____.

List all the ways you helped your group complete this task:

Grading Scale: 10–A

          9–B

          8–C

          7–D

          6 and below–F

          0–did not participate

I give my own performance in the group a grade of _____ because _____

I give each member of my group the following grade on the scale of 10 down to 0:

I give _____ a grade of _____ because

I give _____ a grade of _____ because

I give _____ a grade of _____ because

Teacher Evaluation:

Group Grade _____

Individual Grade + _____ = **Overall Grade** _____ **for This Group Work.**

Comments:

President

Franklin D. Roosevelt, 1938:

"Let us never forget

that government is ourselves and not a

[foreign] power

over us. The ultimate rulers

of our democracy are not a President

and senators and congressmen and

government officials, but the voters of

this country."

Guidelines for Use of Documents

Instructions for the Teacher

1. Make copies of the documents so that each group will have one complete set of documents for each election year.

2. Obtain enough 9 × 12 envelopes with clasp closures so there is one for each group for each day of the lesson where documents are used. (For example, if you will have six groups in the class, you will need a total of thirty-six envelopes since there are six lessons that make use of documents.)

3. Divide the envelopes into six piles. On one group of envelopes, write "1800" with a marker. On the second group, write "1832." On the third group, write "1872." On the fourth group, write "1908." On the fifth group, write "1932." On the final group, write "1972." (If you have six groups, there should be six envelopes marked "1800," six marked "1832," six marked "1872," and so on.)

4. Take the envelopes marked "1800" and all copies of the documents for 1800. Cut apart the documents where they are separated by dotted lines. Put one copy of each document in each envelope and close the clasp. Laminating the documents will make them last much longer.

5. Repeat the above process for each year: 1832, 1872, 1908, 1932, 1972.

6. On the first day of the unit, distribute one envelope marked "1800" to each group. At the end of the lesson, make certain the facilitator for each group replaces all documents in the envelope and returns the envelope to you. Follow the same procedure for subsequent lessons.

Documents for 1800

ARTICLE I, SECTION 2, U.S. CONSTITUTION, 1789

"The House of Representatives shall be composed of Members chosen every second Year by the People of the Several States. . . . No person shall be a Representative who shall not have attained to the Age of twenty-five Years, and been seven Years a Citizen of the United States, and who shall not, when elected, be an Inhabitant of that State in which he shall be chosen."

ARTICLE I, SECTION 3, U.S. CONSTITUTION, 1789

"The Senate of the United States shall be composed of two Senators from each State, chosen by the Legislature thereof, for six Years. . . . No Person shall be a Senator who shall not have attained to the Age of thirty Years, and been nine Years a Citizen of the United States, and who shall not, when elected, be an Inhabitant of that State for which he shall be chosen."

ARTICLE II, SECTION I, U.S. CONSTITUTION, 1789

"The executive Power shall be vested in a President of the United States of America. He shall hold his office during the Term of four Years. . . . No Person except a natural born Citizen. . . shall be eligible to the Office of the President; neither shall any person be eligible to that Office who shall not have attained to the Age of thirty-five Years, and been fourteen Years a Resident within the United States."

FROM *AMERICA AT 1750* BY RICHARD HOFSTADTER

"Once bought and settled, [the slave] had to learn the ways of a system of slavery. . ., he had to respond to the orders and whims of a new master or overseer, had to learn a new system of labor in the cultivation of the unfamiliar crops of tobacco, corn, rice, and indigo. . . . The slaves faced lashes from a driver [overseer] if they did not seem to be doing the labor assigned for their age, sex, and strength. . . ."

"By 1770, the black portion of the population, standing at 21.8 percent, was at its highest in American history."

FROM *A HISTORY OF WOMEN IN AMERICA* BY CAROL HYMOWITZ AND MICHAELE WEISSMAN

Under English common law, in colonial America no woman could vote, be on a jury, hold political office, or be a member of a profession such as law, teaching, or medicine. Married women could not own property. Any property she owned, including the clothes on her back, legally belonged to her husband, and he could sell it at any time without her consent. In addition, married women could not make contracts, sue in court, or obtain a divorce without their husband's permission. Many women hoped the American Revolution would bring a change.

CONGRESSIONAL QUARTERLY'S GUIDE TO U.S. ELECTIONS, 1994

In 1790, all 13 states required property ownership or payment of taxes on land or other property in order to vote. No state allowed women to vote. No state allowed slaves to vote. No state allowed Indians to vote.

ABIGAIL ADAMS, LETTER TO HER HUSBAND JOHN ADAMS WHO WAS A MEMBER OF THE CONTINENTAL CONGRESS FROM MASSACHUSETTS, MARCH 1776

"By the way, in the new code of laws which I suppose it will be necessary for you to make, I desire you would remember the ladies and be more generous and favorable to them than your ancestors! Do not put such unlimited power in the hands of husbands. Remember all men would be tyrants if they could. If particular care and attention is not paid to the ladies, we are determined to foment a rebellion, and will not hold ourselves bound by any laws in which we have no voice or representation."

JOHN ADAMS' REPLY TO HIS WIFE, APRIL 1776

"As to your extraordinary code of laws, I cannot but laugh! . . . . Depend on it, we know better than to repeal our masculine systems."

The laws regarding women did not change under the new American government.

JOHN JAY, NEW YORK DELEGATE TO THE CONSTITUTIONAL CONVENTION AND ONE OF THE AUTHORS OF THE *FEDERALIST PAPERS*

"The mass of men are neither wise nor good—those who own the country ought to govern it."

THOMAS JEFFERSON, VIRGINIA DELEGATE TO THE CONSTITUTIONAL CONVENTION AND AUTHOR OF THE *DECLARATION OF INDEPENDENCE*

Control of the government should belong to "all who had a permanent intention of living in the country."

FROM *THE AMERICAN ELECTORATE* BY BRUCE A. CAMPBELL

Twenty percent of the total population in 1800 were White adult males. About half of those were property-holders or tax payers. So only about ten percent of the total population were eligible to vote. But of those who could vote, only about one-fourth actually did vote. So that means only about three percent of the total U.S. population voted.

ENGLISH COMMON LAW

English common law became the basis for the laws of the colonies and later of the United States. Under common law, a man became an adult with all rights and privileges at the age of 21.

USING THE BALLOT

The first ballots used in American elections were preprinted with the political party and the candidate's name. Often ballots for the two parties were different colors, making it easy to see which party and candidate a voter supported as he placed his ballot in the ballot box. The differently colored ballots also made it unnecessary to be able to read the ballot. An illiterate man could know the candidate for whom he was voting by the color of his ballot.

Free Black Population in the United States, 1800

State	Total Number of Free Blacks	Percentage of Free Blacks and Slaves in the Population
Massachusetts	7,378	100%
Vermont	557	100%
New Hampshire	855	99%
Rhode Island	3,304	90%
Pennsylvania	14,564	89%
Connecticut	5,300	85%
Delaware	8,268	57%
New York	10,374	33%
New Jersey	4,402	26%
Maryland	19,587	16%
Virginia	20,124	6%
North Carolina	7,043	5%
South Carolina	3,185	2%
Georgia	1,019	2%
Kentucky	741	2%
Tennessee	309	2%
UNITED STATES*	108,395	11%

*Total includes population in the District of Columbia, Mississippi Territory, and Northwest Territory, not shown on the chart.
By 1800, one of each 10 persons of African descent in the United States lived free. In the North, only in New Jersey and New York were the majority of the black population still enslaved.
Almost half of the total free black population lived in the South.

Source: U.S. Bureau of the Census

LESSON 2:   Analysis of Voting Rights in the Election of 1832

Objectives

1. Each student will take on a role and participate in a mock presidential election. (psychomotor)
2. Each student, as part of a group, will analyze and evaluate documents relating to the right to vote in 1832. (cognitive)
3. Each student, as part of a group, will form generalizations regarding changes in voting requirements. (cognitive)
4. Each student will help design and implement an analysis of neighborhood voting patterns. (cognitive)
5. Each student will understand that enfranchisement is a fluid process that has led to the expansion and contraction of the electorate throughout U.S. history. (affective)
6. Each student will appreciate the importance of voting in a republican form of government. (affective)

Materials

A transparency of the chart "The United States, 1800–1970,"

a transparency of the Alexis de Tocqueville quote,

name tags from Lesson 1 if following option 1 or use the token characteristics envelopes from Lesson 1 if following option 2,

a ballot box with a sign marked "1832," the 1832 ballot for each student,

a packet of documents on 1832 for each group of three to four students,

an evaluation sheet for each student,

a transparency of the Abraham Lincoln quote.

The packet includes

- Two copies of the "Voting Rights in 1832" graphic organizer;
- One copy of "Analysis of the Election of 1832";
- Documents related to the election of 1832.

Instructional Strategies

Opener

IE 1,   IE 2,   IE 3,   IE 4,   SE 1,   SE 2,
SE 3,   A 1,   A 2

The teacher opens with student volunteers reading their journal entries assigned as homework. The class then reviews the findings of the inquiry into voting rights in the election of 1800.

(If the teacher chooses the second option of incorporating the lessons throughout the year, begin the lesson with a review of student findings and conclusions about the election of 1800.)

Body

SE 1,   SE 2,   SE 3,   A 1

The teacher tells students they will once again be time travelers, going back to 1832. Have students calculate how many years ago 1832 was and how many years since the last mock election. Ask if they think there may have been major changes in the United States. The teacher puts Transparency 1, "The United States, 1800–1970," on the overhead projector and asks students to contrast the United States in 1800 and in 1830 and to guess how changes in those years affected the lives of Americans. The teacher points out that the population was growing rapidly, and people in Europe were curious about our dynamic young country. The teacher places Transparency 2 on the overhead projector and has a student read the observation de Tocqueville made as he traveled across the United States in 1831. Ask a student to recall the class definition of *democracy* from the previous lesson. Remind students how few Americans could vote in 1800. **Teacher:**

- **What did de Tocqueville think about the United States and its citizens?**
- **Why do you think he said "a great democratic revolution is taking place"?**
- **What guesses can you make about events or changes in the U.S. in 1831 that would seem "a democratic revolution"?**

SE 1,   SE 2,   SE 3,   A 1

The teacher points out that in other parts of the world in 1832 people usually did not get to vote for their political leaders, so the United States often was seen as a great example of democracy. Ask students, based on what they learned in the last election, whether they agree that the United States was a democracy in 1800.

SE 1,   SE 4,   SE 5

Teacher has students pass out name tags from Lesson 1. (If teacher uses option 2, he/she may want students to draw characteristics again.) Students pin or tape name tags to their shirts. The teacher asks students to form groups of three or four that share at least one characteristic, but to form groups that are different from the last lesson. The teacher assigns the same group roles (facilitator, manager, archivist, recorder) or allows students to choose, but each student should have a different role from the one they fulfilled in Lesson 1.

SE 1

The teacher recalls that only a few students got to vote in the last election. He/she asks students to predict whether more or fewer students will get to vote in 1832.

SE 2

The teacher passes out ballots for 1832. Students mark their ballots, tearing off the top part to keep in their notebooks. They then form a line to vote. Only those students with the following characteristics are allowed to vote:

male	Caucasian
over 21 years old	can read or not
North or South	own property or not

The teacher directs those who voted to one side of the room and those who didn't to the other. There are 12 males in a class of 24 students, but probably some of them will be disqualified by ethnicity and age, so the number of voters should still remain small.

SE 1,   SE 2

Teacher: Did more students get to vote? Any guesses why there are more in 1832?

The teacher then puts students in their groups and tells them they have an investigation to complete in order to find out why.

IE 1,   IE 2,   IE 3,   IE 4,   SE 1,   SE 2, SE 4,   A 1,   A 2

The facilitators get document packets for "1832." Students will duplicate the process from Lesson 1, analyzing and categorizing the information on Handout 2, "Voting Rights in 1832," and "Analysis of the Election of 1832."

IE 1,   IE 2,   IE 3,   IE 4,   SE 2,   SE 3, A 1,   A 2

Debriefing will follow the same pattern as in Lesson 1. With teacher direction, students analyze each document and what it says about voting, making generalizations about how the election of 1832 was similar to and different from that of 1800. Once again, the votes from the mock election are counted, and students make predictions about how election results, candidates, and issues might change if more people could vote.

The teacher takes up document packets, group written work, and name tags. Students fill in biographical information about Andrew Jackson on the "Presidential Information" chart they kept in their notebooks. Students can supplement the ballot information with their textbooks. The teacher should point out a picture of Jackson as well. On the class "Voting Requirement Changes" chart and on the student individual charts, students will list who was allowed to vote in 1832, who was barred from voting, and then compare this election to 1800 to determine what requirements changed and why. Students will offer questions and guesses about why changes have occurred and probably about why change has not occurred more quickly for other groups. The teacher asks each student to complete the evaluation sheet.

Closing

IE 1,   IE 2,   SE 1,   SE 2,   SE 3

The teacher tells the class that the next election will be 1872. He/she puts Transparency 3, the Abraham Lincoln quotation, on the overhead and asks a student to read the quote for the class. **Teacher: What was Lincoln's idea about who should vote?** (Whoever pays taxes or serves in the military.) **How was his idea different from who voted in 1832?** (He included women.) **Whom did Lincoln leave out?** (African Americans, Native Americans—anyone not "white.")

The teacher points out that Lincoln was a young man in 1836, just beginning his political career. He was elected president in 1860. The next election for the class will be in 1872. Ask if students believe more Americans will be able to vote than voted in 1832? Ask which groups do they predict will be allowed to vote?

Activity: Voter Education Project

IE 1,   IE 3,   IE 4,   SE 1,   SE 2,   SE 4, SE 5,   A 1,   A 3

The teacher tells students that during this unit on voting, they are going to design and carry out a voter education project. They will work on creating bumper stickers and campaign ads and other ways to encourage people to vote. But first they need to collect some data about who votes in their neighborhoods, who does not, and why people either do or do not vote. The first step is to figure out a way to collect that information.

Students may suggest door-to-door questionnaires, telephone polls, setting up data-collection tables at various neighborhood locations, inviting neighborhood leaders/local politicians to the classroom, and many other methods. The class should reach agreement on the method(s) of data collection. The teacher puts students into groups to devise questions to ask. Groups should be heterogeneous with a mix of ability levels, talents, and learning preferences. Questions should seek information on whether a person is registered to vote and his/her attitudes about voter registration. Additionally, the class should ask about frequency of voting and attitudes about voting. The teacher should circulate to keep groups on task and provide clarifying information. After the groups generate questions, the class should evaluate the questions and create a class questionnaire on voting. Also, the students should generate a master chart to use in the classroom for daily tabulation and organization of the raw data.

The teacher assigns the following for homework: Find at least one person 18 years old or older and ask them the questions worked out by the class.

Assessment

Student understanding will be assessed through teacher observation of group work and class discussion, through group written work, and through participation in the voter education project.

THE UNITED STATES, 1800–1970			
Year	Population	Number of States	Major Events
1800	5,308,483	16	1789 Constitution 1791 Bill of Rights
1830	12,866,020	24	1803 Louisiana Purchase 1812–1815 War of 1812
1870	39,818,449	37	1846 Oregon Territory 1846–1848 Mexican War and cession 1861–65 Civil War
1900	75,994,575	45	1870–1900 Industrial Revolution 1898 Spanish–American War: U.S. gained colonies in the Pacific and the Caribbean
1930	122,775,046	48	1917–1918 World War I 1929 Stock Market crash; Great Depression begins
1970	204,765,770	50	1941–1945 World War II 1950–1953 Korean War 1963–1972 Vietnam War

"A great democratic revolution

is taking place in our midst. . . .

[Nothing] . . . struck me more vividly

during my stay in the [United States]

than the equality of conditions. . . .

The people reign over the American political

world as God rules over the universe."

Alexis de Tocqueville, 1831

CANDIDATES

HENRY CLAY—Henry Clay was born in 1777. He was a member of the Whig party, which first appeared in the election of 1832. The Whig party became one of the two major political parties by 1836. Clay had served as Speaker of the House of Representatives, secretary of state, and U.S. senator from Kentucky. He was known as the "Great Compromiser" because he helped find solutions to several serious national conflicts. Clay was a wealthy lawyer before he entered politics.

ANDREW JACKSON—Andrew Jackson was born in 1767. He was a member of the Democratic party. He was a U.S. senator from 1798 to 1804. Jackson was a general in the American army who gained fame by defeating the Creek Indians in Alabama in 1814 and especially through his spectacular victory over a larger British force in the Battle of New Orleans in 1815 at the end of the War of 1812. He became a national hero after the Battle of New Orleans. He served in the Senate again from 1823–1825. He ran for president and lost a very close election in 1828. Jackson was a wealthy plantation owner from Tennessee.

Ballot—Election of 1832

Mark your choice for ONE of the following:

_____ HENRY CLAY

_____ ANDREW JACKSON

Group _____   _____

Members: _____   _____

VOTING RIGHTS IN 1832		
Document Title	One-Sentence Summary of the Document	What Does It Say About Voting Requirements?

Based upon your analysis of the documents, answer the following:

1.   What groups of people were allowed to vote in 1832?

2.   List at least three groups of people who were not allowed to vote in 1832.

3.   Compare and contrast the election of 1832 with the election of 1800. What changed about voting requirements?

   • List the titles of the documents that showed changes in 1832 compared to 1800.
   • List the groups that were affected by the changes.
   • Explain how voting requirements changed.

4.   What contributions were being made by the groups who were still denied the right to vote?

ABRAHAM LINCOLN, 1836:

"I go for all sharing the privileges

of government who assist in sharing its

burdens. Consequently, I go for admitting

all whites to the right of suffrage

who pay taxes or bear arms, by no means

excluding females."

Documents for 1832

ALEXIS DE TOCQUEVILLE, *DEMOCRACY IN AMERICA*

"A great democratic revolution is taking place in our midst. . . . [Nothing]. . . struck me more vividly during my stay in the [United States] than the equality of conditions. . . . The people reign over the American political world as God rules over the universe."

SARAH JOSEPHA HALE, *GODEY'S LADY'S BOOK* (THE MOST POPULAR WOMEN'S MAGAZINE OF THE 1800S), JULY 1832

"A true woman was delicate and timid. She required protection. She possessed a sweet dependency and was above all things modest. A true woman had charming and insinuating [gentle] manners."

   Mrs. Hale advised women to devote themselves to their housekeeping as if it were a fine art. The home was seen as the woman's natural environment. "True" women were supposed to be delicate, passive, helpless, and under the protection of a man.

EDITORIAL, *NILES WEEKLY REGISTER,* OCTOBER 21, 1820

"We hold it to be the natural right of every citizen, who is bound by the law to [serve his government or pay taxes to support it], to vote . . . so that persons so elected are responsible to [the voters] for their good conduct. . . . The possession of a certain amount of property is by no means necessary to [gaining] the right of suffrage."

CONGRESSIONAL QUARTERLY'S GUIDE TO U.S. ELECTIONS, 1994

States gradually relaxed property requirements for voting in the 1820s and 1830s. By 1850, most states had removed the property requirement. Voter participation in presidential elections increased from 3.8% of the total U.S. population in 1824 to 16.7% in 1856.

FROM *THE AMERICAN ELECTORATE* BY BRUCE A. CAMPBELL

None of the new states that entered the Union after the original thirteen had property requirements for voting.

A HISTORY OF SUFFRAGE IN THE UNITED STATES BY KIRK H. PORTER

"Husband and wife were one, and that one was the husband. He assumed all her debts and she was not capable of maintaining legal relationships independent of him. Her property became his, her earnings were his, she could bring no action at law without his aid, and all her dealings with the government had to be through him. Not only could she own no property in her own right, but she had no rights with regard to her children."

ANDREW JACKSON, INDIAN REMOVAL ACT, 1830

"[I propose] a plan of removing the [American Indians] who yet remain within the settled portions of the United States to the country west of the Mississippi River. . . . All preceding experiments for the improvement of the Indians have failed. It seems now to be an established fact that they cannot live in contact with a civilized community. . . . An extensive region in the West has been assigned for their permanent residence."

FREDERICK DOUGLASS, INDEPENDENCE DAY SPEECH AT ROCHESTER, N.Y.

"What, to the American slave, is your Fourth of July? I answer: a day that reveals to him, more than all the other days in the year, the gross injustice and cruelty to which he is the constant victim. To him, your celebration is a sham [fraud]; your boasted liberty, an unholy license; your national greatness, swelling vanity; your sounds of rejoicing are empty and heartless; . . . your shouts of liberty and equality, hollow mockery. . . . There is not a nation on the earth guilty of practices more shocking and bloody than are the people of the United States at this very hour."

GEORGE FITZHUGH, *SOCIOLOGY FOR THE SOUTH*

"The slaves are well fed, well clad [clothed], have plenty of fuel and are happy. They have no dread of the future—no fear of want."

ALEXIS DE TOCQUEVILLE, *DEMOCRACY IN AMERICA*

From 1831 to 1833, 15,000 Choctaws were removed from Mississippi and forced to migrate to Oklahoma. De Tocqueville described a group of them crossing the Mississippi River in the dead of winter:

"The cold was unusually severe; the snow had frozen hard upon the ground, and the river was drifting huge masses of ice. The Indians had their families with them, and they brought in their train the wounded and the sick, with children newly born and old men upon the verge of death. They possessed neither tents nor wagons, but only their arms and some provisions. I saw them embark to pass the mighty river, and never will that solemn spectacle fade from my remembrance. No cry, no sob, was heard among the assembled crowd; all were silent."

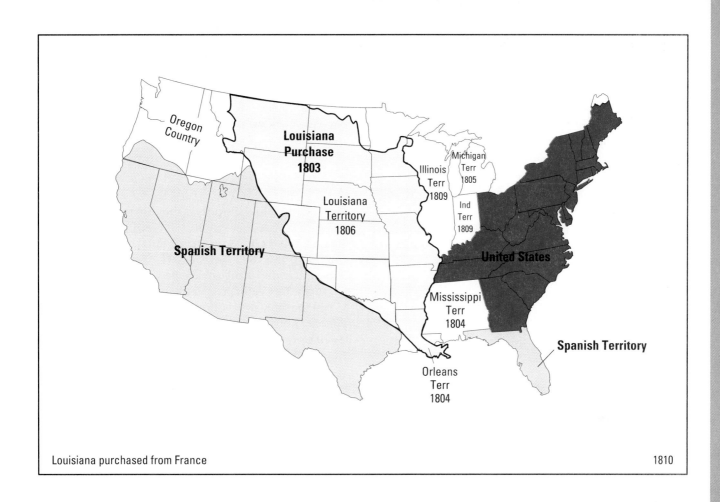

Louisiana purchased from France

1810

LESSON 3:   Analysis of Voting Rights in the Election of 1872

Objectives

1. Each student will take on a role and participate in a mock presidential election. (cognitive)

2. Each student will analyze and evaluate documents relating to the right to vote in 1872. (cognitive)

3. Each student will form generalizations regarding changes in voting requirements. (cognitive)

4. Each student will understand that enfranchisement is a fluid process that has led to the expansion and contraction of the electorate throughout U.S. history. (affective)

5. Each student will appreciate the importance of voting in a republican form of government. (affective)

Materials

Name tags from Lesson 1 if following option one or use the token characteristics envelopes from Lesson 1 if following option two,

an evaluation sheet for each student,

a ballot box with a sign marked "1872,"

a packet of documents on 1872 for each group of three to four students.

The packet includes

- Two copies of the "Voting Rights in 1872" graphic organizer;
- One copy of "Analysis of the Election of 1872";
- Documents related to the election of 1872.

Instructional Strategies

Opener

IE 1,   IE 2,   IE 4,   SE 1,   SE 2,   SE 3

The teacher asks student volunteers to share the data they collected on voting as a result of the homework assignment.

IE 1,   IE 2,   IE 4,   SE 1,   SE 2,   SE 4,
SE 5,   A 1,   A 2,   A 3

The class briefly discusses what they have learned from this small sample. Plans are made for the collection of the rest of the data. Students choose what part to carry out in the ongoing data collection. The teacher checks the students' progress every day and makes adjustments and suggestions as necessary. Data tabulation on the master chart should also occur every day. Data collection should be complete by Lesson 9.

(If the teacher chooses the second option of incorporating the lessons throughout the year, begin the lesson with a review of student findings and conclusions about the election of 1832.)

Body

IE 1,   SE 1,   SE 2,   SE 3

The teacher tells the students they are time traveling today to 1872. Use Transparency 1, Lesson 2, "The United States, 1800–1970," to contrast information about the years 1872 and 1832. **Teacher: What has changed? What effects may the changes have had on the people? How will that affect voting requirements?**

Use the same procedures as in Lesson 1 and Lesson 2. The election for today is 1872. The only students allowed to vote are

male	northern Caucasians
over 21 years old	literate or not
northern or southern African Americans	own property or not

Use the same procedure in having students analyze the documents and in debriefing. Students fill in biographical information about Ulysses S. Grant on the "Presidential Information" chart they kept in their notebooks. Students can supplement the ballot information with their textbooks. The teacher should point out a picture of Grant as well. On the class "Voting Requirement Changes" chart and on the student individual charts, students will list who was allowed to vote in 1872, who was barred from voting, and then compare this election to 1832 to determine what requirements changed and why. Students will offer questions and guesses about why changes have occurred and probably about why change has not occurred more quickly for other groups. The teacher asks each student to complete the evaluation sheet.

Closing

Students should make predictions based on their analysis of the documents. Possibly students will predict troubled times for African American voting and growing rights for women. Ask students to predict whether a larger number of people will vote in the next election. Have them give reasons to support their predictions.

Assessment

Student understanding will be assessed through teacher observation of group work and class discussion, through group written work, and through participation in the voter education project.

CANDIDATES

ULYSSES S. GRANT—Ulysses S. Grant was born in 1822 in Ohio. He was a member of the Republican party, which emerged as the second major political party in 1854. He had attended West Point Military Academy and became a career military officer. Grant was the commanding general for the Union (the North) at the end of the Civil War. He was seen as a hero by the people of the North. Grant served as secretary of war from 1867–1868. He was elected president in 1868. In his first term, there were many instances of corruption and dishonesty among the people he appointed to office, although Grant himself was an honest man.

HORACE GREELEY—Horace Greeley was born in 1811. He was nominated by the Democratic party. Greeley was the wealthy newspaper editor of the *New York Tribune*. He had supported the abolition of slavery before and during the Civil War. He is most famous for an editorial urging Americans to seek their fortunes on the frontier. He wrote: "Go West, young man, go West." He ran for president in 1872 by campaigning against the corruption in the Grant administration.

Ballot — Election of 1872

Mark your choice for ONE of the following:

_____ ULYSSES S. GRANT

_____ HORACE GREELEY

Group _____   _____

Members: _____   _____

VOTING RIGHTS IN 1872		
Document Title	**One-Sentence Summary of the Document**	**What Does It Say About Voting Requirements?**

Based upon your analysis of the documents, answer the following:

1.   What groups of people were allowed to vote in 1872?

2.   List at least three groups of people who were not allowed to vote in 1872.

3.   Compare and contrast the election of 1872 with the elections of 1800 and 1832. What changed about voting requirements?

    • List the titles of the documents that showed changes in 1872 compared to 1800 and 1832.
    • List the groups that were affected by the changes.
    • Explain how voting requirements changed.

4.   What contributions were being made by the groups who were still denied the right to vote?

Documents for 1872

13TH AMENDMENT, *U.S. CONSTITUTION,* 1865

"Neither slavery nor involuntary solitude, except as a punishment for crime whereof the party shall have been duly convicted, shall exist within the United States, or any place subject to their jurisdiction."

14TH AMENDMENT, *U.S. CONSTITUTION,* 1868

"No State shall make or enforce any law which shall abridge [limit] the privileges or immunities of citizens of the United States; nor shall any State deprive any person of life, liberty, or property, without due process of law; nor deny to any person within its jurisdiction the equal protection of the laws."

15TH AMENDMENT, *U.S. CONSTITUTION,* 1870

"The right of citizens of the United States to vote shall not be denied or abridged [limited] by the United States or by any State on account of race, color, or previous condition of servitude."

THE SENECA FALLS DECLARATION, 1848

"We hold these truths to be self-evident: that all men **and women** are created equal. . . . Now in view of this entire disfranchisement [loss of the right to vote] of one half the people in this country . . . and because women do feel themselves aggrieved [injured], oppressed [put down], and fraudulently [unfairly] deprived of their most sacred rights, we insist that they have immediate admission to all the rights and privileges which belong to them as citizens of the United States."

SUSAN B. ANTHONY, SPEECH AT HER TRIAL FOR ILLEGALLY VOTING, JUNE 1873

"I stand before you under indictment for [charged with] the alleged crime of having voted at the last presidential election, without having a lawful right to vote. . . . The women [are dissatisfied] with this form of government, that enforces taxation without representation—that compels [forces] them to obey laws to which they have never given their consent—that imprisons and hangs them without a trial by a jury of their peers—that robs them, in marriage, of the custody of their own persons, wages, and children. . . . It is on this line that we propose to fight our battle for the ballot . . . until we achieve complete triumph and all United States citizens, men and women alike, are recognized as equals in the government."

Anthony was found guilty of illegally voting and fined $100.

A HISTORY OF WOMEN IN AMERICA BY CAROL HYMOWITZ AND MICHELLE WEISSMAN

"In 1860, the New York state legislature finally passed a bill granting married women rights to property and wages. A wife would make contracts with her husband's consent, and she could enter into contracts on her own authority if he were an alcoholic, a convict, or insane."

RECONSTRUCTION ACT, JULY 19, 1867

This act provided that no person who had held office in the government of the Confederate States of America (the South) or who fought in the Confederate army against the United States during the Civil War is now entitled to register to vote. This law took the right to vote away from many white Southern men.

GRAND JURY REPORT, U.S. CIRCUIT COURT, 1869

"We have investigated crimes committed by the Ku Klux Klan by gathering evidence from the victims and the members themselves. The jury has been shocked beyond measure at the number and character of the atrocities [horrible acts of cruelty] committed, producing a state of terror and a sense of utter insecurity among a large portion of the people, especially the black population. We have established . . . that the members must furnish themselves with a pistol, a Ku Klux gown (white recommended) and a signal instrument. Many of the operations of the Klan were executed at night, and were directed against both black and white persons who were members of the Republican party by warnings to leave the country, by whippings, and by murder. . . . The jury has been appalled as much at the number of outrages as at their character, it appearing that 11 murders and over 600 whippings have been committed in York County [Virginia] alone."

THE SECOND SEMINOLE WAR, 1835–1842

During the years 1835 to 1842, the United States spent $20,000,000 and lost 1,500 soldiers, sailors, and marines in an attempt to remove 3,000 Seminole Indians from Florida to Oklahoma. The Seminoles used guerrilla tactics and exploited local geography in their resistance. Some said Florida was a land where only Seminoles, alligators, snakes, and mosquitoes could survive. One white soldier wrote home, "If the Devil owned both Hell and Florida, he would rent out Florida and live in Hell!" Osceola, though not a chief, was a key leader in the Seminole resistance. He was treacherously captured by the U.S. Army under a flag of truce in 1837. In 1838, he died in a Charleston, South Carolina, prison. Ultimately, the U.S. government simply quit fighting, leaving several hundred Seminole survivors in the swamps of Florida.

Political Participation by Race				
State	**Population in 1860**		**Registered Voters in 1867**	
	Caucasian	**African American**	**Caucasian**	**African American**
Alabama	526,000	437,000	61,000	104,000
Florida	77,000	62,000	11,000	16,000
Georgia	591,000	465,000	96,000	95,000
Louisiana	357,000	350,000	45,000	84,000
Mississippi	353,000	437,000	46,000	60,000
North Carolina	629,000	361,000	106,000	72,000
South Carolina	291,000	412,000	46,000	80,000
Virginia	1,100,000	548,000	120,000	105,000

LESSON 4:   Voter Education Project

Objectives

1. Each student will help design and implement an analysis of neighborhood voting patterns. (cognitive)
2. Each student will create and present a contribution to a class voter education project. (cognitive)
3. Each student will discuss the importance of voting in a republican form of government. (affective)

Materials

Materials for students to use in voter education project.

Instructional Strategies

Opener

The teacher asks students to share some of the voting data they have been collecting in their neighborhoods. He/she probes students to help them see patterns.

Body

IE 1,   IE 4,   SE 1,   SE 2,   SE 4,   SE 5,
A 1,   A 2,   A 3

The teacher tells students that today they will work on their project that will be the climax of their study of voting rights. As a class, they will create and implement a voter education project. The project will include the analysis of the data they are collecting on neighborhood voting patterns. Also, either individually or in groups, students will design a variety of materials about why U.S. citizens should vote. Some options include posters, bumper stickers, pamphlets, letters to the editor, news articles, public service announcements, TV commercials recorded on video, multimedia presentations on the computer, a theme song, jingles, flyers, and bulletin boards. Give students some time to think about what they would like to do and to decide whether they will work individually or in small groups. The teacher passes around a sign-up sheet for students to choose their part of the project. He/she circulates to provide further information and feedback and to help students make decisions about their parts on the project. The teacher makes certain the tasks chosen are appropriate for the learners and makes adjustments as necessary.

IE 1,   IE 4,   A 1,   A 2,   A 3

While students are signing up, the teacher discusses how this project will be graded. The teacher outlines his/her criteria for evaluation and the assessment weight the project will have. He/she might encourage students to contribute to determining some of the criteria for evaluation. (A possible assessment form is included.) The teacher also indicates how and where the project will be presented. Some possibilities include presenting it in the cafeteria or auditorium for other classes to experience, at a PTA meeting, at a school board and/or city council meeting, and working with the local Voter Registration office to present it in various locations to encourage voter registration and participation.

Students describe their ideas, with the teacher making suggestions and consolidating plans so there is no overlap and there are a variety of activities planned.

IE 1,   IE 4,   SE 1,   SE 2,   SE 4,   SE 5,
A 1,   A 2,   A 3

For the rest of class, students work on the project. The teacher circulates to provide clarification and feedback and for purposes of formative assessment.

Closing

The teacher tells students to continue working on the project outside of class. They will have one more opportunity to work in the classroom. Close with a quote from former Treasury Secretary William Simon: **"Bad politicians are sent to Washington by good people who don't vote."**

Assessment

The voter education project will count as a major grade for the unit. It may be considered as a summative assessment of student learning.

Sample Evaluation Instrument for Voter Education Project

One way to evaluate the voter education project is to set up criteria such as creativity, originality, workmanship, presentation, and overall effect. You may want to allow students to contribute to determining the criteria for evaluation. A peer evaluation could be included. Generally, it is more effective if peer evaluations are modified by eliminating the highest and the lowest evaluations and averaging the remainder. Combining the peer evaluation with the teacher's on a 50/50 basis tends to produce the best results.

At the time of student presentations, provide each student with an evaluation sheet (half sheets can be used to save paper and copying).

Some possible areas for assessment include

Creativity: Production through use of imaginative skill. Does the product show imagination?

Originality: Are the expressions new or unusual? Is the product unique to the individual? Did the presenter copy others' ideas or are they his/her own?

Workmanship: Is the project constructed well? Has care been taken to use materials carefully? Is there evidence of skill in putting the project together?

Presentation: Is the display of the product well thought out? Is the presenter confident about his/her product? Is the project presented in a way that improves the overall effect?

Overall: What is your overall impression of the project? If you could give only one rating, what would it be?

These criteria should be discussed and understood by all students before starting to generate voter education projects. It is also advisable to review the criteria prior to rating sessions and to display the criteria on an overhead projector while students rate the voter education projects.

Voter Education Project

Individual or _____ _____

Group Members _____ _____

Evaluator's name _____

Rate each of the following criteria with 1 being the lowest rating and 10 the highest. Decimals may be used. (Example: an 8.5 would translate to 85%, a 9.8 would be a 98%) Please be as impartial as possible. Fifty is the highest total possible.

Creativity: Production through use of imaginative skill.

Does the product show imagination?   _____

Originality: Are the expressions new or unusual? Is

the product unique to the individual?

Did the presenter copy others' ideas or are they his/her own?   _____

Workmanship: Is the project constructed well?

Has care been taken to use materials carefully?

Is there evidence of skill in putting the project together?   _____

Presentation: Is the display of the product well thought out?

Is the presenter confident about his/her product?

Is the project presented in a way that improves the overall effect?   _____

Overall: What is your overall impression of the project?

If you could give only one rating, what would it be?   _____

TOTAL: Add your ratings—50 is a perfect score   _____

LESSON 5:   Analysis of Voting Rights in the Election of 1908

Objectives

1. Each student will take on a role and participate in a mock presidential election. (cognitive)
2. Each student will analyze and evaluate documents relating to the right to vote in 1908. (cognitive)
3. Each student will form generalizations regarding changes in voting requirements. (cognitive)
4. Each student will understand that enfranchisement is a fluid process that has led to the expansion and contraction of the electorate throughout U.S. history. (affective)
5. Each student will discuss the importance of voting in a republican form of government. (affective)

Materials

Name tags from Lesson 1 if following option 1 or use the token characteristics envelopes from Lesson 1 following option 2,

a ballot box with a sign marked "1908,"

the 1908 ballot for each student,

an evaluation sheet for each student,

a packet of documents on 1908 for each group of three to four students.

The packet includes

- Two copies of the "Voting Rights in 1908" graphic organizer;
- One copy of "Analysis of the Election of 1908";
- Documents related to the election of 1908;
- A copy of the evaluation sheet.

Instructional Strategies

Opener

IE 1,   IE 2,   IE 3,   IE 4,   SE 1,   SE 2,
A 1

Review what students learned from their inquiry into the election of 1872. Use that review to transition into the election of 1908. Use the table "United States, 1800–1970" to review prior knowledge and help students make guesses about changes that have occurred since 1870.

Body

IE 1,   IE 2,   IE 3,   IE 4,   SE 1,   SE 2,
SE 3,   SE 4,   A 1,   A 2

Use the same procedure as Lesson 1, Lesson 2, and Lesson 3. The only students allowed to vote in the mock election are

male	Caucasians
over 21 years old	literate
Northern or Southern	own property

Use the same procedure in having the students analyze the documents and in debriefing. Students should make predictions based on their analysis of the documents. Students fill in biographical information about William Howard Taft on the "Presidential Information" chart they kept in their notebooks. Students can supplement the ballot information with their textbooks. The teacher should point out a picture of Taft as well. On the class "Voting Requirement Changes" chart and on the student individual charts, students will list who was allowed to vote in 1908, who was barred from voting, and then compare this election to 1872 to determine what requirements changed and why. Students will offer questions and guesses about why changes have occurred and probably about why change has not occurred more quickly for other groups. The teacher asks each student to complete the evaluation sheet.

Closing

Ask students to predict whether a larger number of people will vote in the next election in 1932. Have them give reasons to support their predictions.

Assessment

Student understanding will be assessed through teacher observation of group work and class discussion, through group written work, and through participation in the voter education project.

CANDIDATES

WILLIAM JENNINGS BRYAN—William Jennings Bryan was born in 1860. He was a member of the Democratic party. He ran for president but lost in 1896 and again in 1900. Much of his support came from small farmers and factory workers. He opposed the United States taking colonies in the Caribbean and the Philippines after the Spanish-American War. Bryan was a wealthy lawyer from Illinois.

WILLIAM HOWARD TAFT—William Howard Taft was born in 1857. He was a member of the Republican party. Taft was a wealthy lawyer from Ohio who became a federal judge. He later served as secretary of war under President Theodore Roosevelt. Taft supported reforms such as control of monopolies in industry and the railroads and political changes to give the people more say in their government. Taft was the largest candidate for president, weighing in at more than 300 pounds.

Ballot—Election of 1908

Mark your choice for ONE of the following:

_____ WILLIAM JENNINGS BRYAN

_____ WILLIAM HOWARD TAFT

Group _____   _____

Members: _____   _____

VOTING RIGHTS IN 1908		
Document Title	**One-Sentence Summary of the Document**	**What Does It Say About Voting Requirements?**

Based upon your analysis of the documents, answer the following:

1.   What groups of people were allowed to vote in 1908?

2.   List at least three groups of people who were not allowed to vote in 1908.

3.   Compare and contrast the election of 1908 with the elections of 1800, 1832, and 1872. What changed about voting requirements?

   • List the titles of the documents that showed changes in 1908 compared to 1800, 1832, and 1872.
   • List the groups that were affected by the changes.
   • List how voting requirements changed.

4.   What contributions were being made by the groups who were still denied the right to vote?

Documents for 1908

JAY M. SHAFRITZ, *THE HARPERCOLLINS DICTIONARY OF AMERICAN GOVERNMENT AND POLITICS*

The Australian, or secret, ballot was introduced in the United States in 1888. By the early 1900s, most states had adopted the secret ballot for voting.

ELK v. *WILKINS*, 1884

In April 1880, John Elk, a Native American in Oklahoma, was denied the right to vote. He claimed the Fifteenth Amendment gave him that right. The case eventually went to the Supreme Court. The court said

- Indians are born in the United States. However, they are ruled by their tribe, not by the United States. They owe their allegiance only to the tribe.
- Indians have the same legal status as the children born to foreign visitors while they are in the United States. They are not citizens.
- The only way for John Elk to become a citizen would be for Congress to pass a law setting up ways to make Indians citizens, or by a treaty that agreed they were citizens.

FROM *THE WAY IT WAS IN THE SOUTH: THE BLACK EXPERIENCE IN GEORGIA* BY DONALD GRANT

The annual average income in 1880 for black Georgians was $37.00.

FROM "THE EFFECT OF THE SOUTHERN SYSTEM OF VOTING LAWS ON VOTING PARTICIPATION" BY JERROLD G. RUSK AND JOHN J. STUCKER

"In 1890, Mississippi, in its constitutional convention, required that every citizen between the ages of 21 and 60 must pay a $2.00 poll tax and be able to show the receipt of payment before he could vote. . . . Mississippi followed two years later with a literacy test [that said] that anyone who wished to vote must be able to read the constitution. . . . Thus, in two years' time, Mississippi had set up a model of restrictive legislation for other states to follow. Georgia's poll tax was a required tax which increased each year it was not paid. For example, a person 59 years old who had never paid his poll tax would have to pay $47.47 in order to vote."

By 1910, seven states followed Mississippi's lead and passed laws to disfranchise black voters: South Carolina (1895), Louisiana (1898), North Carolina (1900), Alabama (1901), Virginia (1901), Georgia (1908), and Oklahoma (1910).

FROM "THE POLITICS OF DISFRANCHISEMENT IN GEORGIA" BY RUSSELL KOROBKIN

The Georgia Democratic Party Executive Committee in 1900 adopted a white primary as party policy. They argued that the party was a private organization, so it could set the rules for participation in its primary elections, and only whites were allowed to vote in them.

SENATOR HENRY CABOT LODGE OF MASSACHUSETTS, SPEECH TO THE SENATE, 1894

Lodge spoke against "Italians, Russians, Poles, Hungarians, Greeks, and Asiatics," saying these people were "races with which the English-speaking people have never hitherto assimilated [mixed] and who are most alien [strange] to the great body of the people of the United States."

PRESIDENT CHESTER A. ARTHUR, SPEECH TO CONGRESS, DECEMBER 6, 1881

". . . Prominent among the matters which challenge the attention of Congress at its present session is the management of our Indian affairs. . . . I refer, of course, to the policy of dealing with the various Indian tribes as separate nationalities, of [placing them on] immense reservations in the West, and of encouraging them to live a savage life. . . . [I support the effort] to introduce among the Indians the customs and pursuits of civilized life and gradually to absorb them into the mass of our citizens. . . . I recommend passage of an act making the laws of the various States and Territories applicable to Indian reservations within their borders. . . ."

W.E.B. DUBOIS, *THE SOULS OF BLACK FOLKS,* 1905

"[American Negroes] do not expect that the free right to vote, to enjoy civil rights, and to be educated, will come in a moment; they do not expect to see the biases and prejudices of years disappear at the blast of a trumpet; but they are absolutely certain that the way for people to gain their reasonable rights is not by voluntarily throwing them away and insisting that they do not want them. . . . Negroes must insist continually, in season and out of season, that voting is necessary to modern manhood, that color discrimination is barbarism, and that black boys need education as well as white boys."

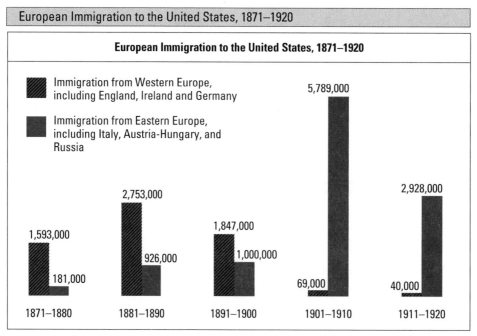

European Immigration to the United States, 1871–1920

Source: U.S. Bureau of the Census

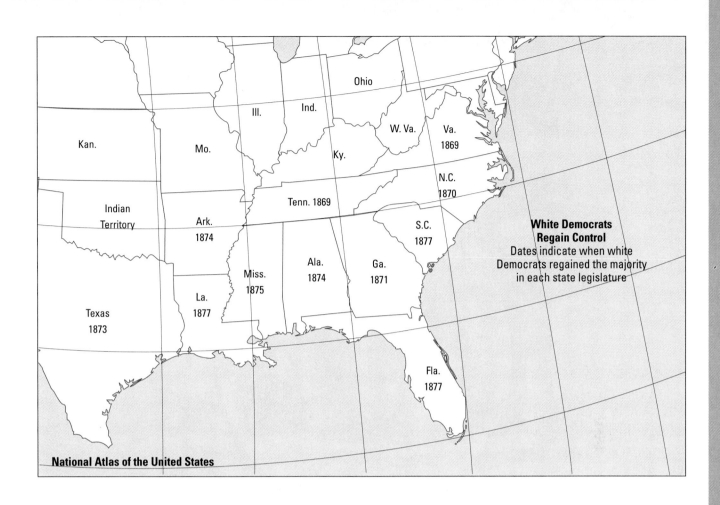

Ohio

Ill.

Ind.

Kan.

Mo.

W. Va.

Va.
1869

Ky.

N.C.
1870

Indian
Territory

Ark.
1874

Tenn. 1869

S.C.
1877

**White Democrats
Regain Control**
Dates indicate when white
Democrats regained the majority
in each state legislature

Miss.
1875

Ala.
1874

Ga.
1871

Texas
1873

La.
1877

Fla.
1877

National Atlas of the United States

Thomas Nast, "The Lost Cause Worse than Slavery," from Harper's Weekly, October 24, 1874. Library of Congress.

LESSON 6:   Analysis of Voting Rights in the Election of 1932

Objectives

1. Each student will take on a role and participate in a mock presidential election. (cognitive)
2. Each student will analyze and evaluate documents relating to the right to vote in 1932. (cognitive)
3. Each student will form generalizations regarding changes in voting requirements. (cognitive)
4. Each student will understand that enfranchisement is a fluid process that has led to the expansion and contraction of the electorate throughout U.S. history. (affective)
5. Each student will discuss the importance of voting in a republican form of government. (affective)

Materials

Name tags from Lesson 1 if following option 1 or use the token characteristics envelopes from Lesson 1 if following option 2,

a ballot box with a sign marked "1932,"

an evaluation sheet for each student,

the 1932 ballot for each student,

a packet of documents on 1932 for each group of three to four students.

The packet includes

- Two copies of the "Voting Rights in 1932" graphic organizer;
- One copy of "Analysis of the Election of 1932";
- Documents related to the election of 1932.

Instructional Strategies

Opener

IE 1,   IE 2,   IE 3,   IE 4,   SE 1,
SE 2,   A 1

Review what students learned from their inquiry into the election of 1908. Use that review to transition into the election of 1932. Use the table "United States, 1800–1970" to review prior knowledge and help students make guesses about changes that have occurred since 1908.

Body

IE 1,   IE 2,   IE 3,   IE 4,   SE 1,   SE 2,
SE 3,   SE 4,   A 1,   A 2

Use the same procedure as in Lessons 1, 2, 3, and 5. The only students allowed to vote are

male or female	Caucasian or
over 21 years old	Native American
Southern or	literate
Northern	own property

Use the same procedure in having the students analyze the documents and in debriefing. Students fill in biographical information about Franklin Roosevelt on the "Presidential Information" chart they kept in their notebooks. Students can supplement the ballot information with their textbooks. The teacher should point out a picture of Roosevelt as well. On the class "Voting Requirement Changes" chart and on the student individual charts, students will list who was allowed to vote in 1932, who was barred from voting, and then compare this election to 1908 to determine what requirements changed and why. Students will offer questions and guesses about why changes have occurred and probably about why change has not occurred more quickly for other groups. The teacher asks each student to complete the evaluation sheet.

Closing

Ask students to predict whether a larger number of people will vote in the next election in 1972. Have them give reasons to support their predictions.

Assessment

Student understanding will be assessed through teacher observation of group work and class discussion, through group written work, and through participation in the voter education project.

CANDIDATES

HERBERT HOOVER—Herbert Hoover was born in 1874. He was a member of the Republican party. Hoover worked during and after World War I (1914–1920) to help provide food and shelter for people displaced by the war. He headed the American Relief Commission and the U.S. Food Commission. Hoover served as secretary of commerce from 1921 to 1928 under both President Warren G. Harding and President Calvin Coolidge. He was elected president in 1928. The stock market crashed in 1929, plunging the United States into the deepest and longest depression in American history. Hoover was a wealthy engineer from Iowa before he entered government service.

FRANKLIN DELANO ROOSEVELT—Franklin D. Roosevelt was born in 1882. He was a member of the Democratic party. He was a lawyer but soon entered politics. Roosevelt was assistant secretary of the navy and ran for vice president in 1920 (but lost). He got sick with polio in the 1920s and became paralyzed from the waist down as a result. He served as governor of New York from 1929 to 1933. Roosevelt promised to help the "forgotten man" during the depression. He came from a very wealthy family in New York.

Ballot—Election of 1932

Mark your choice for ONE of the following:

_____ HERBERT HOOVER

_____ FRANKLIN DELANO ROOSEVELT

Group _____   _____

Members: _____   _____

VOTING RIGHTS IN 1932		
Document Title	**One-Sentence Summary of the Document**	**What Does It Say About Voting Requirements?**

Based upon your analysis of the documents, answer the following:

1.   What groups of people were allowed to vote in 1932?

2.   List at least three groups of people who were not allowed to vote in 1932.

3.   Compare and contrast the election of 1932 with the elections of 1800, 1832, 1872, and 1908. What changed about voting requirements?

    • List the titles of the documents that showed changes in 1932 compared to 1800, 1832, 1872, and 1908.
    • List the groups that were affected by the changes.
    • List how voting requirements changed.

4.   What contributions were being made by the groups who were still denied the right to vote?

Documents for 1932

16TH AMENDMENT, *U.S. CONSTITUTION,* 1913

"The Congress shall have the power to lay and collect taxes in incomes. . . ." Congress enacted a "progressive" income tax, meaning that people with higher incomes paid a higher percentage of their income in taxes to the federal government.

17TH AMENDMENT, *U.S. CONSTITUTION,* 1913

The Seventeenth Amendment gave the people of each state the right to elect U.S. Senators, rather than the Senators being selected by the members of the State Legislature as the Constitution originally provided.

18TH AMENDMENT, *U.S. CONSTITUTION,* 1919

". . . The manufacture, sale, or transportation of intoxicating liquors within, the importation thereof into, or the exportation thereof from the United States . . . is hereby prohibited [made illegal]."

19TH AMENDMENT, *U.S. CONSTITUTION,* 1920

"The right of citizens of the United States to vote shall not be denied or abridged [limited] by the United States or by any State on account of sex."

FOUNDING OF THE NATIONAL ASSOCIATION FOR THE ADVANCEMENT OF COLORED PEOPLE, 1909 (FROM *THE QUEST FOR EQUALITY* BY CHARLES H. WESLEY)

A conference in May 1909 attended by African Americans and Caucasians led to the formation of the NAACP. The five demands that emerged from the conference were

- to ensure voting rights;
- to end "white only" policies in public accommodations;
- to promote free labor relations;
- to urge public education not to educate black youths as "servants and underlings";
- to require equal justice under law.

  By 1914, there were fifty local branches of the NAACP across the United States.

THE IMMIGRATION ACT OF 1924

This law established a quota [set number] for how many people could enter the United States each year. The quota for immigrants from Southern and Eastern Europe, Africa, and Asia were very small numbers, while the quotas for Western European countries were large numbers. As a result, immigration slowed to a trickle, and in 1932, for the first time in American history, more people left the United States than entered it.

1924 INDIAN CITIZENSHIP ACT

"Be it enacted . . . That all non-citizen Indians born within the territorial limits of the United States be, and they are declared to be, citizens of the United States; Provided, That the granting of such citizenship shall not in any manner impair [limit] or otherwise affect the right of any Indian to tribal or other property."

"THE MILL MOTHER'S LAMENT" BY ELLA MAY WIGGINS

Ella May Wiggins worked in a textile mill in Gastonia, North Carolina. The mother of nine children, she never made more than $9 a week. In 1929, she tried to help organize a union for the workers. On the way to a union rally, she was shot in the back by "security guards" hired by the mill owner. She wrote this song about her life.

We leave our homes in the morning
We kiss our children goodbye,
While we slave for the bosses,
Our children scream and cry.

And when we drew our money,
Our grocery bills to pay,
Not a cent to spend for clothing,
Not a cent to lay away.

How it grieves the heart of a mother,
As everyone must know.
But we can't buy for our children,
Our wages are too low.

It is for our little children,
That seem to us so dear,
But for us, nor them, dear workers,
The bosses do not care.

But understand, all workers,
Our union they do fear;
Let's stand together, workers,
And have a union here.

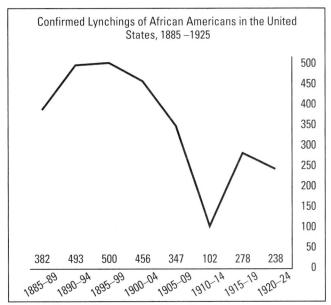

Confirmed Lynchings of African Americans in the United States, 1885–1925

382	493	500	456	347	102	278	238
1885–89	1890–94	1895–99	1900–04	1905–09	1910–14	1915–19	1920–24

Source: *Chicago Defender,* an African American newspaper

Women suffragists picketing the White House, 1917. Library of Congress.

LESSON 7:   Analysis of Voting Rights in the Election of 1972

Objectives

1. Each student will take on a role and participate in a mock presidential election. (cognitive)
2. Each student will analyze and evaluate documents relating to the right to vote in 1972. (cognitive)
3. Each student will form generalizations regarding changes in voting requirements. (cognitive)
4. Each student will understand that enfranchisement is a fluid process that has led to the expansion and contraction of the electorate throughout U.S. history. (affective)
5. Each student will discuss the importance of voting in a republican form of government. (affective)

Materials

Name tags from Lesson 1 if following option 1 or use the token characteristics envelopes from Lesson 1 if following option 2,

a ballot box with a sign marked "1972,"

the 1972 ballot for each student,

an evaluation sheet for each student,

a packet of documents on 1972 for each group of three to four students.

The packet includes

- Two copies of "Voting Rights in 1972" graphic organizer;
- One copy of "Analysis of the Election of 1972";
- Documents related to the election of 1972.

Instructional Strategies

Opener

IE 1,   IE 2,   IE 3,   IE 4,   SE 1,   SE 2, A 1

Review what students learned from their inquiry into the election of 1932. Use that review to transition into the election of 1972. Use the table "United States, 1800–1970" to review prior knowledge and help students make guesses about changes that have occurred since 1932.

Body

IE 1,   IE 2,   IE 3,   IE 4,   SE 1,   SE 2, SE 3,   SE 4,   A 1,   A 2

Use the same procedures as Lessons 1, 2, 3, 5, and 6. The students allowed to vote are

male or female over 18 years old	Caucasian, African American, or Native American
Southern or Northern	literate or not
	own property or not

The only students who cannot vote are those with the characteristics "Recent Immigrant" or "13 years old."

Use the same procedure in having students analyze the documents and in debriefing. Students fill in biographical information about Richard Nixon on the "Presidential Information" chart they kept in their notebooks. Students can supplement the ballot information with their textbooks. The teacher should point out a picture of Nixon as well. On the class "Voting Requirement Changes" chart and on the student individual charts, students will list who was allowed to vote in 1972, who was barred from voting, and then compare this election to 1932 to determine what requirements changed and why. Students will offer questions and guesses about why changes have occurred and probably about why change has not occurred more quickly for other groups. The teacher asks each student to complete the evaluation sheet.

Closing

Ask students to predict whether the number of people who can vote in today's elections is larger than in 1972. Have them give reasons to support their predictions.

Assessment

Student understanding will be assessed through teacher observation of group work and class discussion, through group written work, and through participation in the voter education project.

CANDIDATES

GEORGE MCGOVERN—George McGovern was born in 1922. He was a member of the Democratic party. Born in South Dakota, he served in the House of Representatives from 1957 to 1961 and the U.S. Senate from 1963 to 1972. McGovern favored immediate and unconditional withdrawal from the Vietnam conflict. Under his leadership, the Democratic party rules were rewritten to give more representation to young people, women, and minorities. McGovern had been an upper-middle class lawyer before entering politics.

RICHARD M. NIXON—Richard M. Nixon was born in 1913. He was a member of the Republican party. He served as congressman and senator from California and as vice president under President Dwight Eisenhower in the 1950s. He had won election to the presidency in 1968 with a promise to end the war in Vietnam and to promote law and order in America. The United States signed an agreement to withdraw from Vietnam early in 1972. The U.S. economy experienced high inflation during Nixon's first term, which led to economic hardships for many Americans. Nixon was a wealthy lawyer from California.

Ballot—Election of 1972

Mark your choice for ONE of the following:

_____ GEORGE MCGOVERN

_____ RICHARD M. NIXON

Group _____   _____

Members: _____   _____

VOTING RIGHTS IN 1972		
Document Title	One-Sentence Summary of the Document	What Does It Say About Voting Requirements?

Based upon your analysis of the documents, answer the following:

1.   What groups of people were allowed to vote in 1972?

2.   List at least three groups of people who were not allowed to vote in 1972.

3.   Compare and contrast the election of 1972 with the elections of 1800, 1832, 1872, 1908, and 1932. What changed about voting requirements?
   - List the titles of the documents that showed changes in 1972 compared to 1800, 1832, 1872, 1908, and 1932.
   - List the groups that were affected by the changes.
   - List how voting requirements changed.

4.   What contributions were being made by the groups who were still denied the right to vote?

Documents for 1972

24TH AMENDMENT, *U.S. CONSTITUTION*, 1964

"The right of citizens of the United States to vote in any primary or other election for President or Vice President, for electors for President or Vice President, or for any Senator or Representative in Congress, shall not be denied or abridged [limited] by the United States or by any State by reason of failure to pay any poll tax or other tax."

26TH AMENDMENT, *U.S. CONSTITUTION*, 1971

"The right of citizens of the United States, who are eighteen years of age or older, to vote shall not be denied or abridged [limited] by the United States or by any State on account of age."

SMITH v. *ALLRIGHT*, 1944

The Supreme Court found that the use of the white primary in Texas violated the Fourteenth and Fifteenth Amendments. It ordered Texas to stop the use of the white primary.

MALCOLM X, BLACK MUSLIM MINISTER, SPEECH TO AN AFRICAN AMERICAN AUDIENCE ON APRIL 3, 1964

". . . It's time for you and me to become more politically mature and realize . . . that if we don't cast a ballot, it's going to end up in a situation where we're going to have to cast a bullet. It's either a ballot or a bullet."

EQUAL RIGHTS AMENDMENT, PROPOSED BY CONGRESS IN 1972

"Equality of rights under the law shall not be denied or abridged [limited] by the United States or by any State on account of sex."

The amendment required approval by thirty-six state legislatures in order to become part of the Constitution. In 1982, it died after winning approval from thirty-three states. It is not part of the Constitution today.

MARTIN LUTHER KING, "LETTER FROM BIRMINGHAM CITY JAIL," 1963

"An unjust law is a code inflicted upon a minority which that minority had no part in enacting or creating because it did not have the unhampered right to vote. Who can say the Legislature of Alabama which set up the segregation laws was democratically elected? Throughout the state of Alabama all types of conniving methods are used to prevent Negroes from becoming registered voters and there are some counties without a single Negro registered to vote despite the fact that the Negro constitutes a majority of the population."

WENDELL CHINO, PRESIDENT OF THE MESCALERO APACHE TRIBE, SPEECH AT THE NATIONAL CONGRESS OF AMERICAN INDIANS ON OCTOBER 6, 1969

"Most of our Indian people do not now have, nor have we ever had political or legal relations with state governments. . . . Only recently have [American Indians] been allowed the vote in many states and today few of our Indian people do vote in state elections and have no power base in the state political machines."

VOTING RIGHTS ACT OF 1965

"No voting qualification . . . shall be imposed or applied by any State or political subdivision to deny or abridge [limit] the right of any citizen of the United States to vote on account of race.
. . . [The federal court will not allow] a test or device . . . used for the purpose or with the effect of denying or abridging the right of any citizen of the United States to vote on account of race or color. . . . The phrase 'test or device' shall mean any requirement that a person . . . [shall] (1) demonstrate the ability to read, write, understand, or interpret any matter; (2) demonstrate any educational achievement or his knowledge on any particular subject; (3) possess good moral character. . . ."

STOKELEY CARMICHAEL AND CHARLES V. HAMILTON, *BLACK POWER—THE POLITICS OF LIBERATION IN AMERICA,* 1967

"[The act of registering to vote] gives one a sense of being. The black man who goes to register is saying to the white man, 'No.' He is saying: 'You have said that I cannot vote. You have said that this is my place. This is where I should remain. You have contained me and I am saying 'No' to you and thereby I am creating a better life for myself. . . .' The black person begins to live. He begins to create his own experience when he says 'No' to someone who contains him."

Black voter registration, Atlanta, Georgia, 1946. Special Collections Department, Pullen Library, Georgia State University, Atlanta, Georgia.

Western Defense Command and Fourth Army
Wartime Civil Control Administration
Presidio of San Francisco, California
May 3, 1942

INSTRUCTIONS TO ALL PERSONS OF JAPANESE ANCESTRY:

Pursuant to the provisions of Civilian Exclusion Order No. 33, dated May 3, 1942, all persons of Japanese ancestry, both alien and non-alien,* will be evacuated [removed] by 12 o'clock noon, Saturday, May 9, 1942.

The Following Instructions Must Be Observed:

1. A responsible member of each family, preferably the head of the family, or the person in whose name most of the property is held, and each individual living alone, will report to the Civil Control Station to receive further instructions. This must be done between 8:00 A.M. and 5:00 P.M. on Monday, May 4, 1942, or between 8:00 A.M. and 5:00 P.M. on Tuesday, May 5, 1942.

2. Evacuees [the people being removed] must carry with them the following property:
    (a) Bedding and linens (no mattress) for each member of the family;
    (b) Toilet articles for each member of the family;
    (c) Extra clothing for each member of the family;
    (d) Sufficient knives, forks, spoons, plates, bowls and cups for each member of the family;
    (e) Essential personal effects for each member of the family.
    The size and number of packages is limited to that which can be carried by the individual or family group.

3. No pets of any kind will be permitted.

4. No personal items and no household goods will be shipped to the Assembly Center.

J. L. DeWIT, Lieutenant General, U. S. Army Commanding.

*A non-alien was a U.S. citizen with Japanese ancestry. Japanese Americans were referred to as aliens and non-aliens, rather than as noncitizens and citizens.

The United States government during World War II placed approximately 110,000 Japanese Americans in detention camps. Two-thirds of those incarcerated were native-born U.S. citizens.

LESSON 8:   Synthesis of Inquiry Data on Voting Rights, 1800–Present

Objectives

1. Each student will analyze the impact of demographic changes in the electorate on persons elected to political office. (cognitive)
2. Each student will help design and implement an analysis of neighborhood voting patterns. (cognitive)
3. Each student, either individually or as part of a group, will create and present a contribution to a class voter education project. (cognitive)
4. Each student will appreciate the importance of voting in a republican form of government. (affective)

Materials

Pictures of presidents, class and individual charts of voting requirement changes, ballots for mock presidential election, a transparency of "Voter Turnout 1932–1996," materials for voter education project

Instructional Strategies

Opener

IE 1,   IE 2,   IE 4,   SE 1,   SE 3

The teacher opens with the following quotation from Supreme Court Justice Harlan in 1896: **"In view of the Constitution, in the eye of the law, there is in this country no superior, dominant, ruling class of citizens. There is no caste here. Our Constitution is color-blind, and neither knows nor tolerates classes among citizens. In respect of civil rights, all citizens are equal before the law."**
Teacher: Do you agree with this statement? Are all citizens equal before the law? Are all citizens equal when it comes to voting?

Body

IE 3,   IE 4,   SE 1,   SE 2,   SE 3

The teacher leads the organization of information on changes in voting requirements from 1800 to 1972. He/she asks students to refer to their "Voting Requirement Changes" charts, the ballots in their notebooks, and the "Presidential Information" chart. He/she uses the large class chart showing suffrage changes from 1800 to 1972.

Teacher: Compare the groups who could vote by 1972 with those who could vote in 1800. What observations and generalizations can you make?

The teacher asks students to look at pictures of Jefferson, Jackson, Grant, Taft, FDR, and Nixon, either in their textbooks or from another source.
Teacher: You've discovered that many more people were able to vote as time went on. Yet these presidents have a lot in common. Look at them. Look at your "Presidential Information" chart and review what we've learned about them. What are some characteristics these presidents share? Students should notice that all are older male Caucasians. Students may point out that all were members of one of the major parties, all were relatively wealthy, all were political or military leaders before their election to the presidency.

IE 1,   IE 2,   IE 3,   SE 1,   SE 2,   SE 3

Teacher: So what difference has it made that more people have gotten the right to vote? If African Americans and women and poor people and young people can vote, why haven't we had an African American or female or poor or young president? The teacher should encourage expression of many opinions, asking students to back up their opinions with evidence.

IE 1,   IE 2,   IE 4,   SE 1,   SE 2,   SE 3,
SE 5

The teacher then leads students in a mock election for the next scheduled presidential election. The teacher leads a discussion of possible candidates and writes their names on the board. On the ballot, also include some current issue-oriented questions with local, state, national, and international perspectives. The teacher may want students to have done research on these issues prior to this lesson. The teacher distributes ballots, students vote, and students tabulate the results. The class discusses the outcomes.

A possible extension activity would be for students to create their own political parties, establish their own platforms, do research on important issues, and design and simulate campaigns for public office. They could also identify people in public life whom they believe would be attractive candidates for the presidency.

Closing

IE 1,   IE 3,   SE 1,   SE 2,   SE 3

The teacher points out that 100 percent of the voters in the classroom voted in their mock election. But typically, one-half or fewer eligible voters participate in U.S. elections. He/she places Transparency 1, "Voter Turnout," on the overhead projector with the bottom half of the transparency covered up. After discussing the low rate of voter turnout, the teacher uncovers the bottom half of the transparency. **Teacher: Why do you think so few Americans bother to vote? Why do you think young people and people of color and Southerners and lower-income people are less likely to vote? Do you think it is important to vote? Why or why not? What can be done to get more of our citizens to participate in choosing our leaders?**

IE 1,   IE 2,   IE 3,   IE 4,   SE 1,   SE 2,   SE 4,   SE 5,   A 1,   A 2, A 3

The teacher suggests that the class voter education project might influence people to be more active voters. The class spends the rest of the period working on their projects. The teacher circulates to provide clarification and feedback and to engage in formative assessment.

Assessment

Student understanding will be assessed through teacher observation of class discussion, through written work, and through participation in the voter education project.

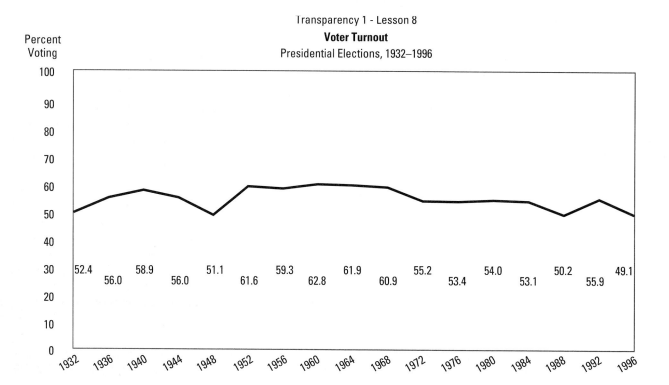

Transparency 1 - Lesson 8
Voter Turnout
Presidential Elections, 1932–1996

The Highest Voter Participation Is Among

- Caucasians
- Persons age 45 to 65
- Non-Southerners
- Skilled and professional workers
- Persons with higher income levels

Source: Federal Election Commission

LESSON 9: Voter Education Project

Objectives

1. Each student will help design and implement an analysis of neighborhood voting patterns. (cognitive)
2. Each student, either individually or as part of a group, will create and present a contribution to a class voter education project. (cognitive)
3. Each student will appreciate the importance of voting in a republican form of government. (affective)

Materials

Materials for students to use in voter education project.

Optional: Invite a guest speaker to talk about voter registration procedures or a local politician or a representative from the League of Women Voters.

Instructional Strategies

Opener

IE 1,   IE 2,   IE 3,   IE 4,   SE 1,   SE 2,
SE 3,   A 1

The students will continue to work on the voter education project. **Teacher: Share the most important data you have discovered in this research project. Relate the generaliza-** tions formed in the previous lesson about why people vote (or don't) and the results of the expanding franchise.

Body

IE 1,   IE 2,   IE 3,   IE 4,   SE 1,   SE 2,
SE 3,   SE 4,   SE 5,   A 1,   A 2,   A 3

Continue the work on the voter education project. By today, students should have collected all data on neighborhood voting patterns. Begin with students analyzing the raw data and looking for patterns and trends. Either in large or small group, facilitate students organizing the information into one or more visual presentations. Possibilities include a table, graph, chart, or other visual representation, along with a written analysis by the students. The teacher might choose to have students do research on how to register to vote and on political party organizations or political activist groups, such as the League of Women Voters, or political action committees or advocacy groups. The teacher might invite a speaker from the Office of Voter Registration in the county to meet with the class and give feedback on the project.

Assessment

The voter education project would count as a major grade, possibly as the summative assessment for the unit.

LESSON 10: Voter Education Project

Objectives

1. Each student, either individually or as part of a group, will create and present a contribution to a class voter education project. (cognitive)
2. Each student will appreciate the importance of voting in a republican form of government. (affective)

Materials

Evaluation forms for voter education project for each student.

Instructional Strategies

Opener

IE 3,   IE 4,   SE 1,   SE 3

This day is devoted to the presentations of the completed voter education project. The teacher should open by discussing where the projects can be displayed so members of the students' community will learn more about voting.

Body

IE 1,   IE 2,   IE 3,   IE 4,   SE 1,   SE 2,
SE 3,   SE 4,   SE 5,   A 1,   A 2,   A 3

Students present their projects to the class. The teacher and students evaluate student creative contributions to the project according to the guidelines established. After this initial presentation, students might present to the PTA, a school assembly, the Board of Education, or the city council. The projects might also make good social science fair projects.

Assessment

The voter education project would count as a major grade, possibly as the summative assessment for the unit.

Suggested Activities

1. Conduct research in your state to find out what your first state constitution stipulated regarding voting requirements. Create an activity where students compare/contrast your state's initial requirements to those indicated in the documents for Lesson 1.

2. Choose one of the following groups and do in-depth research to learn more about how they gained the vote:

    White men without property

    African American men

    Women

    Native Americans

    18-year-olds

    Create a series of lessons or a unit in which students explore the enfranchisement of the group you chose. Include primary sources and instructional approaches that appeal to multiple learning preferences.

3. Create a technology-based lesson or series of lessons where students use the Internet to research contemporary efforts by groups to exercise political power. See the "Resources and References" list for web addresses for political action and advocacy groups.

4. Design a series of lessons in which students create their own political parties, establish their own platforms, do research on important issues, and design and simulate campaigns for public office. Include decision-making activities for students to form judgments on the critical issues.

5. Organize a local oral history project to interview community activists. Take photographs and use videotape or audiotape to record the interviews. Use the data from the interviews to create a multimedia project on effective civic action in your community. Alternately, design a classroom activity where students carry out the oral history project. Have students present their projects to an audience beyond the classroom.

Andrews, J. R., and David Zarefsky. 1992. *Contemporary American voices: Significant speeches in American history, 1945–present.* New York: Longman.

Campbell, B. A. 1979. *The American electorate: Attitudes and actions.* New York: Holt, Rinehard, & Winston.

Commager, H. S. 1973. *Documents of American history.* 9th ed. 2 vols. Englewood Cliffs, NJ: Prentice Hall.

Congressional Quarterly's guide to U.S. elections. 1994. 3rd ed. Washington, DC: Congressional Quarterly.

Expect excellence: Curriculum standards for social studies. 1994. Washington, DC: National Council for the Social Studies. http://www.ncss.org

Finkelstein, M. J., A. Sandifer, and E. S. Wright. 1976. *Minorities: USA.* New York: Globe Book Company.

Grant, D. 1993. *The way it was in the South: The black experience in Georgia.* New York: Birch Lane Press.

Hymowitz, C., and M. Weissman. 1978. *A history of women in America.* New York: Bantam Books.

Japanese American Citizens League Web Page. http://jacl.org/

Korobkin, R. The politics of disfranchisement in Georgia. *Georgia Historical Quarterly* 74 (Spring 1990): 20–58.

League of Women Voters Web Page. http://www.lwv.org/

Library of Congress Web Page. American memory. http://www.lcweb2.loc.gov/ammem/

National Archives Web Page. Includes digital classroom activities and online exhibit hall. http://www.nara.gov

National Association for the Advancement of Colored People (NAACP) Web Page. http://www.naacp.org/

National Congress of American Indians Web Page. http://www.ncai.org/

National Council of La Raza Web Page. http://www.nclr.org/

National standards for civics and government. 1994. Washington, DC: Center for Civic Education. http://www.civiced.org/

National standards for United States history. 1994. UCLA: National Center for History in the Schools. http://www.sscnet.ucla.edu/nchs/

National Organization for Women Web Page. http://www.now.org/

National Political Congress of Black Women Web Page. http://www.npcbw.org/

National Puerto Rican Coalition Web Page. http://www.incacorp.com/nprc

National Urban League Web Page. http://nul.org/

National Women's Political Caucus Web Page. http://www.incacorp.com/nwpc

Organization of Chinese Americans Web Page. http://www.ocanatl.org

People of the American Way Web Page. http://www.pfaw.org/

Porter, K. H. 1918. *A history of suffrage in the United States.* New York: AMS Press.

Ravitch, D., ed. 1990. *The American reader: Words that moved a nation.* New York: HarperCollins.

Shafritz, J. M. 1992. *The HarperCollins dictionary of American government and politics.* New York: HarperPerennial.

Wesley, C. H. 1978. *The quest for equality: From Civil War to civil rights.* Cornwell Heights, PA: The Publishers Agency, under the auspices of The Association for the Study of Afro-American Life and History.

Conclusion
Reflecting on Culturally Responsive Pedagogy

Beverly Jeanne Armento

Georgia State University

To be culturally responsive in one's teaching, educators must be child centered and fully aware of the prior knowledge, language, and experiences of the children in their classes. In addition, educators must be fully aware of the academic content and the achievement goals intended for students. In part, the task of the culturally responsive educator is to bridge the gap between prior knowledge and the academic learning tasks. This can be done by starting with examples, vocabulary, and experiences that are familiar to the students and then using these to build a bridge or scaffold toward the new learning processes and content. The teacher's role is to minimize the cultural and academic mismatch between the current and new knowledge, the current and new ways of thinking, and the current and new ways of problem solving. Culturally responsive pedagogy applies to all curricular areas and provides a way for educators to consider methods for maximizing learning for all students. The culturally responsive instructional units in this book emphasize the range of ways educators can actively engage learners, the ways we can meaningfully assess student learning, and the ways we can adapt curriculum so that it is more inclusive and accurate.

Why do educators need to be child centered and aware of prior knowledge? Think about the definition for *learning* that is used in this book: Learning is a reorganization of prior knowledge. One's prior knowledge forms a platform or a foundation for all future learning. Children come to school with rich foundations, full of the experiences, language, symbols, images, and tools of their home, community and culture. This platform is a good place to start building the bridge to new ideas. For the new ideas to rest firmly on the foundation the child brings to school from the home and community, the new ideas must be anchored securely on the foundation. Teachers can build on this foundation by starting with examples known to the child and by including cultural knowledge in the content of instruction.

Continuing with this metaphor of construction, if there is no connection between the foundation and the building, the new construction will not stand. Analogously, if there is no connection between the child's home and community (the foundation) and the new knowledge acquired in school (the building), the students will fail to learn. In such cases, learners grapple with figuring out just what the new knowledge means and how it relates to them. In addition, since the building (new learning) is not secured to the foundation (prior knowledge of the child), the building can be easily destroyed (or forgotten, not used). This metaphor of building on a firm foundation is a useful one to think of when considering the child, the academic demands of today's society, and the role of the culturally responsive educator.

The "gap" between current and new learning could involve cultural terms and vocabulary, literacy or mathematical skills, known and unknown examples and experiences, or errors and misconceptions in thinking. The job of the culturally responsive educator is to "narrow the gap" so that meaningful learning occurs.

A big part of narrowing the gap has to do with the students and the ways educators invite students to "own" the new learning. All students must feel that they are learning something important, something that they can use, and something that makes sense to them. Of course, it would be great if students were curious about the topic, if they were eager to figure out a problem, or so puzzled about something that they could not wait to do some research to ease the intellectual tension. Teachers in all types of schools and with students of every ethnic group often report that many of their students do not bring this intellectual curiosity and enthusiasm to learning. The task of the culturally responsive educator is to try to create a level of anticipation and excitement for learning that propels students into the learning tasks. Wanting to communicate with students in another city, for example, creates a purpose for writing and expressing thoughts about oneself (Frasher, in the language arts unit in this book). Trying to figure out the factors a forecaster would use to predict weather patterns creates the motivation for investigation and research for students in the science class (Weinburgh, in the science unit in this book). Once students "own" a reason for learning, their curiosity and motivation can be activated to help bridge the cultural and academic gaps that might exist. Motivation to learn and having a purpose for learning are really the first steps to effective teaching and academic achievement. The culturally responsive educator must pay a great deal of attention to this important factor, for without motivation and active engagement of the learners, nothing of any consequence will occur.

"Helping all students reach high standards" has become an important goal for educators. In order for this goal to mean more than a slogan, educators must have the tools and the belief system that will enable them to work effectively with all students and their families. In part, the belief system presented in this book suggests that educators must be dynamically responsive to their students, must custom design instruction for students in order to bridge any gaps that exist between the current knowledge, beliefs, and skills of the student and the desired learning goals. At the minimum, educators need to be aware of the cultural and experiential richness that is a part of each child and should expect that each child can and wants to learn.

The units of instruction presented in this book are not intended to be singular solutions to the complex issues associated with academic achievement of diverse learners. However, the authors believe that attention to the principles of culturally responsive pedagogy will strengthen educators' abilities to meet the needs of diverse learners. It is critically important that educators hold certain basic beliefs about the nature of children and about their roles and responsibilities as teachers. Such beliefs empower educators to act in more purposeful and sustained ways to attend to the individual needs of students. In addition, educators must understand the essence of meaningful learning, thus placing the emphasis on students and the ways they are engaged in the processes of building new knowledge and skills. Educators must open their eyes to the images that surround them and their students: Are all students included in the visual and verbal messages that are being sent to students? If not, how can these images be supplemented? Are students learning that there are opinions different from their own? If not, how can this be done? And, educators must have a wide repertoire of evaluative tools at their disposal so that they can accurately understand just what the child is comprehending.

Armed with the beliefs and tools of the culturally responsive educator, we can more effectively address the goals of equity and excellence in the education of all children.

Index

Eye contact, 8

F

Facilitators, 149
Families, assistance from, 21
Family stories, 44–46
Fast Sam, Cool Clyde, and Stuff, 215–16
Feldman, R. S., 8
Field-dependent learning, 9
Field study lesson, 216–20
Field trips, 99
Fifteenth Amendment, 142–43, 178
Fitzhugh, G., 172
Flinders, D. J., 5, 8
Folktales, 48, 99
Forms and handouts
    area lessons, 83, 86–88
    1800 election lesson, 151–57
    1832 election lesson, 165–73
    1872 election lesson, 175–79
    1908 election lesson, 184–90
    1932 election lesson, 192–97
    1972 election lesson, 199–205
    field study lesson, 219–20
    M&Ms lesson, 228–29
    precipitation lesson, 130, 132
    severe weather, 134–36
    storytelling evaluation, 50
    temperature, 113–15, 121
    time capsule lesson, 224–25
    voter education project, 182
Fourteenth Amendment, 178
Foxfire principles, 13
Fractions, 62
Free black population, 161
Friendship lesson, 215–16
Fronts, 125
Frostbite, 121
Functions, 63

G

Gemake, J. G., 9
Geography lessons, 221–25
Geometry, in textiles, 55–56. *See also*
        Interdisciplinary unit
Geometry standards, 62, 64
Giroux, H. A., 14
Global connections, 146
Gollnick, D. M., 7
Grain of Rice, A, 226
Grant, D., 187
Grant, Ulysses S., 175

Graphic organizers, 106
Gray, T., 9
Greeley, Horace, 175
Greene, M., 22
Grossman, H., 9
Group work goals, 30–31, 65, 66

H

Hale, Sarah Josepha, 171
Hale-Benson, J. E., 9
Hamilton, C. V., 203
Handouts. *See* Forms and handouts
Heat cramps, 121
Heat exhaustion, 121
Heatstroke, 121
Heat syncope, 121
Hierarchical cultures, 29
High expectations, 11–13, 20
High pressure systems, 127–28
Hilliard, A. G., 9
Hintz, M., 58
Hispanic stories, 52
History, changes in, 24
Hofstadter, R., 159
Hoopes, D. S., 6
Hoover, Herbert, 192
Hoover-Dempsey, K. V., 21
Huitzilopochti, 137
Humidity
    effects on weather, 104–5
    lesson outlines, 108
    lessons about, 128–29
Hygrometers, 128–29
Hymowitz, C., 159, 178
Hypothermia, 121

I

Immigrants
    family stories of, 45
    literature of, 37
    origins by decade, 188
Immigration Act of 1924, 195
Inclusiveness
    in citizenship education, 140
    in curricula, 25, 26
    of science standards, 109
Income taxes, 195
Independent reading, 37
Indian Citizenship Act, 143, 196
Indian Removal Act, 172
Individual differences, 12, 20–21
Individualistic cultures, 29

M

McClelland, A., 7, 9
McGovern, George, 199
Mack, J., 58
Mainstream culture in schools, 6–7
Malloy, C. E., 65, 66
Managers, 149
M&Ms lesson, 226–29
Manning, M. L., 9
Maritime winds, 123
Martin, J. R., 15
Mathematics
    achievement discrepancies, 55
    curriculum standards, 61–68
    lessons for, 226–29 (*see*
        Interdisciplinary unit)
Measurement, math standards for, 62, 64
Meteorologists, 104
Meyer, L., 59
Migrations, 24–25
Military Reconstruction Act, 142
"Mill Mother's Lament," 196
Moore, C. G., 8
Motivation
    intrinsic, 28
    principles of, 30, 214
    relevance and, 21
Multiple interpretations, 139–40
Music, 57, 147
Mutual understanding, 140

N

Nash, G., 24
National Association for the
    Advancement of Colored People
    (NAACP), 195
National Council for the Social Studies
    (NCSS) standards, 139–41,
    145–46, 210
National Council of Teachers of English
    (NCTE) standards, 39–40
National Council of Teachers of
    Mathematics (NCTM) standards,
    61–68
National Science Education Standards,
    109–10
Nations, interdependence of, 24–25

Native American rights, 187, 188, 196
Native American stories, 52–53
Navajo rugs
    in area lesson, 59, 81–82
    discussion questions, 99
    history of, 57–58
    Internet resources, 101
    in perimeter lesson, 59, 79–80
    sample designs, 73–78
Neighborhood voting patterns, 180–82,
    209
Nettles, M. T., 3
News stories, 40–42
Nieto, S., 21
Nineteenth Amendment, 195
Nixon, Richard M., 199
Nonverbal communications, 8, 48–49
Number sense, 61, 63
Number systems, 63

O

Oakes, J., 22, 31
Ogbu, J., 6
Old Farmer's Almanac, 117
Osceola, 179
Owens, R. G., 6

P

Padron, Y. N., 7
Parallelograms, 85, 88
Partner classes, 40–41
Pattern recognition
    lesson outline, 60
    lesson plans for, 69–70, 96–97
    math standards for, 62, 63
Perimeter
    lesson outlines, 59–60
    lesson plans for, 79–80, 84
Personal narratives, 43
Perspective taking, 26–27
Physical science standards, 110
Polar winds, 123
Poll taxes, 143, 187, 202
Polygon similarity, 60, 89–90
Porter, K. H., 171
Potato printing, 99